CW00347899

THE HISTORY OF JERUSALEM

ITS ORIGINS TO THE EARLY MIDDLE AGES

THE HISTORY OF JERUSALEM

ITS ORIGINS TO THE EARLY MIDDLE AGES

ALAN J. POTTER

To Laura
With very best wishes
Alan

PEN & SWORD HISTORY

AN IMPRINT OF PEN & SWORD BOOKS LTD.
YORKSHIRE – PHILADELPHIA

First published in Great Britain in 2020 by
Pen & Sword History
An imprint of
Pen & Sword Books Ltd
Yorkshire - Philadelphia

Copyright © 2020 Alan J. Potter

ISBN 978 1 52678 329 5

The right of Alan J. Potter to be identified as Author of this work has been asserted
by him in accordance with the Copyright, Designs and Patents Act 1988.

A CIP catalogue record for this book is available from the British Library.

All rights reserved. No part of this book may be reproduced or transmitted
in any form or by any means, electronic or mechanical including
photocopying, recording or by any information storage and retrieval system,
without permission from the Publisher in writing.

Printed and bound in England
By TJ Books Ltd.

Pen & Sword Books Ltd incorporates the Imprints of Pen & Sword Archaeology,
Atlas, Aviation, Battleground, Discovery, Family History, History, Maritime,
Military, Naval, Politics, Railways, Select, Transport, True Crime, Fiction,
Frontline Books, Leo Cooper, Praetorian Press, Seaforth Publishing,
Wharncliffe and White Owl.

For a complete list of Pen & Sword titles please contact
PEN & SWORD BOOKS LIMITED
47 Church Street, Barnsley, South Yorkshire, S70 2AS, England
E-mail: enquiries@pen-and-sword.co.uk
Website: www.pen-and-sword.co.uk

Or

PEN AND SWORD BOOKS
1950 Lawrence Rd, Havertown, PA 19083, USA
E-mail: uspen-and-sword@casematepublishers.com
Website: www.penandswordbooks.com

Contents

Author's Statement

Ten years ago, as I began the countdown to my retirement, I thought I would like to embark on a project that was very different from my long-term commitment to company accounts, stocks, shares, indices and increasingly arduous anti-money laundering regulations. That is not so say that my preceding decades had not been interesting, nor worthwhile, but enough was enough and I now craved mental stimulation of a very different kind.

History seemed a natural choice – real stories about real people – and after a number of false starts, I decided upon Jerusalem. My wife of thirty-seven years had been born in Bethlehem, where the Roman Catholic community is treated mostly with disdain by the majority Muslim population and with caution by the Israeli authorities, and I had visited nearby Jerusalem with my wife and children during the 1990s.

I was fascinated by Jerusalem's Old City and why this tiny place was so important to so many of today's religious groups – Jews, Muslims and a variety of Christians creeds such as Roman Catholics, Armenians and Greek Orthodox. It was not until I began my 'Jerusalem project' that I realized how little I knew and this enabled me to arrive at an inescapable conclusion: as a self-respecting pedant, I had to start at the very beginning.

In order to annotate to the depth that I felt would make the project worthwhile, I have concluded just before the well-documented subsequent periods, which others have chronicled. I hope that any readers of this book will enjoy the overall story of Jerusalem in antiquity, and perhaps even find it helpful as a volume that may be occasionally used for reference purposes.

I would like to record the invaluable assistance of my daughter Alison, who, in spite of leading a very busy life, found time to read and re-read my drafts in order to ensure good English and clarity of expression. The maps and diagrams in this book are essentially the result of the conscientious endeavours of Ben Charles, to whom I am also very grateful.

Alan J. Potter
September 2019

Abbreviations

BAR	*Biblical Archaeology Review*
BASOR	*Bulletin of the American Schools of Oriental Research*
DOP	*Dumbarton Oaks Papers*
ERH	*English Historical Review*
Eu. Jud.	*European Judaism: A Journal for the New Europe*
HTR	*The Harvard Theological Review*
IEJ	*Israel Exploration Journal*
JQR	*Jewish Quarterly Review*
JRS	*Journal of Roman Studies*
NAPNF 2	*The Nicene and Post-Nicene Fathers of the Church*, Series 2
NEAEHL	*The New Encyclopedia of Archaeological Excavations in the Holy Land*, Ephraim Stern (ed.), 1993–2008, Jerusalem
NEArch	*Near Eastern Archaeology*
PEQ	*Palestine Exploration Quarterly*
SHA	*Scriptores Historiae Augustae* (see Primary Sources)
SOAS	*Bulletin of the School of Oriental and African Studies*
WCJS	*A World Congress of Jewish Studies*

List of Maps and Diagrams

Chapter 1

Foundations

Palestine forms a small section of the Fertile Crescent that extends from the Persian Gulf, along the plains and valleys of the Tigris and the Euphrates rivers to the Anatolian plateau, before bending south-westerly along the eastern coast of the Mediterranean Sea. The cultivatable land of this crescent was the birthplace of some of the earliest Asian civilizations. Wedged between the Mediterranean in the west and the Transjordanian highlands in the east, Palestine was the land bridge forming the trade routes between Africa and Asia.

The principal international highway, the *Way of the Sea*[1] or *via maris*, meandered northwards from Egypt along Palestine's Mediterranean coast (see figure 1). At Megiddo there was an intersection with the main Transjordan trade route, before the *Way of the Sea* continued its coastal path to destinations that included Anatolia, Syria and Mesopotamia. The road was, however, fraught with danger, as travellers and traders were exposed to pirates and thieves and possible aggression from any ill-disposed peoples residing along the route.

The Judean hill country afforded a greater degree of security for interchange between the south and north along a ridge, on either side of which were steep meandering valleys. This key secondary road followed the north–south watershed from Shechem to Hebron and on to Beer-Sheba. There were intersecting crossroads where valleys cut into the hills from the coastal plains to the west and the Jordan Rift Valley to the east. Sited on this route, just to the south of where the column of hills turns slightly to the west, was Jerusalem.

In its earliest manifestation, what in the passage of time was to become the south-eastern hill (the Ophel) of Jerusalem, was the home of its first known settlers. The Ophel was well protected on the east by the precipitous Kidron Valley, which joined the deep Hinnom Valley on the southern side. To the west was the Tyropoeon Valley and to the north

1

was a low saddle leading to another hill, which later became known as Mt Moriah.

Precipitation in Palestine is quite predictable, with hardly any rainfall between May and October, but fairly plentiful from November through to March. Jerusalem receives approximately twenty-five inches of rain annually, but this is absorbed by the abundant soft porous limestone rock, obviating the materialization of any local brooks or ponds. The so-called late rains comprise moderate showers during April and early May, which help local crops to reach full maturity. As well as the defensive qualities afforded by the surrounding steep valleys, a primary reason for the development of a settlement in Jerusalem was the proximity of an enduring source of water – the Gihon Spring.[2]

A relatively unimportant spring, En Rogel,[3] was situated close to the convergence of the Hinnom and Kidron Valleys, but for most of the year it had to be used as a well.[4] It was of limited value to any permanent settlement, as the amount of water it provided was small and it would have been difficult to defend.[5] Discounting the small yield from En Rogel, ancient Jerusalem's only stable water supply was the Gihon Spring,[6] situated on the banks of the Kidron Valley, at the foot of the eastern slope of the early Jerusalem settlement. The Gihon Spring is fed by groundwater that accumulates in a subterranean cave, and each time that it fills to the brim, it empties through cracks in the rock and is siphoned to the surface. This natural feature made it necessary to accumulate water in a pool, to be available when the spring was not gushing forth.

There is archaeological evidence demonstrating the existence of a 'presence' on the Ophel in the Early Bronze Age (c.3200–2300 BCE), with further indications of habitation in caves or mud huts lower down on the eastern slope.[7] Archaeological remains indicate a similar situation in the Middle Bronze Age (c.2200–1550 BCE), with probably a small settlement on the Ophel, extending down the eastern incline to the Gihon Spring. This changed dramatically during the Late Bronze Age (c.1550–1200 BCE) with the construction of a system of artificial terraces that enabled more sophisticated houses to be built on the slopes leading down to the Kidron Valley. As the terraces were, however, prone to subsidence, they needed constant maintenance.[8]

In the mid-fifteenth century BCE, Egyptian Pharaoh Thutmose III began military action against a number of small city-states who viewed the alternative north-eastern Syrian superpower, the Mitanni, as their ultimate overlord. The dual purpose of the campaign was to ensure access to resources such as cedar, copper and tin from the coastal regions of *Djahy*,[9] and also to gain control over the vital trade routes that passed through the Levant.[10] At the Battle of Megiddo, Thutmose defeated a coalition of Canaanite tribes and established Egyptian dominance over Palestine.[11] In order to ensure the continuation of Egyptian authority, local vassal governors were appointed to the individual Syro-Palestinian city-states.

The power and influence of the Mitanni, however, had not been dissipated and there were numerous rebellions by city-states seeking to switch their allegiances. Thutmose III and his late-fifteenth-century successor, Amenhotep II, had to undertake regular military excursions in order to maintain Egyptian hegemony over Palestine. The emergence of a rival regional super-power, the Hittites, fostered a change in the relationship between the Egyptians and the Mitanni from conflict to peaceful alliance and, for the former, an era of peace and prosperity ensued. Insights into the international system in place during the fourteenth century BCE have been afforded by the discovery of an archive referred to as the Amarna Letters.[12]

A number of these clay tablets, providing the earliest known literary references to Jerusalem and Bethlehem, were written to the rulers of Egypt by their client prince in Jerusalem, Abdi-Heba. The Jerusalem dignitary begs for assistance against of marauding outlaws, complains that Egyptian slave-troops (or mercenaries) have burgled his own house, and describes the anarchic conditions prevailing in Palestine in general and locally in Bethlehem:

> [...] *the hostility against me is strong* [...] *send me garrison troops* [...] *The 'Apiru plunder all the lands of the king. If there are archers (here) in this year, the lands of the king, my lord, will remain (intact)* [...] *I was almost killed by the men of the land of Nubia in my own house* [...] *There is not a single governor (remaining) to the king* [...] *The entire land of the king has revolted* [...] *a town of the land of Jerusalem, Bit-Lahmi by name, a town belonging to the king, has gone over to the people of Keilah.*[13]

Notwithstanding intermittent conflicts between nations, the cohesion of the eastern Mediterranean region during the Late Bronze Age, depended upon a system of mutually respectful diplomatic relations between the so-called *Great Kings*, who received tribute from numerous lesser rulers. In Palestine, city-states operating under Egyptian sovereignty were predominant. However, during the thirteenth and the twelfth centuries BCE, as the Iron Age unfolded, the entire system began to collapse, in response to a combination of demographic and technological changes and aggression from overseas invaders.

Probably emanating from the north-west, an alliance of Mediterranean peoples, which included the Philistines, initiated the demise of the Anatolian Hittite empire.[14] Egypt was also compelled to defend itself against invasion by so-called 'Sea-Peoples' and in the process lost control of its Palestinian territories, at a time when the Assyrian empire was relatively impotent and unable to step into the political vacuum.

Much of the northern Palestinian coast comprised Phoenician city-states such as Acco,[15] Tyre and Sidon. In towns such as Gaza and Ashkelon, the Philistines established themselves on the southern Palestinian coast and it is not unreasonable to suppose that the very arrival of the 'Sea-Peoples' caused population movements away from the coast. In addition, the Aramaeans, who had previously occupied the fringes of the arable land around the Fertile Crescent, began to spread into the lower more productive regions.[16] Other ethnically, politically and religiously diverse clans and tribes were also present, particularly in the central hill country. Some may have been Semites who had lived in Palestine for centuries and there were newer settlers that included escapees from Egypt and sundry economic migrants, all contributing further to the diverse mix of races and cultures in Palestine.

Not surprisingly, the inhabitants of the settlement on the eastern slopes of Jerusalem were wholly dependent upon farming and their domestic livestock. In the semi-arid climate where even the winter rain was unreliable, technological innovations such as iron tools and improvements in the construction of terraces, gave impetus to the husbandry of fruit trees and vines, for harvesting at a different time of the year to the cereal crops grown in the plains and valley floors.[17]

The combination of the various stresses resulting from the inflows of dissimilar cultures, political disturbances, technological adjustments and the termination of Egyptian authority, altered the North-Syrian and Canaanite city-state system beyond recognition. The entire region experienced a period of political autonomy, in which the urban centres were replaced by new ethno-political configurations and various regions of the Levant were inhabited by different societies. The realignment of the socio-political structures resulted in new smaller settlements on the sites of the old cities and new villages springing up in the previously sparsely inhabited hill country.

The Early Iron Age villagers of the central hill country perhaps included the Israelite clans and tribes described in the Book of Judges, and *in those days there was no king in Israel; every man did what was right in his own eyes.*[18]

Chapter 2

David

The traditional source of our understanding of this period is the Old Testament. The biblical narratives, however, were written from religious rather than historical perspectives. They were compiled long after the actual events had taken place and are subject to inconsistencies. Understandably, the biblical accounts have been subjected to rigorous academic challenges, and the material referring to David, the first king of the supposed United Monarchy of Judah and Israel, does not submit easily to critical historical examination.[1] Attempts to verify or add to the Old Testament version of events with archaeological evidence and or non-biblical records have largely disappointed, leading some to conclude that the populations of Judah and Israel were not sufficiently stable during the tenth century BCE to support a comprehensive regional political entity.[2]

In biblical terms, the pre-Israelite inhabitants of Jerusalem were a Canaanite tribe called Jebusites and their settlement was referred to as Jebus.[3] Whether or not the occupants of the hill country comprised the original twelve tribes of Israel, they were certainly in fierce conflict with the Philistines who were attempting to extend their sphere of influence.[4] It was against this backdrop of struggle that Saul emerged as leader of the anti-Philistine factions. Saul's kingdom was a loosely defined and administered territory, the inhabitants of which looked to him for protection.[5] The court was based about six miles north-east of Jerusalem, in a settlement/village known as Gibeah, and it was here that he was joined by David, a native of Bethlehem. The manner of David joining Saul's court varies in different biblical stories, from innocent shepherd boy selected by Samuel, to musician, to giant slayer, but probably, he was simply a young professional soldier who became Saul's armour bearer.[6]

Although the exact dates are uncertain, towards the conclusion of the eleventh century and the early years of the tenth century BCE, events occurred that culminated with David taking Jerusalem. At some point

David fell out of favour at the royal household, and before the demise of Saul, David was variously a fugitive in hiding, leader of a private roaming army, and a mercenary serving A'chish, the king of the Philistine city-state of Gath.[7] The Philistine army crushed Saul's forces at the battle of Mount Gilboa[8] in the Jezreel Valley, and although Abner and Ish-bosheth, surviving relatives of Saul, attempted to maintain leadership, effectively the reign of the house of Saul had ended with his death. For safety reasons the administration centre moved eastwards from Gibeah to Mananaim in the Transjordan.[9]

Perhaps fortunately for the later legitimacy of his reign, due to fears that they might switch sides, David and his mercenaries were not allowed to fight alongside the Philistines at the battle which ended Saul's life.[10] David took advantage of the power vacuum that then existed and established a base eighteen miles south of Jerusalem, in the town of Hebron, where the southern Judean tribes appointed him to be their king.[11] Hostilities existed for some years between David and the house of Saul, but as time went on, the latter became increasingly impotent. Eventually both Abner and Ish-bosheth were assassinated, and in the end the northern Israelite tribes were left with no alternative other than to make peace with David and also anoint him as their king.[12]

The independent city of Jerusalem, situated on the central north-south watershed, dominated the mountain crest route between David's northern and southern kingdoms. Unsurprisingly, it became evident to David that this location would be ideal as his headquarters and administrative centre for both kingdoms. There were no apparent political ties between the Jebusites, who occupied Jerusalem's south-eastern hill and any of the Jewish tribes. Accordingly, neither those in the north nor those in the south would have reason to be jealous or resent the founding of a new capital at Jerusalem.

On the eastern slope of the Ophel ridge was the vitally important Gihon Spring. Although Jerusalem was fortified and protected by steep valleys on three sides, there is no mention of a siege or battle that enabled David to capture the city. The hypothesis that David's army managed to gain surprise access to Jerusalem from the vicinity of the Gihon Spring stems from the biblical phrase: *whoever would strike the Jeb'usites, let him get up the water shaft to attack.*[13] The mountain is formed from soluble limestone and dolomite and characterized by underground drainage systems and caves. During the latter years of the eighth century BCE, engineers were to adapt the natural fissures and crevices in the rock formation to facilitate the construction of a tunnel to divert the waters of the Gihon Spring. It is quite feasible, therefore, that David's army found a way through these caves into Jerusalem to secure an easily defendable, populated and undamaged city.[14]

Jebusite Jerusalem now became the City of David situated on the Ophel (see figure 2). Some confusion was created by a first-century CE source maintaining that David's *stronghold* was on the *far higher* hill,[15] which can only mean the Western Hill. This assertion is mistaken as, of course, were later works that perpetuated the error. Numerous subsequent excavations have confirmed that the City of David was located east of the Tyropoeon Valley.[16]

Estimates of the area of the City of David have included 10.87 acres[17] and also *less than nine acres*.[18] An alternative estimate of *a bare 12 acres at most* has been used together with an assumed density figure of 160–200 persons per acre, to conclude that the population *cannot have been much more than 2,400 (12×200) and probably numbered somewhat less, say 2,000.*[19] In this hypothesis, no distinction was made between the inhabitants of the Jebusite settlement and David's Jerusalem. If David's army had captured the city without a bloody battle or mass exodus of Jebusites, neither of which are mentioned in the Old Testament, then the population would have been expanded by David's soldiers and subsequently their wives and children.

Notwithstanding that the Gihon Spring was outside the city walls, it is difficult to minimize the importance to Jerusalem of having its own supply of water. A different approach to the population question could be taken by considering how many people this source of spring water could support. After taking into account the amount that could reasonably be collected in buckets for domestic use, excluding natural wastage and irrigational outflows, and making a judicious estimate of daily consumption per head, a maximum population figure of 2,500 is indicated.[20]

Tradition has it that the ancient Israelites maintained a tented shrine containing Moses' Ark of the Covenant. In the tenth century BCE the shrine was situated possibly c.20 miles to the north of Jerusalem in the archaic walled city of Shiloh,[21] or possibly c.10 miles to the west in Kiriath-jearim. Wherever it was located, soon after the conquest, David organized the transfer of the Ark to a specially erected tent in Jerusalem.[22] This not only reinforced David's position as protector of a unified Judean/Israelite cult, but also symbolized that henceforth the focal point and hub of the Jewish religion was in Jerusalem. Historically, threshing floors served as sites for holy rituals[23] and on the high hill to the north of the existing city walls, David built an altar on a threshing floor that he purchased from Araunah the Jebusite,[24] who was possibly the king or ruler of Jerusalem when it fell to David.[25] David's payment of fifty shekels of silver suggests that this was a place of special significance, and it was here on Mt Moriah that David's son Solomon would construct a temple complex to emphasize the might of the king and to worship Yahweh.

The lack of a centralized controlling power following the twelfth-century CE collapse of Egyptian authority had possibly ended, or at least drastically curtailed state slavery and the corvée in Palestine.[26] However, state slavery and civil obligations to carry out work for the crown became integral to David's system of governance. Partly in order to facilitate such projects as the construction of his palace within the old Jebusite Ophel precinct, David instigated a census to register those liable for taxes, corvée and forced labour. An overseer named Adoram was assigned to take charge of the corvée and the coerced slave gangs, which included conquered peoples such as the Ammonites.[27]

The traditional view is that David was the great warrior and his son Solomon was the accomplished builder and although these attributes did exist, the construction of David's palace indicates that they were not mutually exclusive. David demonstrated his military prowess by successfully defending himself against the Philistines and conducted successful campaigns against the peoples of various surrounding territories such as the Moabs, the Edomites and the Ammonites, supported by Syrian mercenaries. In particular David conducted a successful war against Hadadezer, king of Zobah,[28] and the kingdom of Aram-Damascus, which sent an army to assist Hadadezer. David bolstered his treasury with large amounts of bronze and shields made of gold, which he looted from Zobah. Additionally, the Syrians of Hamath, who had also been in conflict with Hadadezer, further rewarded David with articles of gold, silver and bronze.[29] Nevertheless, David's contribution to the development of Jerusalem was principally political and it was left to Solomon to elevate the Iron Age town into an imposing city, principally by extending the city to the north and overseeing the construction of a magnificent Temple–Palace complex.

David was not viewed by the various settlements and tribal groups throughout Judah and Israel in the same way that they looked to Saul for protection against a common enemy. His kingdom was more of a city-state based in Jerusalem and, of course, there undoubtedly would have been some resentment of his rule. In an attempt to make his position more secure, David appointed loyal Levite priests from his original capital, Hebron, as administrators of the unified kingdom.[30] His ruthlessness is illustrated by the handing over of seven of Saul's male descendants to be executed by the Gibeonites.[31] The biblical narrative[32] suggests that this was done to appease God and end a three-year famine or alternatively as retribution for the *bloodguilt*[33] incurred by Saul's murderous treatment of the Gibeonites. Nevertheless, the elimination of so many of Saul's lineage did eradicate a potential threat to David's position, although this episode was bound to cause further bitterness.

A revolt led by David's son Absalom had such widespread support that David was obliged to temporarily leave Jerusalem, and even after the defeat and death of Absalom there was some uncertainty over whether or not David had enough support amongst the tribal leaders of Judah and Israel to assure his reinstatement.[34] A malcontent named Sheba from the tribe of Benjamin led yet another rebellion that had to be suppressed before David's rule in Jerusalem could once again be deemed secure.[35] Henceforth the underlying divisions within the united monarchy became more pronounced as the northern Israelite clans were subjected to discrimination in the form of punitive taxes and the imposition of forced labour.[36]

As David neared the end of his life, his eldest surviving son Adonijah made a determined effort to ensure that it was he that was to accede to his Father's throne. A very public and extravagant ceremony was arranged near En Rogel to sanction the progression of David's eldest surviving son to the throne of Israel and Judah.[37] Nevertheless, David chose to grant his more favoured son, Solomon, the royal title of king.[38] Effectively, David and Solomon were co-rulers for a short period until David died in around 972 BCE, but, importantly, Adonijah's attempt to seize the throne had been circumvented and Solomon's succession was ensured.

Chapter 3

Solomon

As David neared the end of his life the political situation in the 'United Monarchy' was delicately poised, and significantly Solomon was not publicly proclaimed king in Jerusalem with the general agreement of the Judean and Israelite leaders. Instead, in approximately 973 BCE, Solomon was anointed as his father's co-regent at the Gihon Spring by a select few of David's priests and courtiers.[1] Following the demise and burial of David, Solomon's sole rule commenced in around 972 BCE. Emulating his father's ruthlessness, Solomon immediately consolidated his position by ordering the deaths of his elder brother Adonijah and his supporters.[2]

The Mt Moriah threshing floor, where an altar had been erected, was the chosen site for a grand temple. Even while David was on the throne, plans were made for the edifice, with stores of iron, bronze, cedar timbers and dressed stones being made ready.[3] The fulfilment of the task, however, fell to Solomon who, in the fourth year of his reign,[4] levelled off the northern hill to make a platform for work to commence on the new palace and temple compound.

The Temple dimensions are given as sixty cubits long, twenty cubits wide and thirty cubits high[5] (approximately 105×35×52½ feet), but despite these details a precise plan cannot be reconstructed, as, for example, there is no information regarding the width of the walls. Clearly, however, the Temple was too small for general public use, and was intended as a house for Yahweh and a chapel for the royal family and senior priests. The Temple was fronted by a large vestibule, beyond which stood the main temple hall with the inner sanctuary situated at the western end. The building comprised three storeys, each five cubits (c.9 feet) high, surrounded by side chambers, and the tripartite plan, as well as the decorations and furnishings, appears to have been typical of the day, with eclectic features paralleling those from Egypt to Mesopotamia. This was partially due to the lack of building skills

11

amongst the inhabitants of Jerusalem, which meant that Solomon had to rely on hired external labour, and is what one would have expected for a sacred precinct constructed and decorated by Phoenician craftsmen.[6]

To preclude any stonework from being seen inside the temple, the walls were lined with boards of cedar that had fruit and flowers carved into it and the floor was covered with cypress wood. The inner sanctuary housed two cherubim made of olivewood and overlaid with gold. Each stood ten cubits (c.17 feet) high with wingspans also of ten cubits that touched in the centre of the sanctuary. The wooden walls and doors were covered with carvings of cherubim, palm trees and flowers overlaid with gold.[7]

For his bronze embellishments to the temple, Solomon once again needed skills that were not to be found amongst the artisans of Jerusalem. He hired Hiram, an expert craftsman from the city of Tyre, to cast two huge hollow bronze pillars to be placed in the temple vestibule. Including the ornate capitals, decorated with sculptured pomegranates, on the crest of the pillars, the columns were forty feet high. Echoing the symbolism of the images of the fruits and flowers carved into the cedar wall coverings, the pomegranate engravings represented fertility. The twin bronze pillars at the northern and southern ends of the entrance to the Temple, had a standard ancient Near Eastern temple significance marking the entrance to the heavens.[8] In the south-east corner of the inner court stood a great bronze bowl (the *molten* or *brazen sea*) resting upon twelve bulls, three facing each of the four corners of the world. Additionally, ten ornate bronze stands were constructed with wheels to give them the appearance of chariots. These stands supported large bronze lavers,[9] which were more practicable for priestly ablutions than the vast *molten sea* bowl.

The chronology of the biblical narrative is almost certainly contrived to fit the religious message of the Jewish scribes. Additionally, bearing in mind that the authors were writing while in exile in Babylon some four hundred years later, the description of Solomon's Temple is likely to be more faithful to the situation that existed just before the destruction wrought in 586 BCE, than when the temple was initially constructed. In the absence of alternative sources, however, our perceptions of this period of time in Jerusalem must necessarily be guided by the accounts given in the books of the Old Testament.

The Temple took seven years to complete, but it took a further thirteen years to finish the work on the palace complex.[10] Before the palace stood a magnificent Hall of Pillars and a Throne Hall where Solomon would hand down his arbitrary judgements.[11] Six steps with ornate lions on either side, led up to Solomon's ivory throne, which was overlaid with gold. There were two further lions either side of the armrests and a calf's head at the back of the throne.[12]

One of Solomon's many wives was reputedly the daughter of an Egyptian pharaoh, possibly the offspring of Siamun (978–959 BCE) or Psusennes II (959–945 BCE). Either because she was a favoured wife and/or owing to her royal Egyptian status, she was endowed with her own palace within the complex. It is reasonable to assume that her palace was adjacent to Solomon's and the most likely site of the royal living quarters was south of the Temple in the area between it and the original City of David.[13] Notwithstanding the half dozen Biblical references to Solomon's Egyptian wife,[14] it could be argued that such a marriage was unlikely on the grounds that foreign princes who married Egyptian princesses were obliged to move to the Egyptian court, because Egyptian princesses were never sent away to a foreign country.

Another of Solomon's constructions within the Temple/Palace compound was the *House of the Forest of Lebanon*, with its cedar beams and pillars.[15] Its purpose is unknown and possibly it was simply the repository for Solomon's golden drinking vessels as well as his shields made of gold.[16]

Solomon's expansion onto Mount Moriah to build his temple and palace compound more than doubled the size of Jerusalem (see figure 3). One estimate of the area of the city suggests almost 32 acres, with a density of between 160 and 200 inhabitants per acre and a 'not far off' total population of between 4,500 and 5,000.[17] The selected density coefficients do, however, seem to suggest a total population residing in Solomon's Jerusalem of somewhere between 5,120 and 6,400.

Solomon's architectural exploits were by no means confined to Jerusalem, as he has been credited with major constructions in places such as Hazor, Megiddo and Gezer. He is also mentioned as the builder of the earth-filled terrace walls, which served as the northern defence line of the Ophel, and which were known as the Millo.[18] However, the Millo is also mentioned following David's capture of Jerusalem, in the context of David building the city from the Millo inward.[19] It seems probable that the Millo existed during at least the latter part of Jebusite rule, and that Solomon adapted it to take account of the northwards expansion of Jerusalem onto Mount Moriah.

Using the same chief slave master[20] that David had employed, Solomon made very extensive use of forced labour to achieve his building projects.[21] The numbers of forced labourers quoted in the biblical accounts is almost certainly exaggerated, but, nevertheless, indicate that forced labour gangs had become an important aspect of state policy. The major source of the slaves was, of course, prisoners of war,[22] but following the failed rebellion of Sheba against King David, the state slavery structure began to be supplemented by the corvée imposed upon the northern Israelite clans. Solomon greatly extended this divisive practice, ultimately contributing significantly to the northern tribes' rejection of his son as successor to the throne of the united monarchy.

Crucial to Solomon's contribution to the development of Jerusalem were the labour-intensive activities of mining, quarrying and construction, into which slavery and the accumulation of wealth were inexorably interwoven. Forced labour enabled the metallurgical industry, the quarrying of stone and the erection of buildings and walls to proceed at little cost and the economic benefits of the enterprises were maximized accordingly.[23]

Biblical accounts lead us to believe that great wealth was accumulated in Jerusalem during the reign of Solomon.[24] Consistent with the authors' idealization of Solomon, before he was corrupted by his foreign wives, these accounts are likely to be exaggerated. Nevertheless, it is reasonable to assume that Solomon's Jerusalem did benefit from various sources of income. The extent of the kingdom meant that it had jurisdiction over at least significant parts of the coastal passage between Egypt and the Jezreel Valley, the Transjordan road between the Red Sea and Damascus, and the important secondary route between the Gulf of Aqabah and the Mediterranean ports of the Phoenicians. Control of these highways would have allowed Solomon to levy customs duties and transit taxes. Additional sources of wealth would have arisen from a joint shipping/commercial enterprise with the Phoenicians,[25] and perhaps gifts from overseas rulers, such as the fabled Queen of Sheba![26]

Once again, it is difficult to place too much reliance on the biblical accounts, which initially portray a wise, wealthy and expansionist leader, and later, having been led astray by foreign wives, a polytheistic king that displeases his god.[27] This criticism is highly artificial as in the heterogeneous Jerusalem population ruled by David, and then Solomon, it would be regarded as quite normal for there to be shrines to other gods. Although Yahweh had emerged as the national god, and had been formalized by Solomon through the inclusion of the Temple within the complex of royal buildings, Yahwistic monotheism was a concept belonging to an age far into the future.[28]

Solomon's death occurred in around 931 BCE and although we will never know just how truly unified the monarchy of Judah and Israel was under David and Solomon, the early years of the tenth century BCE did at least end the isolation of the hill people of central Palestine. Henceforth the international culture of the Near East and its commercial activities would interact with the Palestinian hill people, especially those in the developing city of Jerusalem.

Chapter 4

Separate Kingdoms

The Levite priests from the region of David's original power base in Hebron dominated the administration of the unified monarchy, and while reference is made to Solomon's vast contingents of forced labour comprising solely foreigners,[1] this does not reconcile with Jeroboam, an Ephraimite officer, being placed in charge *over all the forced labor of the house of Joseph.*[2] The house of Joseph comprised the Ephraim/Israel tribes, who made up Saul's old powerbase, and to have some of their number used as virtual slaves gave rise to a feeling of alienation. The prophet, Ahijah, is reported to have proclaimed to Jeroboam that Yahweh was *about to tear the kingdom from the hand of Solomon, and give you ten tribes.*[3] Jeroboam fled to Egypt, possibly due to Ahijah's prophesy, but most likely because he had fallen out of favour with Solomon, who feared his ambition.

With his capital at Jerusalem, King David had united the Israelite tribes and his son Solomon had extended the power and opulence of the city. There was, however, an undercurrent of resentment fuelled by the unequal treatment of the clans. The people of the north had been treated as a vassal nation ever since Sheba's unsuccessful attempt to overthrow David, and the discrimination had increased during Solomon's reign. The imposition of forced labour and punitive taxes brought about an unexpected backlash in the wake of Solomon's death in c.931 BCE.[4]

Although not specifically mentioned in the Old Testament, Solomon's son Rehoboam would have been ratified as the new king in Jerusalem, as the legitimate heir of the kingdom established by David. Perhaps as a sign of their dissension, the northern tribes had not sent representatives to Jerusalem to acknowledge Rehoboam as Solomon's successor. In view of this Rehoboam was obliged to travel to Shechem to seek confirmation that all the tribes accepted him as the new king. The aspirations of Jeroboam, combined with the high regard with which he was held, led to him returning from Egypt to rule the breakaway northern kingdom of Israel. With an almost unbelievable lack of subtly, Rehoboam appointed David's and Solomon's hated senior slave master, Adoram, as his lead negotiator. The discussions failed completely, with Adoram being stoned to death and Rehoboam being forced to retreat to his capital.[5]

Jerusalem was now the religious and political centre of the weakened state of Judah (see figure 4), presided over by Rehoboam between approximately 931 and 914 BCE – if he ruled for seventeen years.[6] Extending northwards to Galilee and the town of Dan was Jeroboam's larger Ephraimite/Israelite state, henceforth known as the Kingdom of Israel. To the west, the new breakaway state encompassed the Plain of Sharon, which gave it access to the Mediterranean, and in the east were large tracts of Transjordan including the cities of Ramoth-gilead and Dibon.[7] In the south were the borders with Judah and the disputed, and perhaps reduced, territory of the tribe of Benjamin,[8] which for the next four decades, was the scene of intermittent warfare between Judah and Israel.

Israel had control parts of the coastal road (The Way of the Sea or *via maris*) and the Transjordan highway, two of the major north/south trade routes. Additionally, the Dothan Plain and the Shechem Pass allowed for the passage of traffic from the east to the west and *vice versa*. Not surprising therefore, Israel was economically and militaristically more powerful than Judah.

The territorial disputes between Judah and Israel were not their only boundary concerns. The partition of the 'United Monarchy' facilitated greater independence for the neighbouring kingdoms of Ammon, Moab and particularly Edom, whose border with Judah became quite fluid. Additionally, to the north was Syria, growing in military strength and increasingly hostile, and to the south was Egypt's relatively new twenty-second Dynasty.[9] Both Judah and Israel lost territory to other kingdoms during the forty years following their separation.[10]

The Old Testament lists fifteen cities[11] that Rehoboam fortified for the defence of Judah. One of these was the Philistine city of Gath, where previously his grandfather David had served as a mercenary. Probably, Gath was under the control of Judah at this point in time and, together with the buttress town of Aijalon, protected Judah's north-west frontier. Further south on the western fringes of Judah, Soco and Lachish were strengthened as a deterrent against Philistine aggression. Most of the towns that were reinforced, however, protected the southern approaches to Jerusalem. This group included Bethlehem and Hebron, and served to discourage incursions from Edom, as well as enforcing the power base of Jerusalem and its control over the countryside, thus preventing any further splintering of the state of Judah.

An early major ordeal for the divided kingdoms came about when the Egyptian Pharaoh Sheshonq undertook a military campaign in Palestine to secure domestic prestige and to reassert Egyptian influence over the important trade routes of the region. In accordance with the custom established by his predecessors, Sheshonq recorded the names of the cities he conquered or claimed dominion over. The lists, found in the Temple of Amon at the Karnak temple complex near Luxor, are only partially legible and there are translational difficulties. Nevertheless, it seems that the northern kingdom suffered the main thrust of the Egyptian crusade, and Judah was relatively unscathed. After subduing a number of Judah's southern fortified towns, Sheshonq arrived at Jerusalem *in the fifth year of King Rehobo'am*.[12] To save the city Rehoboam succumbed without resistance and allowed the Pharaoh to remove treasures from the Temple and the royal palace, including Solomon's shields of gold.[13] The Egyptian records accord with the biblical sources in dating Sheshonq's Palestinian campaign in around 926/925 BCE.[14]

Rehoboam died c.914 BCE and was succeeded by his son Abijah (Abijam). The hostilities in the form of occasional border skirmishes that had been experienced between Judah and Israel throughout Rehoboam's kingship continued during Abijah's relatively short reign of three years.[15] Abijah is reported to have had a major military triumph over Jeroboam's Israelite army, capturing a number of towns and villages, including Bethel. However, the exaggerated account of Abijah's victory is typical of the biblical bias promoting the Jerusalem-based Yahwistic cult over the less favoured polytheistic northern kingdom. The Old Testament tells us little else of Abijah's time as king in Jerusalem other than that he had fourteen wives and thirty-eight children![16]

As Abijah's son Asa *reigned forty-one years in Jerusalem* (c.911–870 BCE), he became king of Judah at a relatively young age. He is credited with various acts which suited the theological and political aspirations of the compilers of the Old Testament. These included banishing male prostitutes, removing the apostate queen mother, casting out idols and bringing votive gifts into the Temple.[17]

A sizeable Ethiopian incursion into southern Judah was reported to have been repulsed by Asa's army[18] in around 896 BCE, near the town of Mareshah, which his grandfather Rehoboam had fortified thirty or so years earlier. The authenticity of this narrative is questionable, however, and it is possibly a transposition of a later sixth-century BCE event.[19] Although both Judah and Israel had many other actual and potential enemies to contend with throughout the reigns of Rehoboam and Abijah, and the majority of the Asa's monarchy, hostilities still existed between the two Jewish kingdoms. Notwithstanding Old Testament hyperbole, however, the belligerence primarily took the form of fairly minor encounters on the border between Benjamin and Ephraim (Israel).

The Israel/Judean aggression reached a peak in c.895 BCE when the king of Israel, Baasha, fortified the town of Ramah about ten miles north of Jerusalem.[20] This was an extension of his predecessors' aims to curtail religious defections from Israel, and was also a direct threat to the commercial and military viability of Jerusalem. Asa responded by appealing to, and paying bribes to Ben-hadad I, the king of the Aram-Damascus Syrians. To relieve the pressure on Asa, the Syrians occupied Galilee causing Baasha to redeploy his forces, thus allowing Asa to dismantle the fortifications. The continued use of the corvée that David had reintroduced to Palestine is demonstrated by Asa's proclamation that no Judean was exempt from the task of recycling the stones and timbers from the disassembled Ramah ramparts to shore up Judean defences in the nearby towns of Mizpah and Geba.[21]

Asa's long-lasting administration of Judah from his capital in Jerusalem contrasted with a ferocious maelstrom of regicides, civil wars and rival monarchies in Israel, especially during the period from 885 until 880 BCE, when a former army field commander named Omri finally emerged as the sole undisputed king of Israel. In a fairly standard Old Testament format, the commendable deeds of Asa as a new king diverge from the actions at the end of his reign that were considered ideologically unsound. In particular, when he was in poor health Asa sought help from physicians rather than from Yahweh.[22] Asa's debilitating illness was the catalyst for the 873 BCE appointment of his son as co-regent, and three years later Jehoshaphat became sole monarch upon his father's death.

Notwithstanding a measure of inconsistency and one particular criticism, the biblical texts generally afford Jehoshaphat a favourable and pious role, occasionally with exaggerations that detract from their reliability as historical sources. The inconsistency concerns Jehoshaphat's effectiveness in eliminating non-Yahwistic idol worship: He did *what was right in the sight of the Lord; yet the high places were not taken away, and the people still sacrificed and burned incense on the high places*, conflicts with *he took the high places and the Asherim out of Judah*.[23] The criticism relates to his co-operation with the Israelites, who were considered to be apostate.[24] On the plus side, however, Jehoshaphat is credited with legal reforms to ensure that there were competent, honest and impartial judges, both in Jerusalem and Judah's other main cities.[25] Additionally, Jehoshaphat dispatched preachers to the Judean towns and cities, travelled extensively himself to disseminate spirituality and also completed the task begun by his father to rid the land of male prostitutes.[26]

Rapprochement between the southern and northern kingdoms had begun c.880 BCE after Omri had secured full control in Israel and established a new capital in the city of Samaria. At this point in time Asa was still on the Judean throne, but Jehoshaphat initially appears to have had reservations and took measures to bolster Judah's defences against Israel.[27] The mistrust diminished, however, especially after Ahab succeeded his father as king of Israel in c.873 BCE. A marriage was arranged between Athaliah, the daughter of Ahab and his infamous Phoenician wife Jezebel, to Jehoshaphat's son Jehoram, thus creating a bond between the two royal families.

The close ties between Israel and Judah initiated by Omri enabled benefits to accrue to both kingdoms, particularly during the contemporaneous reigns of his son, Ahab and Jehoshaphat. The Omride dynasty prevailed in Israel for around four decades, and its internal stability, military strength and international policies enabled the Jerusalem based kingdom of Judah to thrive economically,[28] and probably for the first time since the days of Solomon, merchants could once again move freely overland from Jerusalem to Phoenicia.

Each kingdom, free from the burden of defending itself against the other, grew strong militarily. Notwithstanding self-evident hyperbole, the number of fighting units in Jerusalem made impressive reading,[29] but, nevertheless, in matters of military cooperation, Judah was Israel's junior partner. In July/August 853 BCE,[30] Jehoshaphat's army took part in the Battle of Qarqar, on the west bank of the Orontes River in western Syria. Imperialistic Assyrian expansion led by Shalmaneser III provoked the Syrian (Aramaean) and Palestinian states into a defensive coalition, but Jehoshaphat's soldiers were presumably deemed to be part of Ahab's forces, as Judah's military contribution fails to be listed in the Assyrian record, *the Monolith Inscription*.[31]

Jehoshaphat appears to have embarked on a proposed maritime expedition, but the biblical details are hazy and contradictory, and in any case the venture failed.[32] Somewhat mystifying is the report of an attempted invasion of Jerusalem from a number of neighbouring states, which was ultimately confounded by the intervention of Yahweh.[33] A military action of greater historical veracity occurred later in 853 BCE, when Jehoshaphat supported Ahab in a war to retake Ramoth-gilead from Hadadezer,[34] the king of the Aram-Damascus Syrians. There is a hint of a deferential role in Jehoshaphat's reply to Ahab when asked to join the campaign: *I am as you are, my people as your people, my horses as your horses.*[35] Nevertheless, the Syrians were successful at the battle of Ramoth-gilead, during which Ahab sustained a wound from which he would not recover. Jehoshaphat was forced to flee back to the safety of his palace in Jerusalem and, in the following year, he appointed his son Jehoram as co-regent.

Ahab's son Ahaziah reigned as king of Israel for about one year, but in 852 BCE he died with no male heir and was therefore succeeded by his brother Jehoram (Joram).[36] The sister of Ahaziah and Jehoram (Joram) was, of course, Athaliah, the wife of Jehoram of Judah, who had been elevated from co-regent to sole monarch when Jehoshaphat died in Jerusalem in 848 BCE. To ensure his sovereignty against any possible challenges, immediately upon his ascension to the throne, king Jehoram of Judah arranged for the murder of his six brothers *and also some of the princes of Israel.*[37]

The Book of the Chronicles of the Kings of Judah and *The Book of the Chronicles of the Kings of Israel* were records kept by scribes in Jerusalem and Samaria respectively, detailing the activities of the kings of the separate kingdoms of Judah and Israel. These now unfortunately missing and unavailable royal archives were used on numerous occasions as source material by the compilers of the Old Testament books 1 and 2 Kings and 1 and 2 Chronicles. The Old Testament portrays the respective king Jehorams of Judah and Israel as distinct entities, but this may result from separate transcripts being kept by the royal archivers.

At the point of Ahaziah's demise and the subsequent succession of Jehoram (Joram) as king of Israel, 2 Kings 1:17 (RSV) describes them as brothers. Neither equivalent passage in the Greek Septuagint[38] nor the Hebrew Tanakh[39] specifically refer to Jehoram (Joram) as the brother of Ahaziah, leading to some speculation that perhaps the thrones of Judah and Israel were occupied by the same person.[40] Most likely, however, they were separate individuals, at a time of friendship when the two royal houses were naming heirs to the throne after each other (see figure 5).[41] Jehoram of Israel was also known as Joram and to avoid confusion from this point forward, these kings of Judah and Israel will be referred to as Jehoram and Joram respectively.

Both kingdoms began to decline in the mid-ninth century BCE, as territories under their control began to revolt. Judah also suffered the loss of income from the trade routes to Arabia as Edom regained its independence, and this, in turn, encouraged the city of Libnah to rebel against the hegemony of Jerusalem.[42]

Additionally, threats to the independence of Israel and Judah loomed large from the Assyrian and the Aram-Damascus Syrian empires. Between 849 and 845 BCE, Shalmaneser III's Assyrian army attempted further military ventures into Palestine, but just as in 853 BCE, these failed to progress beyond the region of Qarqar.

During the period between his success at the 853 BCE Battle of Ramoth-gilead, and his eventual overthrow in 842 BCE, Hadadezer, the Syrian king, pursued very aggressive policies in Samaria, which experienced famine, inflation and even cannibalism.[43] Even making the assumption that the Kingdom of Israel bore the brunt of Syrian aggression, life during this period would still have been very harsh in the other Palestine territories, including Judah and its capital city of Jerusalem.

Chapter 5

Syrians and Assyrians

841 BCE was to prove to be a fundamentally important year in the history of the whole Near Eastern region. For Jerusalem, it began with the death of Jehoram, king of Judah, and the ascension to the throne of his twenty-two-year-old son, Ahaziah.

Further east, Shalmaneser III launched yet another military campaign to secure control of the territory bordering the eastern Mediterranean. During the preceding year, Hazael had murdered and replaced Hadadezer as king of the Aram-Damascus Syrians and he now led the anti-Assyrian coalition, which on this occasion was no match for the Assyrian army. Hazael retreated to the safe haven of the virtually unassailable strongly walled city of Damascus, while Shalmaneser devastated the surrounding area, before marching into the Transjordan region of Hauran, to the east of Ramoth-gilead.

In the meantime, Israel's king Joram and his troops had been guarding Ramoth-gilead against a possible attack by Hazael's Syrian army. Reportedly, Joram was wounded in battle against the Syrians and had retired to Jezreel in order to recuperate.[1] It seems improbable that Hazael would take his army seventy-five miles through Assyrian occupied territory, from his refuge in Damascus to Ramoth-gilead to fight against the Israelite army. It has been speculated that a skirmish with Assyrian troops seems more likely to have caused Joram's wounds.[2] The injured Joram was visited in Jezreel by his nephew, Judah's new king Ahaziah, who, as it transpired, found himself very much in the wrong place at the wrong time.

It would have been necessary for Jehu, Joram's chief of staff, to have obtained the agreement of Shalmaneser III for what happened next. Israel's Omride era ended with an extremely brutal takeover by Jehu, who murdered the kings of both Judah and Israel at Jezreel. Jehu assumed the kingship of Israel amid an enormous amount of bloodletting.[3] Probably taking the route along the Jezreel Valley, Shalmaneser III marched through Israel to the Mediterranean coast to receive gold and silver tributes from the kings of Tyre and Sidon and from the new king of Israel at the commencement of his reign in 841 BCE. Jehu is depicted bowing before Shalmaneser on one of the panels of the Assyrian stele, *The Black Obelisk*.[4]

Following the death of Ahaziah and the return of his body for burial in Jerusalem, the rightful heir to the throne of Judah was Joash.[5] As, however, Joash was a newly born baby boy, there was a power void in the royal city and the one to act decisively to fill the vacuum was the Queen Mother, Athaliah. She opportunistically seized the throne of Judah in a *coup d'état* almost as violent as that perpetrated by Jehu in Israel. Athaliah may have been the widow of king Jehoram and the mother of the recently murdered king Ahaziah, but she was not of Davidic descent – she was a half-Israelite half-Phoenician, non-Jewish, Baal-worshipping foreign princess. There was opposition, particularly from the Jewish Temple hierarchy and, if Athaliah were to rule Judah, her only chance of success would be to act with speed and alacrity to eradicate every male of Davidic lineage. Accordingly, Athaliah *arose and destroyed all the royal family of the house of Judah*.[6]

There were not as many royal princes to be dispensed with as there might have been, because forty-two had been killed by Jehu during the murderous rampage carried out while he secured control of Israel. Leaving Jezreel on his way to Samaria, Jehu encountered the forty-two relatives of Ahaziah, who were on their way to Jezreel to visit Ahaziah and Joram, unaware that they had been assassinated. The would-be visitors were taken to a pit and slaughtered.[7]

Apparently, however, there was one royal prince that survived the purges of Athaliah and Jehu – the baby Joash, who had been secreted away by Ahaziah's sister, the princess Jehosheba, with the help of Jehoiada, her husband, and a prominent temple priest, possibly Jerusalem's high priest.

In 838 BCE, while the four-year-old Joash remained out of sight and Athaliah held sway in Jerusalem, Shalmaneser III undertook his final western campaign aimed primarily against Hazael's Syrian kingdom. The Assyrian threat to Syria/Palestine then subsided as Shalmaneser, and his successor Shamshi-Adad V (c.823–810 BCE), were preoccupied by internal civil strife, as well as aggressive posturing from the kingdoms of Urartu (Armenia) in the north and Babylonia in the east.

The lull in Assyrian imperialistic ventures allowed Hazael to emerge as the dominant force in Syria/Palestine. The Syrian pre-eminence was to last for more than thirty years before the Assyrians once again sought to control the lands adjacent to the eastern seaboard of the Mediterranean Sea.

Jehosheba and Jehoiada hid the infant Joash for six years and the fact that Athaliah was unable to find and kill her grandson for so many years indicates that her tenure as Judean ruler was a period of unrest and intrigue in Jerusalem.[8] Joash was concealed and protected until he was seven years old, when Jehoiada orchestrated a *coup d'état* in around 835 BCE, with Joash being anointed king of Judah.[9] Scholars have speculated that Joash did not survive Athaliah's purge and that the seven-year-old boy had been put forward as a puppet by Jehoiada to wrest control from Athaliah. Perhaps even that the boy was the son of Jehoiada and Jehosheba. Athaliah's Baal-worshipping tendencies and her alien ancestry, not to mention the massacre of the royal family, had engendered considerable antipathy towards her and, in these circumstances, the people of Jerusalem readily accepted the new boy king as Joash, the son of Ahaziah.[10] In either case Athaliah's days were numbered and the king's guard took her *through the horses' entrance to the king's house* and slew her.[11]

The priestly Jehoiada's guardianship of Joash obviously influenced the young king, whose Yahwistic credentials were confirmed as he grew older and became interested in making repairs to the Temple. It had been well in excess of one hundred years since the Temple had been built during the time of Solomon and inevitably some renovation work had become necessary. Although funding was put in place, it seems that for many years no actual repairs were undertaken and eventually the restoration monies had to be paid directly to the craftsmen (carpenters, builders, masons and stonecutters), who *dealt honestly*,[12] and presumably more so than the priests who originally collected the funding.

In Israel in around 814 BCE, Jehu was succeeded by his son, Jehoahaz. In the face of relentless aggression Israel became subservient to the Syrians, who imposed rigid military restrictions and reduced Israel's territory to little more than the Ephraim hill country. With Israel geographically and militarily decimated, the Syrian army had free rein to pass through and take possession of the Philistine plains. They devastated the city of Gath and now posed a grave threat to Jerusalem. In order to avoid an attack on

Jerusalem and a possible sack of the city, Joash handed over the treasure from the Temple and his own palace to Hazael.[13]

The Old Testament books known as Chronicles occasionally adjust and elaborate material from the OT manuscripts entitled Kings and this additional material, the intention of which is often to provide theological and political interpretations of events, should be indulged cautiously. Obviously into this category is the assertion that Joash's mentor Jehoiada eventually died at the age of 130 years. Perhaps also Joash's subsequent apostasy, murder of Jehoiada's son and wounds inflicted by the Syrian army[14] should all be treated with a healthy dose of scepticism.

Nevertheless, both biblical sources record that Joash was murdered by his own people, and this was in around 796 BCE. The assassination was possibly motivated by revenge, because Joash had upset the priests over the handling of the Temple repairs funding and/or the murder of Jehoiada's son. Additionally, it is possible once again to speculate that Joash was an impostor, put in place by Jerusalem's priests to circumvent Athaliah's rule, and that he had simply outlived his usefulness by attempting to exert too much of his own authority.[15]

Thus, at the beginning of the eighth century BCE Joash was succeeded by his twenty-five-year-old son Amaziah. When Amaziah was initially crowned king, he would not have had sufficient strength of command to be able to deal promptly with his father's assassins. However, *as soon as the royal power was firmly in his hand he killed his servants who had slain the king his father.*[16] Assyria was now ruled by Adad-nirari III, who had ascended the throne in 810 BCE. He revived Assyrian imperialistic ambitions and instigated a series of western campaigns. Subsequently, the Assyrians began to extract tributes from many regions, including the countries of Palestine.[17]

As the Assyrians were once again growing in military strength, Syrian power was weakening commensurately and ceased to be a threat to the Kingdom of Judah. Amaziah was therefore free to raise an army for a savage attack on Edom to regain control of the trade routes to Arabia and the Red Sea Port of Eilat (Elath). The army that Amaziah put in place originally included mercenaries from Israel, but with second thoughts, he discharged these soldiers of fortune before attacking Edom. *In fierce anger* the mercenaries looted Judean towns on their way back to Samaria.[18]

Jehoash, king of Israel, had begun his reign in 797 BCE, one year before Amaziah was crowned in Jerusalem. Initially their relationship was fairly amicable and Amaziah had proposed a treaty to be sealed by the marriage of his son to Jehoash's daughter.[19] The treaty and the marriage did not materialize and after the rampage by the Israelite mercenaries, the relationship between Judah and Israel soured to such an extent that hostilities soon ensued. The cause of the war may have been that one or other of the antagonists simply felt that they could take advantage of the power vacuum created by the Syrian decline to secure domination of the region.

As a precautionary measure, king Jehoash appointed his son Jeroboam II as co-regent in 793 BCE. Jehoash then invaded Judah and some twelve miles west of Jerusalem overwhelmed Amaziah's army at Beth-shemesh, where Amaziah was taken captive. The Israelites marched on Jerusalem and gained entry to the city by destroying about six hundred feet of the north-western wall *from the Ephraim Gate to the Corner Gate*.[20] Previously when Amaziah was an infant, his father king Joash had circumvented a Syrian invasion by handing over the palace and temple treasures, and now what had accumulated since then was looted by the Israelite king Jehoash. Hostages, almost certainly including members of the royal family, were then taken back to Samaria,[21] and for the remainder of Jehoash's reign, Judah was effectively a vassal state of Israel.

With Amaziah being held prisoner in Samaria, in 791 BCE the people of Jerusalem crowned his sixteen-year-old son Azariah king of Judah.[22] Semantically, with his father still alive, Azariah might be referred to as co-regent, but in all practicable senses he was the king in charge of Judah. This situation prevailed even when Amaziah was allowed to return to Jerusalem in 781 BCE, upon the death of Jehoash. Having been responsible for the subjugation of Judah to Israel had made Amaziah deeply and lastingly unpopular. A further fifteen years passed, but in 767 BCE Amaziah got wind of a plot to assassinate him. Fearing for his life, he fled from Jerusalem to Lachish, but even there he was not safe and the conspirators caught up with him. He was murdered and his body was then returned to Jerusalem for burial. The Biblical chronology is unsound when it places the crowning of the sixteen-year-old Azariah after the death of his father.[23] Azariah's fifty-two-year long reign[24] has to be counted from 791 BCE, rather than 767 BCE.

Azariah reinforced Jerusalem's walls by building fortified towers at key points, including *the Corner Gate*,[25] at the southern end of the section of the wall destroyed by the Israelites a generation earlier when his father, Amaziah was on the throne. Understandably this incident had left an indelible mark on Azariah, who was determined to rectify a perceived weakness in Jerusalem's defensive wall. As well as bolstering the numbers of armed soldiers and making sure that they were well equipped, *In Jerusalem he made engines, invented by skilful men, to be on the towers and the corners, to shoot arrows and great stones.*[26]

Under the prolonged leadership of king Jeroboam II,[27] Israel enjoyed a remarkable resurgence and expansion, and Judah's revival was at least in part dependent upon the revitalization of its northern neighbour. The return of Edom to Judah's sphere of influence was indicative of the recovery in the fortunes of Jerusalem during the reign of Azariah. Judean power once again extended to the shores of the Red Sea and control of the port of Elath.[28] Azariah's armies also fought victoriously against the Philistines and local Arab tribes, and success against Ammon resulted in the latter being forced to make tribute payments.[29]

As Jerusalem returned to a period of prosperity, the population naturally increased. New homes had to be found outside the confines of the walls of the City of David, and as expansion to the east was inhibited by the precipitous Kidron Valley, beginning around 770 BCE, dwellings began to spring up on Jerusalem's Western Hill.[30]

However, for Azariah, his time in power was abruptly interrupted as in 750 BCE he contracted leprosy. The old king had to be quarantined and his son Jotham assumed authority as co-regent.[31] The unfortunate Azariah lived for another eleven years before Jotham became the sole monarch, but in practical terms, Jotham had been in command ever since the onset of his father's illness in 750 BCE. Jerusalem continued to flourish, both within the walled city as well as further settlement on its Western Hill. Jotham contributed building projects such as a new gate to the temple compound and reinforcing Jerusalem's wall at the Ophel.[32] The prosperity enjoyed by Jerusalem during his reign allowed Jotham to enhance the fortifications in the Judean countryside and to pursue territorial expansion east of the river Jordan. Following the death of Azariah in 739 BCE, Jotham fought a successful war against the Ammonites to ensure the continuation of their tribute obligations,[33] which continued until 735 BCE, when a change in the power structure in Jerusalem gave Ammon the opportunity to reassert its independence.

Assyria, now led by Tiglath-pileser III (744–727 BCE), was once again dominating the eastern Mediterranean seaboard as far south as Gaza, to the south of which a stele was erected to commemorate a new Assyrian/ Egyptian border. Gaza became an Assyrian port and customs post, and the coastal plain north of Philistia became an Assyrian province. Both Azariah and Jotham had provided Judean support to regional anti-Assyrian alliances, but in 735 BCE a pro-Assyrian faction in Jerusalem became dominant and instigated the elevation of Jotham's son Ahaz to the position of co-regent. Perhaps Jotham was not in good health as he only survived for a further three years, but in any case, the reins of power in Jerusalem now lay firmly in the hands of Ahaz. The aggressive Assyrian presence in the region escalated the movement of people into Jerusalem and its developing settlements on the Western Hill.

Assyrian inscriptions record that Tiglath-pileser III was extracting tributes from Ahaz (referred to as Jehoahaz), the kings of Syria and Israel and many other local rulers, including those of Transjordan.[34] The disbursements to Tiglath-pileser would have been made under duress, except perhaps those made by Ahaz, who was regarded by the other Syrian and Palestinian rulers as an Assyrian collaborator. The internal popularity of Ahaz is also questionable and certainly the compilers of the Old Testament regarded his apostate practices with disdain.[35]

Assyria had been at war with Urartu in the north and Media in the east, but the conclusion of these wars in 734 BCE allowed Tiglath-pileser to return to his quest to control the eastern Mediterranean seaboard and to deal with the anti-Assyrian alliance. The leaders of the anti-Assyrian coalition, the Syrian king Rezin and the Israelite king Pekah, reacted to Ahaz' refusal to join their alliance by attacking Jerusalem.[36] The Biblical chronology of the assault is unclear,[37] however, the synchronization implies that this occurred during the period between 735 and 732 BCE when Jotham was alive, but his co-regent Ahaz was in absolute control.

Assailed by Syria and Israel in the north, Judah was in a vulnerable position and its traditional southern enemies, the Edomites and the Philistines also began to encroach upon its territory.[38] Ahaz sent messengers asking Tiglath-pileser for help and accompanied the request with treasure from his palace and the Temple.[39] Jerusalem survived because in 732 BCE Tiglath-pileser III destroyed the anti-Assyrian coalition, overran Damascus and killed Rezin. Much of Syria/Palestine was assimilated into the Assyrian provincial system. The assertion that Ahaz' salvation resulted from his bribery and pleas for help seems implausible as Tiglath-pileser was a compellingly powerful sovereign leader, unlikely to play the role of paid mercenary.

Fortunately for Ahaz, the conclusion of the Assyrian wars with Urartu and Media had brought the conquest of the east Mediterranean seaboard once again onto the Assyrian agenda and Tiglath-pileser III's military intervention against Syria was providentially coincidental. The price to pay was, however, that Judah retained only nominal independence and was in effect an Assyrian satellite state. The extent of the reassertion of its authority was such that Assyria became predominant in the Middle East for the next one hundred years.

Chapter 6

Hezekiah

At first sight, the Old Testament references to the reigns of Ahaz and his son Hezekiah, who was only fifteen years younger than his father, present some chronological difficulties. They were co-regents from 729 until 715 BCE, when Ahaz died and Hezekiah began his sole monarchy, which lasted until 697 BCE. This was superseded by the ten-year co-regency of Hezekiah with his son Manasseh, until the death of Hezekiah in 686 BCE.[1]

The compilers of the Old Testament were well disposed towards Hezekiah, who they viewed as a pious monarch that discouraged non-Yahwistic idol worship.[2] The praise heaped upon Hezekiah should, however, be viewed in the context of the authors' desire to present him in the best possible light. He is credited with renovating the Temple doors, organizing a re-purification of the Temple and overseeing the restoration of traditional worship. Hezekiah reorganized *the priests and the Levites, division by division, each according to his service*, reintroduced the tithe system and even commanded that Temple chambers be prepared for the surplus tithes of grain, wine, oil and honey etc.[3]

The Feast of the Passover had been neglected in Jerusalem, but Hezekiah arranged for the return of this tradition and invited Jews throughout Judah and Israel to attend, following which pagan shrines were widely destroyed.[4] Centralizing Yahwistic worship in Jerusalem had political and economic overtones, for this would increase the reliance of the Judeans upon their capital city and its ruler. Allegiance to Hezekiah and the Davidic lineage would be enhanced, providing Hezekiah with firmer control both religiously and politically. It may be speculated that there was an additional benefit resulting from rallying the Jews from the Israelite kingdom to support Hezekiah's eventual clash with Assyria.

Tiglath-pileser III had created a great Assyrian empire and upon his death in 727 BCE he was succeeded by his son Shalmaneser V and once again political events to the north began to significantly impact upon Jerusalem. Encouraged by vague promises of help from Egypt, there was a general feeling amongst the vassal states of Syria and Palestine that the time was right to attempt to escape the shackles of Assyria. A Phoenician revolt against the Assyrians[5] was followed by a rebellion by the Kingdom of Israel. Although their king, Hoshea, was captured and imprisoned, the Israelites continued to resist the Assyrians from within their well-equipped and strongly fortified capital city of Samaria.

The Assyrians launched an assault on the city of Samaria in an attempt to bring an end to Israel's rebellion. The siege became protracted, partly due to a temporary distraction when the army was recalled to Assyria during an internal coup d'état. Once the Assyrian army returned, however, it was only a matter of time before Samaria was eventually forced to surrender in around 722 BCE. Large numbers of refugees had already been fleeing the conflicts in northern Palestine and the flight southwards now increased dramatically, as the local Jewish residents sought to avoid the ethnic cleansing regime instigated by the Assyrians. Those who did not escape were deported beyond the river Euphrates and replaced by *people from Babylon, Cu'thah, Avva, Ha'math and Sepharv'im*.[6]

Judah had been an Assyrian satellite state since 732 BCE and there is little evidence to suggest that initially Hezekiah caused any serious concern to Shalmaneser or his successor, Sargon II (722–705 BCE). A Nimrud Inscription, dated around 717 BCE, makes mention of Sargon as the *subduer of the country Judah*,[7] but there was no indication that this was anything other than a record that Judah was obliged to pay tribute to Assyria. The Assyrians carried out further military campaigns to suppress rebellions in southern Syria and Palestine during 720, 716 and 713–711 BCE. The last of these culminated in the appointment of an Assyrian governor to the Philistine cities of Ashdod, Gath and Asdudimmu and their inhabitants being declared Assyrian citizens.[8] On the northern border of Judah stood the Assyrian province of Samerina and to the south there were Assyrian outposts on the border with Egypt and Arab groups acting as special Assyrian appointees. Now that Ashdod was under direct Assyrian rule, Judah was now almost completely encircled by Assyrian forces of one kind or another.

With the benefit of hindsight, many of the seemingly innocent administrative changes and natural reforms instigated by Hezekiah point towards careful preparations for eventual war against Assyria. Hezekiah had witnessed sufficient spontaneous neighbouring uprisings fail at great cost to the insurgents. He knew that he had to lay careful groundwork to ensure that he had any chance of success against the might of Assyria and would certainly have wished to avoid the fate of Ilubi'id (Ia'ubidi) of Hamath, who had been flayed alive as a warning to others contemplating rebellion.[9]

There was a Judean tax collection/administrative system in place to facilitate the distribution and storage of goods. Arrangements were made to ensure food reserves and supplies as storehouses were established for *grain, wine and oil; and stalls for all kinds of cattle, and sheepfolds.* Again, the precautions were not restricted to Jerusalem as Hezekiah *provided cities for himself, and flocks and herds in abundance.*[10] At numerous sites, the remains of hundreds of large four-handled storage jars have been found. These all bear one of three emblems made from a very limited number of seals and the Hebrew inscription *lmlk* (of, to or belonging to the king). The jars were also marked with one of four place names, three of which referred to regional centres and one to *mmsht* or the government in Jerusalem, representing the centre for the northern hill country. The goods collected in the jars were sent to one of the four district centres for storage, redistribution and administrative or military use.[11]

On the military front, Hezekiah made sure that weapons were in good supply and that the army had a proper chain of command.[12] Numerous towns and cities in the surrounding countryside were fortified and Jerusalem's defences were strengthened with the introduction of elite special forces.

Hezekiah had a dual strategy for dealing with the commodity that neither aggressors nor defenders could survive without. To deny any external enemy access to water he *planned with his officers and his mighty men to stop the water of the springs that were outside the city … and they stopped all the springs and the brook that flowed through the land.*[13] To ensure continued access to water inside the city an 'S' shaped tunnel was carved through 533 metres of bedrock from the Gihon Spring to the Siloam Pool by Hezekiah's artisans, who *tunneled the sheer rock with iron and built pools for water.*[14] In 1880 CE, towards the lower entrance of the tunnel, an accidental discovery was made of an incomplete inscription, the contents and script of which confirm that the tunnel dates to the reign of Hezekiah.[15]

Refugees, seeking safety from the various conflicts with the Assyrians, flooded into Jerusalem, adding to the burden which the influx of Samaritans had already created on the crowded City of David. Although there was some settlement of the extramural area to the north,[16] the steep Kidron and Hinnom valleys precluded any major developments to the east and the south of Jerusalem. There was, however, a strong acceleration in migration to the west, and the previously relatively low population density of the Western Hill increased to the extent that newly named suburbs emerged. The *Mishneh* ('Second Quarter')[17] developed in the proximity of the modern-day Jewish Quarter of Jerusalem's Old City, while the dwellings of the *Makhtesh* ('the Mortar')[18] were also situated on the Western Hill and possibly parts of the Tyropoeon Valley.

Hezekiah strengthened the eastern wall of Jerusalem utilizing stones of nearby houses.[19] Within the walls, buildings were separated by alleyways with drainage channels emptying into the Kidron Valley. Outside the eastern wall of the City of David, Hezekiah *built another wall*,[20] the purpose of which was to enclose the Pool of Siloam.

Even more importantly, Hezekiah encompassed the Western Hill within the city walls. The defensive intent underlying this construction is evidenced by the discovery of a particularly broad wall between 6.4 and 7.2 metres thick, situated 275 metres to the west of the southern end of the Temple enclosure.[21] The westernmost reaches of Hezekiah's defensive wall extended as far south so as to enclose the summit of Mount Zion, before eventually inclining eastwards to meet the southern precinct of the City of David. With Hezekiah's tunnel and the Pool of Siloam, together with the new settlements on the Western Hill, all within the confines of the walls, Jerusalem's defences were complete (see figure 6).

The scholarly estimates made of the total population of the metropolis of Jerusalem at the end of the eighth century BCE differ considerably.[22] The variables include population density coefficients, whether extramural areas are included in the figures or just the residents within the walls and indeed exactly what areas were walled. Taking into account the nature of the 'guesstimates' that have been made, and assuming that Hezekiah's wall extensively incorporated the Western Hill, a total population figure of around 25,000 (including extramural areas) seems reasonable.

During the last few years of the eighth century BCE, the armies of the Assyrian Empire were preoccupied with a Babylonian rebellion in its south-eastern reaches and incursions into its northern territories from the kingdom of Urartu and the semi-nomadic barbarian groups known as Cimmerians. This was an opportunistic time for Hezekiah to begin his rebellion, supported by other Syrian and Palestinian leaders and with the promise Egyptian assistance. Reliance upon Egypt, however, did not have unanimous approval in Jerusalem and the contemporaneous religious figure Isaiah, voiced particularly strong objections: *Woe to those who go down to Egypt for help.*[23] The timing of the Urartu and Cimmerian hostilities may have been entirely coincidental, but in around 703 BCE, Hezekiah had met with a delegation from the king of Babylon, Merodach-baladan II,[24] prior to the anti-Assyrian insurrection in Babylon.

The Assyrian king Sennacherib put down the Babylonian insurgency and in 701 BCE moved to reassert his authority in Palestine. The Assyrian army travelled along the Mediterranean coast, receiving tribute from the kings who knew better than to resist, and vanquishing those that did not readily acquiesce. The cities of Sidon and Ashkelon were amongst those forced to capitulate and have their kings replaced by new vassal monarchs. Egyptian bowmen and chariots, supported by Ethiopian cavalry, arrived to engage the Assyrians on the outskirts of Eltekeh. The Egyptian forces were defeated, however, and once the Assyrians had besieged and taken the town of Eltekeh, they moved on to capture the city-state of Ekron.[25] It was here that earlier the Ekron king, Padi, had been ousted because he would not join the alliance against Assyria, and he was now Hezekiah's prisoner in Jerusalem.

After the surrender of Ekron, the Assyrians entered Judah and claimed to have *laid siege to 46 of his strong cities, walled forts and to the countless small villages* and that Hezekiah's *irregular and elite troops which he had brought into Jerusalem* [...] *deserted him.*[26] Lachish and Libnah were main centres of resistance to the Assyrian army, and while these towns were being subdued, Sennacherib sent envoys to negotiate the surrender of Hezekiah in Jerusalem. This may have been when Hezekiah attempted to buy off the Assyrians with *all the silver that was found in the house of the Lord, and in the treasuries of the king's house.*[27] It is also plausible that this was when Hezekiah released Padi, who the Assyrians restored to the throne of Ekron. Despite the cajoling of the Assyrians, Hezekiah, with moral support from the prophet Isaiah, did not surrender and Sennacherib besieged Jerusalem making Hezekiah *a prisoner* [...] *like a bird in a cage* [...] *surrounded him with earthwork in order to molest those who were leaving his city's gate.*[28]

Allegedly, Jerusalem enjoyed a miraculous salvation as *the angel of the Lord went forth, and slew a hundred and eighty-five thousand in the camp of the Assyrians [...] Sennacherib king of Assyria departed, and went home.*[29] This account bears a strong resemblance to the legend concerning the miraculous outcome of Egyptian pharaoh, Sethos' (Shabataka c.721–706 BCE) confrontation with Sennacherib at Pelusium.[30] While it is possible that a plague of some kind infected the Assyrian army and acted as a catalyst for their departure,[31] it is equally feasible that this is no more than a retelling of a folk story that suited the motives of the compilers of the Old Testament. Without surrendering the city, Hezekiah had conceded, saying: *I have done wrong; withdraw from me; whatever you impose on me I will bear.*[32]

From the Assyrian point of view, there was security in leaving a subservient Judean state in place, not to mention the avoidance of the great loss of life that taking Jerusalem by force would have entailed. Although twenty years previously, Samaria had been made an Assyrian province, the Phoenician and Philistine seaport kingdoms as well as Moab, Ammon, Edom and Judah were all allowed to remain as semi-independent states, probably as it served Assyrian interests to have buffer territories in place, administered by local subservient client princes (see figure 7). With all his objectives achieved, it was therefore entirely logical for Sennacherib and his army to return to his palace at Ninevah.

The Assyrian Annals recorded that Sennacherib expelled 200,150 people from the kingdom of Judah. This figure is clearly an exaggeration, but nevertheless, large numbers were deported or at least displaced. Sennacherib also imposed excessive tribute liabilities upon Hezekiah and importantly, a more even balance of power amongst the vassal Palestinian states was brought about by a redistribution of much of Judah's territory *to Mitinti, king of Ashdod, Padi, king of Ekron and Sillibel, king of Gaza.*[33] A consequence of the reduction in Judah's western lands in c.701 BCE, was a further migration to Jerusalem. Rather than live under Philistine rule, many Jews left their towns and villages and headed to Jerusalem, just as those from Samaria had done twenty years earlier to avoid deportation by the Assyrians.

Whether or not due to his trials and tribulations with the Assyrians, Hezekiah became seriously ill and apparently was close to death.[34] Nevertheless he recovered and went on to live for a further fifteen years. Possibly still not in the best of health, Hezekiah needed to groom his future successor and probably because at the age of twelve Manasseh was deemed to have reached adulthood, he was appointed as his father's co-regent in 697 BCE. It is not clear whether Manasseh was the only surviving son or whether he was chosen by Sennacherib or his supporters in Jerusalem, but the reported words of Isaiah to Hezekiah resonate: *And some of your own sons, who are born to you, shall be taken away; and they shall be eunuchs in the palace of the king in Babylon.*[35]

Chapter 7

Babylon

Manasseh spent eleven years as co-regent with his father until 686 BCE, when Hezekiah died and Manasseh began his long reign as sole monarch. The two Old Testament observations that *he reigned fifty-five years in Jerusalem*[1] include the period spent as co-regent. Despite the expansion experienced by the city of Jerusalem during the latter years of the eighth century BCE, Manasseh's kingdom endured hardships that included an overwhelming debt burden and, outside the capital city, a war-ravaged land with a decimated population. Isaiah's reproach of his people includes a pithy observation of the ruinous conditions following the war with Assyria: *Your country lies desolate, your cities are burned with fire.*[2]

The Hinnom Valley,[3] which formed an L-shaped gorge on the western and southern perimeters of Jerusalem's Western Hill and Mount Zion, incorporated an area known as the *Topheth*. This was used as the repository for the bodies of executed criminals and the dumping of unwanted rubbish for incineration in an unceasing fiery inferno. The *Topheth* was also a place of punishment and burning during pagan rituals to venerate the Ammonite god Melech.[4] The Old Testament associates a sinful Manasseh with the practice of child sacrifice by fire in the Valley of Hinnom.[5] He is portrayed as a wicked king so beyond redemption that he was responsible for the eventual destruction of Jerusalem.[6]

In 2 Chronicles there is also a story unsubstantiated by any other record, whereby the king's evil actions are interrupted by Assyrian commanders *who took Manas'seh with hooks and bound him with fetters of bronze and brought him to Babylon.*[7] Repentance and reaffirmation of Yahwistic principles facilitated the return of Manasseh to Jerusalem, whereupon he carried out building works and military reorganizations, which are very reminiscent of Hezekiah' s earlier war preparations.[8] Manasseh is also credited with carrying out religious reforms upon his enlightened return from Babylon, but his role as a Yahwistic reformer is, however, later contradicted.[9]

Judah had been an Assyrian satellite state since the beginning of the seventh century BCE, but it was now subject to firmer control, with the effective government almost certainly in the hands of a pro-Assyrian faction and possibly receiving advice/instruction from an Assyrian High Commissioner. Manasseh is very briefly mentioned in Assyrian records as a contemporary and loyal subject of Sennacherib's son and successor, Esarhaddon,[10] and he would have been one of the vassal kings forced to confirm their loyalty to their Assyrian overlords by submission to Esarhaddon's Vassal Treaties of 672 BCE.[11]

Both 2 Kings and 2 Chronicles describe how Manasseh, before *the visit* to Babylon, reversed some of the religious reforms enacted by his father and restored polytheistic worship and built altars to pagan gods in the Temple.[12] Manasseh had little choice other than to conduct the affairs of Judah and Jerusalem in accordance with policies favoured by his Assyrian overlords. If this resulted in the encroachment of supplication to Assyrian gods (e.g. Ashur and Ishtar) into the Yahwistic culture, then this must have been viewed by Manasseh as a price worth paying for being allowed to regenerate the war-torn Judean economy. Understandably, conflicts arose between the pro-Assyrian faction and the Yahwistic traditionalists, necessitating the suppression of opposition by Manasseh.[13]

Manasseh's subservience to his Assyrian masters was exhibited in 664 BCE. This was the year that the Assyrians reasserted their military control in Egypt and in celebration Manasseh named his new-born son Amon, after the Egyptian sun god Amun. The very elderly Manasseh died in 642 BCE, and Amon succeeded his father in Jerusalem. Amon was, however, unable to emulate his father's lengthy reign and a court intrigue soon resulted in his assassination. The conspirators themselves were put to death and in 640 BCE, Amon's eight-year-old son, Josiah, was appointed to rule by *the people of the land*.[14]

The compilers of 2 Kings depict Josiah as one of the most righteous rulers of Jerusalem, who undertook religious reforms, including destroying the apostate altar erected at Bethel by Jeroboam, the first king of Israel following the division of the Davidic kingdom.[15] The somewhat flawless depiction of Josiah raises the question of the validity of the Old Testament view of Josiah as a reliable historical source.

The Old Testament relates that in *the eighteenth year* (c.622 BCE) of Josiah's reign there was a discovery in the Temple of *the book of the law*, which was deemed to be of great spiritual significance and led to a widespread purge of Jewish religious practices. Scholarly opinions differ, but it is generally thought that portions of the present book of Deuteronomy are based on *the book of the law*. Allowing that the Old Testament idealized representation of Josiah was prone to some exaggeration, his reported reforms were extensive and began with a covenant made by Josiah *and all the men of Judah and all the inhabitants of Jerusalem, and the priests and the prophets* to uphold the commandments of the book of the law.[16]

Non-Yahwistic vessels, probably relating to Assyrian cult rituals, were removed from the Temple and the priests associated with these artefacts were banished. The image of Asherah[17] was removed from the Temple and the rooms used by the male prostitutes were demolished. The non-Yahwistic images of horses and chariots at the Temple entrance were removed, as were false altars constructed by previous kings on the roof and in the courts of the Temple. Topheth, the site of child sacrifice in the Hinnom Valley, was purged along with other pagan shrines around Jerusalem. Following the changes to the Yahwistic practices in Jerusalem, the scope of the reforms spread throughout Judah *from Geba to Beer-sheba*, culminating in the destruction of a sacrilegious shrine at Bethel. Probably Josiah had extended his territory a few miles to the north of Geba so that Bethel was now part of Judah.

At the beginning of Josiah's reign, Judah was controlled by Assyria, but later it became subservient to both Assyria and Egypt, and then to Egypt alone as Assyrian power declined. In 616 BCE, Egyptian troops were assisting the Assyrian army east of the Euphrates,[18] and accordingly they would have had to be confident of their position in Palestine in order to extend their supply lines to such an extent. The transition from Assyrian vassal to Egyptian subservience was accompanied by more internal freedom, as the Egyptians were much less interested in exercising close control over affairs that had no commercial or military significance. Against this backdrop, Josiah was able to effect religious reforms in Jerusalem and in Judah generally.

In the final years of the seventh century BCE, the older super-powers of Egypt and Assyria were co-operating against an insurgent alliance of emerging nation-states that included Medes and Babylonians. This alliance had driven the Assyrians firstly from their capital at Nineveh and then secondly from the strategically important city of Harran.[19] The Egyptian pharaoh Neco II was on his way to Carchemish on the Euphrates to assist the Assyrians, but in the summer of 609 BCE he was intercepted by Josiah at Megiddo. Whatever the motive might have been for Josiah's intervention, he paid the ultimate price. The Old Testament has two slightly differing accounts of Josiah's death, but substantively he was mortally wounded or killed in battle at Megiddo.[20]

Josiah had four sons, three of whom were to reign in Jerusalem as kings of Judah, as was one of his grandsons. The order in which these future kings succeeded to the throne owed more to political expediency than to age or seniority (see figure 8). After Josiah's burial in Jerusalem *the people of the land*[21] anointed Jehoahaz II as the new king of Judah. He was Josiah's fourth son, originally named Shallum.

Later in 609 BCE, Neco II joined forces with the army of the Assyrian king, Ashur-uballit II and together they made an unsuccessful attempt to retake Harran from the Babylonians.[22] After a humiliating defeat at the hands of the Babylonians, Neco established a headquarters on the eastern bank of the Orontes River at Riblah. Notwithstanding the altercation at Megiddo, Egypt's position in Palestine was still very much that of overlord and three months after his succession, Jehoahaz was summoned to present himself to Neco, who presumably was not in the best of moods. Certainly, he was unwilling to countenance a Judean ruler chosen without his permission and the unfortunate Jehoahaz was taken in chains to Egypt, where he died.

Neco II exacted tribute of one hundred talents of silver and one talent of gold and chose Josiah's second son, Eliakim, to be king of Judah, renaming him Jehoiakim. Rather than deplete the royal coffers, the new vassal king levied a tax on his people to pay the tribute to his Egyptian masters.[23] Jehoiakim's loyalty to Egypt did not go unquestioned in Jerusalem, with strong and persistent opposition being voiced by many, including the prophets Jeremiah and Uriah. In addition to criticizing his foreign and cultic policies, Jeremiah denounced Jehoiakim's use of forced labour to build a new royal palace.[24] Jeremiah appears to have avoided the ultimate punishment for his seditiousness, but Uriah, having fled to Egypt, was duly extradited and put to death.[25]

The allied Assyrian and Egyptian forces had been routed by the Babylonian army near Harran. Subsequently in 605 BCE, the Babylonian crown prince, Nebuchadnezzar, secured a decisive victory over the Egyptians and the surviving remnants of the Assyrian army, at the Battle of Carchemish on the banks of the Euphrates River.[26] Ashur-uballit II may have survived or been killed at either battle, but whatever his fate, he disappears from history and the Assyrian empire ceases to exist. The consequence of this for Palestine was the emergence of a violent struggle for supremacy of the eastern Mediterranean seaboard between Babylonia and Egypt.

Nabopolassar, the first king of the Neo-Babylonian Empire (the Chaldean Dynasty) died in 605 BCE, and was duly succeeded by his son, Nebuchadnezzar.[27] Initially, the new king was unopposed in Syria and Palestine, which were referred to as *Hattu* in the Neo-Babylonian chronicles. Nebuchadnezzar *marched about victoriously in Hattu. All the kings of Hattu came into his presence and he received their vast tribute.*[28] Nebuchadnezzar's displays of military strength, including the destruction of the Philistine city of Ashkelon in 604 BCE, induced Jehoiakim to forsake his Egyptian overlords and to begin paying homage to the Babylonians.

It looked as if the tide had turned against Nebuchadnezzar, however, as his attempt to invade Egypt in 600 BCE was repulsed. Even the compilers of the Babylonian chronicles found it difficult to present the defeat in a positive light. It is recorded that Neco took his army to meet the invaders and *both sides suffered severe losses* before the Babylonian army *turned and [went back] to Babylon.*[29] The fifth-century BCE Greek historian Herodotus puts the Babylonian failure in stronger terms, recounting that Neco *engaged the Syrians* (Babylonians) *in a land battle and won a victory at Magdolos* (possibly Migdol). *After this, he captured Cadytis* (Gaza).[30] The fall of Gaza to the Egyptian forces is also mentioned in the Old Testament.[31]

Evidently, following this defeat, Nebuchadnezzar found it necessary to refurbish his military machine and during the subsequent year he *stayed home* (and*) refitted his numerous horses and chariotry.*[32] Jehoiakim had been paying tributes to Babylonia for three years, but now decided to rebel,[33] the most likely causes of which were the Egyptian victory over the Babylonian army and the absence of the main Babylonian militia during its period of refurbishment. Nebuchadnezzar's return to Palestine, in 599 BCE, was noted for a campaign against the desert Arab tribes,[34] and although Jerusalem was not immediately threatened by his core army, the city was troubled by nearby Babylonian garrisons and auxiliary troops from Syria, Moab and Ammon.[35]

At the end of 598 BCE, however, Nebuchadnezzar laid siege to Jerusalem, whose resistance was broken in the mid-March 597 BCE. There are diverse reports concerning the demise of Jehoiakim, suggesting that Nebuchadnezzar had him killed or taken in fetters to Babylon.[36] However, it is more likely that before Nebuchadnezzar reached Jerusalem, Jehoiakim died naturally and in December 598 BCE was succeeded by his eighteen-year-old son Jehoiachin, who had been his co-regent for the past ten years.[37]

Jehoiachin's reign as sole monarch lasted only three months, as when it became clear that no assistance would be forthcoming from the Egyptian army, Jehoiachin surrendered to Nebuchadnezzar on 16 March, 597 BCE.[38] Nebuchadnezzar deported the Judean royal family and all other surviving useful male members of the population for resettlement in Babylonia, so that *none remained, except the poorest people of the land.* The number of male deportees mentioned in the Old Testament is 10,000 and 8,000,[39] although there is possibly some duplication in these figures.

If at least 10,000 males were deported, and postulating that the proportion of male adults in ancient societies was 28 per cent,[40] the total number of people in Jerusalem, before Jehoiachin's capitulation, could conceivably have reached as many as 36,000. Of course, as ever during times of ancient warfare, the normal population figure was inflated by people from the surrounding areas seeking the perceived safety of the city walls. The widespread concern in the countryside was evident as, for example, the nomadic Rechabite clan sought refuge in Jerusalem *for fear of the army of the Chaldeans and the army of the Syrians.*[41]

The Temple and the Palace were looted and in 597 BCE, Nebuchadnezzar appointed Josiah's third son, Mattaniah, as the new king of Judah. He was renamed Zedekiah and made to swear loyalty to the Babylon king and promise never to conspire with Egypt.[42] Notwithstanding this holy oath and the fact that there was a pro-Babylonian faction in the city, rebellion never seemed far from the minds of many in Jerusalem. Even at the beginning of Zedekiah's reign, emissaries from the Palestinian regions of Edom, Moab, Ammon, Tyre and Sidon met with him in Jerusalem to discuss a joint political strategy.

In 596/5 BCE, the authority of Nebuchadnezzar was challenged, albeit unsuccessfully, by the south-eastern neighbouring state of Elam, and in December 595 BCE, a domestic rebellion necessitated drastic action against his own army.[43] In the meantime, Psammetichus II (595–589 BCE) had succeeded his father, Neco II, as the Egyptian pharaoh, and following a decisive military campaign against Nubia (Ethiopia), Psammetichus II undertook a victory tour in Palestine in 591 BCE. Some or all of these events must have contributed to Zedekiah's decision to rebel and withhold his annual tribute to Babylonia, with the result that in 588 BCE, Nebuchadnezzar *came with all his army against Jerusalem and laid siege to it.*[44]

A direct assault on the city was by no means an easy option. There were steep valleys on three sides of the city and there were solidly constructed defensive walls. This was particularly so on the eastern side of Jerusalem, where the strong walls had solid packing and were on steep slopes and thus almost impervious to both launched weaponry and battering rams. The northern wall would have provided an easier target, but the most undemanding tactic was to attempt to starve the city into submission.

Just as previous Judean kings had relied upon Egyptian support to thwart aggressors against Jerusalem, Zedekiah expected military assistance from the son of Psammetichus II, Apries (589–570 BCE). It is recorded on inscribed potsherds discovered at the site of biblical Lachish and dated c.589–588 BCE, that a Judean army general named Coniah had visited Egypt.[45] Apries did send an army into Palestine causing the Babylonians to temporarily suspend their siege of Jerusalem.

The siege was resumed once the Pharaoh's army returned to Egypt, but the respite had enabled the Judeans to replenish their food reserves, thus prolonging the inevitable outcome. Eventually, in the summer of 586 BCE, Zedekiah fled from the famine-stricken city, only to be captured by the pursuing Babylonian army on the plains of Jericho. Zedekiah was taken to the Syrian town of Riblah, where Nebuchadnezzar ordered his punishment, which may well have been stipulated in the terms of the oath sworn when appointed king of Judah. The last thing that Zedekiah saw was the murder of his sons, following which he was blinded and taken in chains to Babylon and placed in prison *till the day of his death.*[46] Conversely, many years later, Jehoiachin, the legitimate king of Judah, was released from prison in Babylon, not to return to Jerusalem, but to live with dignity at the Babylonian royal court.[47]

As Jerusalem had rebelled twice during Nebuchadnezzar's reign, it was inconceivable that he would allow its defences to remain in place, and accordingly the Babylonian army demolished the city walls.[48] The terraces on the eastern slopes were dependent on retaining walls, which were ultimately reliant on the city wall at the base, and the dismantling of these walls resulted in the complete crumbling and erosion of all the east side of Jerusalem.[49] Homes, public buildings, the Palace and the Temple were also burned down.[50] The massive destruction of Jerusalem is apparent both in the layers of charred remains and in the thick layer of rubble from collapsed buildings on the eastern slope of the City of David revealed during modern day excavations.

The wholesale devastation of Jerusalem included Solomon's great Temple, from which its many bronze artefacts and its bronze pillars were taken to Babylon for recycling. Gold and silver were also taken from the Temple.[51] Perhaps for the compilers of the Old Testament it was too sensitive an issue to acknowledge, but presumably the Ark was destroyed when the Temple was consumed by fire.

Even more of the population were exiled to Babylon and the effects of this and the extensive destruction had far reaching repercussions on the future evolution of life and cult practices in the city. With the demolition of the City of David came its effective elimination from the future development of the larger city of Jerusalem. As the Millo, the earth-filled terrace walls serving as the northern defence line of the Ophel, had been torn down, the south-eastern spur of the Jerusalem mountain complex could no longer be easily defended. Consequentially, the Ophel became an inconsequential suburb, sometimes inside and sometimes outside the city wall, but never again a very important or prosperous part of the city's life.

Chapter 8

The Second Temple

A number of towns, particularly to the north of Jerusalem in the Benjamite area, survived the invasion of Judah. That these towns were left intact was because they offered no resistance and capitulated to the Babylonian army fairly early during the conflict. But it was not just Jerusalem that had to pay the penalty for the second uprising against Babylonia, as the destruction extended to many other Judean towns, from Lachish in the west, En-gedi in the east and as far south as Arad. The full extent of the destruction in Jerusalem is, however, open to question, as was the extent of the damage to the Judean economy generally.

Thousands of Jews were deported from Jerusalem to Babylon, but this was not merely retribution. Due in part to Nebuchadnezzar's building projects, the Babylonian economy was booming and the skills of Jerusalem's artisans were very much needed. Understandably, those remaining in the city tended to be *the poorest of the land to be vinedressers and plowmen*.[1] However, those left behind would also have included some priests, scribes, tradesmen and workmen as well as peasants, thus ensuring that a degree of a functioning society would have existed.[2] Benefits accrued to the enduring population in the form of a redistribution of land[3] and additionally the relief of debts owed to affluent Jews who had been deported. The reduced population would also have been augmented by the return to Jerusalem of many of those who had fled to the relative safety of the countryside, while the victorious army was setting fire to the city and forcibly transporting great numbers of people hundreds of miles away to an uncertain future in a foreign land.

Bearing in mind the devastation and plundering wrought in Jerusalem and other towns, the huge number of casualties and the deportation of much of the population, it is conceivable that Judah had been left in ruins, with little more than an agricultural subsistence economy. Perhaps, however, the reality was that the complete demolition of Jerusalem was too vast a task for the Babylonian army and, in the circumstances, even unnecessary. Judah was not without economic significance to the Babylonian empire, because Palestine's agricultural production exceeded what was required by its own population. In particular, vines and olives were important exports to regions such as Mesopotamia, where these products were unable to grow and therefore it made sense for the Babylonians to maintain Judah as a functioning economy.[4] This would certainly be an explanation for the attempt to rejuvenate the economy by giving vineyards and fields to the destitute.[5]

Jerusalem was no longer the capital city, and the head of the Judean state was no longer a descendant of David. The pro-Babylonian faction, which previously had been a minority in Jerusalem, became prominent as Nebuchadnezzar appointed one of their number as the new Judean leader. This was Gedaliah, from an important family that had served in high government positions since the rule of Josiah, some forty years earlier. Josiah's royal secretary who was handed *the book of the law* discovered in the Temple, was Gedaliah's grandfather, Shaphan.[6] It is unclear whether Nebuchadnezzar appointed Gedaliah as the new king of Judah or merely governor. If the former, perhaps the compilers of the Old Testament simply could not acknowledge a king that was not of Davidic lineage.

The new Judean capital city was Mizpah, a town that had not been destroyed during the war and which stood about ten miles north of Jerusalem, in the territory of the tribe of Benjamin. Initially the prominent Judeans gave Gedaliah their backing,[7] but within months Ishmael, a military officer with distant links to Davidic lineage, led an assassination group, who murdered Gedaliah in around 586 BCE, and *slew all the Jews who were with Gedaliah at Mizpah, and the Chaldean soldiers who happened to be there.*[8] Lacking popular support, Ishmael fled to Ammon, while other military commanders fearing Babylonian reprisals, made for Egypt.

Nebuchadnezzar died in 561 BCE, to be succeeded by his son Amel-marduk (Evil-merodach). For the next six years Babylonia experienced a period of upheaval and revolution, during which no king was able to survive for any length of time: Amel-marduk was killed in 560 BCE, Neriglissar died in 556 BCE, and Labashi-marduk was replaced in 555 BCE by Nabonidus, a Babylonian military commander. For various reasons, including long periods of absence from Babylonia, Nabonidus was not a popular monarch. In 540 BCE, he returned from a lengthy stay in Arabia in a vain attempt to strengthen Babylon against the growing military threat from Persia. The Babylonian empire was, however, to come to an end in September 539 BCE, when the Persian king, Cyrus, was successful in campaigns against a number of Babylonian cities. Also known as Cyrus the Great, finally he *entered Babylon without a battle*.[9]

Jerusalem, Judah and indeed all Palestine, as territories previously ruled by Babylonia, became part of the Persian Achaemenid Empire and remained so for the next two centuries. Under Cyrus, Persia became the largest empire the world had yet seen, stretching from the Mediterranean Sea in the west to the Indus River in the east. The religion of the Achaemenian kings was Zoroastrianism, which imposed an obligation to rule justly and in accordance with the core concept of *asha* (truth and righteousness). Cyrus ruled adhered to Zoroastrian beliefs, but made no attempt to impose the Achaemenian ideology on the people of his subject territories. He used the politically expedient and not uncommon philosophy of allowing subjected peoples to exercise religious freedom, and even to promote himself as a restorer of gods and their sanctuaries.

Jewish exiles began to return to Jerusalem following the proclamation *in the first year of Cyrus king of Persia* (c.539/8 BCE, after the fall of Babylon):

> *The Lord, the God of heaven ... has charged me to build*
> *him a house at Jerusalem ... Whoever is among you of all*
> *his people... let him go up to Jerusalem ... and rebuild the*
> *House of the Lord.*[10]

Cyrus suggested that such returnees should be assisted with money and supplies by those who remained, and instructed that the gold and silver vessels, which the Babylonians had looted from the Temple in 586 BCE, should be returned and these were duly handed over to Shesh-bazzar, *the prince of Judah*.[11]

The veracity and the chronology of the Old Testament lists of returnees are open to question and undoubtedly there was not a single mass movement back to Jerusalem, but rather groups returned during the reigns of various Persian kings, from Cyrus II through to Artaxerxes II (405–359 BCE). The evidence is not abundantly clear, but the first main wave was led by Shesh-bazzar in about 538 BCE, and the last possibly as late as 398 BCE, when Ezra led a further significant group back to Jerusalem.[12] As the Babylonians had never resettled Jerusalem, the large numbers of returnees were not faced with insurmountable hurdles to their social, political and religious rejuvenation of the city.[13]

It has been suggested that Shesh-bazzar is an alternative name for Zerubbabel, who was the Governor of Judah under Darius, the king of Persia between 522 and 486 BCE. The confusion of the names is partly due to the conflicting reports in the Old Testament surrounding the laying of the foundations of the new Temple.[14] However, it is much more likely that Shesh-bazzar, *the prince of Judah*, was a Babylonian appointee and that post-539 BCE, Cyrus allowed Shesh-bazzar to continue in office, but now simply as the Governor of Judah.[15]

Cyrus was killed fighting in the east in 530 BCE, and was succeeded by his unpopular *harsh and scornful* son Cambyses.[16] The Persian Empire was extended even further when Cambyses undertook an invasion of Egypt in 526/5 BCE. It was indicative of the control that Persia now enjoyed over the Eastern Mediterranean seaboard that Cambyses and his army had unencumbered passage through Palestine, and used the port of Acco as the assembly point of the Persian forces invading Egypt. By 523 BCE, Cambyses was dead and the Persian royal family was experiencing an internecine war. The ultimate resolution of the civil strife came in 522 BCE, with the crowning of Cambyses' brother-in-law, Darius, and *All the people of Asia whom Cyrus and later Cambyses had conquered were subject to him.*[17]

The Old Testament lists of important Jews returning to Jerusalem[18] included the high priest, Joshua, and Zerubbabel. Seventeen years had passed since the return of Shesh-bazzar and the initial contingent of returnees to the holy city. Subsequently, in around 521 BCE, a second major influx of previously exiled Jews was led back to Jerusalem by Zerubbabel. Because he was a grandson of Jehoiachin,[19] the king of Judah taken to Babylon by Nebuchadnezzar, Zerubbabel was of royal Davidic lineage (see figure 9) and by 521 BCE he had been installed as the governor of Judah.[20]

Joshua (Jeshua) and Zerubbabel were pre-eminent in the Temple rebuilding project including giving *money to the masons and carpenters, and food, drink and oil to the Sidonians and the Tyrians to bring cedar trees from Lebanon to the sea, to Joppa, according to the grant which they had from Cyrus king of Persia.*[21] The principal material used to erect the temple was the same as that used by the people of Jerusalem for their houses and the city walls. This was the abundant local Turonian limestone, or *meleke*, that accounted for much of the geological formation of the city plateau.

The actual reconstruction of the new Temple was a tortuous and protracted business and at one stage, in around 519 BCE, was called into question by Tattenai, the governor of the Persian province west of the Euphrates. Tattenai sent a report to Darius, which led to the Persian king ordering a search of the archives in the city of Ecbatana. A scroll was unearthed that recorded Cyrus' decree that the Temple in Jerusalem should be rebuilt and proposed the dimensions of the mooted new Temple, noted that it should be funded *from the royal treasury*, and that *the gold and silver vessels* taken from the old Temple by Nebuchadnezzar should be returned. Darius made a further decree concerning the rebuilding of the Jerusalem: *let it be done with all diligence.*[22]

The extraordinary delay in the rebuilding of the Temple has been variously attributed to the Judeans being too busy tending their own homes, a lack of resources and funding and even a drought. In his castigation of the people, the contemporary religious figure, Haggai, blames the drought on the Judeans failure to proceed with the building.[23]

There was possibly resistance to the rebuilding from the Samaritans now living in Jerusalem as well as a lack of numbers of the Jews who had returned, and their reluctance to accept assistance because Cyrus had granted his remit solely to the Jews.[24] As historical documents, however, the Biblical accounts must be treated with some scepticism, and there is a view that the first six chapters of Ezra show bias, inconsistencies and historical anomalies to such an extent that it is difficult to ascertain how much work, if any, was carried out on the Temple rebuilding during the reign of Cyrus.[25]

It is likely that the Jews had sound ideological reasons for the delay in rebuilding. From a religious viewpoint, the destruction of the original Temple in 587/586 BCE came about because *the Sons of Israel had sinned against the Lord their God.*[26] The Jews felt that God's anger must be assuaged before the Temple could be rebuilt and a number of early post-monarchical texts pose the question how long before God will return to His people?[27] Seventy years is mentioned in a number of biblical works[28] and logically seems to be the answer, as probably all those who had offended their God would have since died.

Possibly on the same site as the original Temple, the building of the Second Temple (Zerubbabel's Temple) was eventually completed in 516 BCE on *the third day of the month of Adar', in the sixth year of the reign of Dari'us the king.*[29] To dedicate the new Temple to God, the Jews of Jerusalem celebrated with an elaborate service that included the traditional animal sacrifice. The burnt offerings on this occasion are listed as *one hundred bulls, two hundred rams, four hundred lambs, and as a sin offering for all Israel twelve he-goats.*[30]

Chapter 9

Nehemiah

Jerusalem lay at the centre of what was now a much-reduced Judah, comprising little more than the plateau between the Dead Sea in the east and the Shephelah lowlands to the west. Together Judah, Palestine, Phoenicia, Cyprus and Syria formed the administrative Persian *satrapy* of Abar-Nahara (Beyond the River). Judah itself was divided into a number of districts, in which the strictly local affairs were overseen by Persian appointed Jewish governors. Some of these districts, such as Jerusalem, had subdivisions, each with its own person in charge.[1]

It should be noted that the Old Testament books of Ezra and Nehemiah (The First and Second Books of Esdras) were originally one and were probably written by the same compiler of Chronicles. The author's main purpose is to describe the religious and political reorganizations following the return of the exiled Jews. There is some uncertainty as to the chronology and order of the events described because the two main sources, the memoirs of Ezra and those of Nehemiah are intermingled.[2]

Although the new Temple in Jerusalem had been completed in 516 BCE, the scale of the 586 BCE Babylonian destruction continued to impact life in and around Jerusalem for many generations. Nehemiah, serving in the royal household in the Persian capital of Susa was told:

> *The survivors there in the province who escaped exile are in great trouble and shame; the wall of Jerusalem is broken down, and its gates are destroyed by fire.*[3]

and

> *the surrounding nations were inflicting many injuries on the Jews, overrunning the country and plundering it by day and*

doing mischief by night, so that many had been carried off
as captives from the country and from Jerusalem itself, and
every day the roads were full of corpses.[4]

However, the placing of Nehemiah's return to Jerusalem in the twenty-fifth year of the reign of king Xerxes[5] is erroneous, not the least because Xerxes I ruled Persia for no more than twenty years (486–465 BCE). Xerxes was murdered and, eventually, after a struggle at the Persian court, was succeeded by his son Artaxerxes I (465–425 BCE). The wrangling for the throne of Persia provided the impetus for yet another Egyptian rebellion, on this occasion supported by the Athenian navy. A prolonged war ensued and it was not until 455 BCE that Egypt was once again under secure Persian control. In 449 BCE Athens and Persia signed a peace treaty, pledging no further Athenian interference in Egypt and Cyprus and no further Persian activity along the southern and western coasts of Asia Minor.

In the context of mistrust within the royal court and unease abroad, in 445 BCE Artaxerxes I despatched Nehemiah to Jerusalem in order to cement Jewish support for the Persians in the region. Thus, approximately seventy years after the completion of Zerubbabel's Temple in 516 BCE, Nehemiah arrived in Jerusalem during the twentieth year of the reign of Artaxerxes I.[6]

Nehemiah's remit as the new Governor of Judah was to rebuild Jerusalem, including the reconstruction of the city walls and gates. As a stronger Jerusalem would necessarily diminish the influence and authority of neighbouring states, opposition to the project was voiced by the Samaritans, the Ammonites, Arabs and the people of Ashdod. Threats ensued and the walls had to be restored under the watchful eyes of Jewish armed guards.[7]

A few of the old broken gates were repaired and, where applicable, completely new gates were built. The gates were connected with towers and walls, again some of which were renovations and other new constructions (see figure 10).[8]

Originally, the eastern side of the City of David had been fortified on the lower part of the slope leading to the Kidron Valley. As a result of the Babylonian dismantling of the city walls, the slopes were probably blanketed with rubble and impassable in some places.[9] Where repairs were made to the previous wall, these were generally on the western side and although the line of Nehemiah's eastern wall cannot be determined with strict accuracy, this was higher up, on the crest of the slope leading down to the valley.[10] Under Nehemiah's direction, the wall that Hezekiah erected around Siloam's Pool, approximately two hundred and fifty years earlier, was rebuilt as the *wall of the Pool of She'lah of the king's garden, as far as the stairs that go down from the city of David.*[11]

Possibly, Nehemiah was also involved with the building or renovation of the fortress designed to provide protection for the Jewish Temple. At some stage, during either the First or Second Temple Periods, a defensive structure was erected at the north-eastern corner of the Temple Mount. Subsequently this became known as the *baris* during the Hasmonean era and later as Fortress Antonia during the time of Herod the Great. References to *the fortress of the temple* and *the governor of the castle* hint at Nehemiah's possible involvement with its development.[12]

The Western Hill and Mount Zion did not form part of Nehemiah's restoration project. Nevertheless, the construction of the city walls, towers and gates would have taken some considerable time, although neither of the ancient source estimates of *fifty-two days* nor *two years and four months* appear particularly reliable.[13]

Inevitably, following the deportation of so many people at the end of the sixth century and the contraction of the land-area comprising the city, mid-fifth-century Jerusalem contained far fewer people than the large conurbations of the earlier eighth and sixth centuries. Before the waves of returnees had begun in about 538 BCE, it would not be unreasonable to surmise that the ruined city had only a few thousand residents. Following the restoration work and strengthening of the city defences, however, it was logical for a significant increase in the population of Jerusalem to take place.[14] Nevertheless, the population of Jerusalem in the middle of the fifth century BCE was probably less than 15,000, some of whom were priests with families living on small estates outside the city walls.[15]

As well as his efforts concerning the structural renovation of the city, Nehemiah also addressed the socio-economic problems faced by the people of Jerusalem. During a time of famine, the poorest peasants struggled to pay the interest levied on loans and mortgages taken out to finance their tax payments or even to purchase grain, and in some cases, this had led to the selling of their children into slavery. Nehemiah took issue with the wealthier Jews, berating them with the message:

> *Let us leave off this interest. Return to them this very day their fields, their vineyards, their olive orchards, and their houses, and the hundredth of money, grain, wine, and oil which you have been exacting of them.*[16]

As the governor of Judah, it was Nehemiah's duty to collect taxes on behalf of the Persian government. The imposition of taxes for the upkeep of their own households was an additional task carried out by the Persian-appointed regional governors, many of whom applied this toll to excess. Nehemiah acted to lessen the tax burden on the people by foregoing the taxes that would maintain his palace.[17]

In around 433 BCE Nehemiah rejoined the court of Artaxerxes I, before once again returning to Jerusalem, where he took objection to the lack of observance of strict Jewish religious laws. He took measures to prevent foreigners entering the Temple, preached against the marriages of Jews to foreigners, reinstated the tithe payments to the Levites, and reinforced the sanctity of the Sabbath.[18]

Not all local governors were as supportive of Jerusalem's religious observations as Nehemiah had been, and one particular governor caused controversy towards the end of the fifth century BCE. This was Bagoas,[19] who had championed Jesus in his claim to be Jerusalem's high priest in place of the incumbent, Johanan. Despite Jesus and Johanan being brothers, the latter had murdered the former during a quarrel in the temple. Bagoas' support for Jesus had its roots in the belief that the established Jewish priesthood harboured pro-Babylonian sentiments and were therefore anti-Persian. Coincidentally, the Jewish community based at Elephantine[20] in Egypt were petitioning to rebuild their temple and resume the offerings of grain, incense and animal sacrifice. The response to the Jews of Elephantine appears to have been used opportunistically to impose a punishment on the Jerusalem priests for the murder of Jesus and exact a tax, which effectively banned animal sacrifice in the Jewish Temple of Jerusalem for the next seven years.[21]

The Persians lost control of the Delta region of Egypt during the final years of the fifth century, and early in the fourth century the Egyptians began to extend their sphere of influence along the coastal plain of Palestine into Phoenicia. At this point in time, Persia was ruled by Artaxerxes II, who preferring to have allies rather than rebellious vassals in Palestine, orchestrated the return to Jerusalem of a further assembly of Jewish exiles in around 398 BCE. To lead the returnees Artaxerxes appointed a learned priestly Jewish scribe named Ezra, who left Babylon with the full authority of the Persian king *to make inquiries about Judah and Jerusalem according to the law of your God, which is in your hand.*[22]

Ezra led the wave of exiled Jews back to Jerusalem with finance provided by Artaxerxes and contributions freely offered by any Jews that were still in Babylon. Instructions were issued to the authorities in the Persian *satrapy* of Abar-Nahara to assist and not hinder Ezra's return to Jerusalem and, as the new Governor of Judah, Ezra was given the authority to appoint magistrates and judges and impose penalties on lawbreakers.[23]

Ezra played an important role in teaching the people of Jerusalem to understand Jewish religious law. He would preach *the book of the law of Moses ... facing the square before the Water Gate from early morning until midday.*[24] In his opposition to the marriage of Jews to foreigners, Ezra took a stronger line than Nehemiah and went as far as suggesting that Jewish men actually divorce their foreign wives and disown the children of such unions.[25]

There is little available historical data shedding light on events in Jerusalem during the sixty years or so between Ezra's governorship and Alexander the Great's invasion of Persia in 334 BCE. On occasions life in the city may have been impacted by the power politics of the Egyptians and the Persians, but generally the whole of Palestine enjoyed a period of relative calm under the benign rule of the Persians and little *disturbed its regular and slow moving manner of life.*[26] Natural increases in the population of Jerusalem would have occurred, but more so in settlements outside the walls that had been restored by Nehemiah.

Chapter 10

The Greeks

Jerusalem remained under Persian jurisdiction until Alexander the Great invaded Persia in 334 BCE. At the battle of Issus[1] in November 333 BCE, Alexander routed the Persian army of Darius III (336–331 BCE) and then, intending to march south to Egypt, entered Phoenicia. Most of the cities and strongholds failed to resist and immediately surrendered. Tyre, however, defied Alexander and resisted a land and sea siege for seven months.[2] The main involvement of Jerusalem in Alexander's activities in Palestine was probably confined to the supply of materials for the massive siege-works at Tyre and of provisions for the army. The Phoenician city-state finally succumbed in July 332 BCE, but Alexander's progress towards Egypt was once again delayed, this time by a Persian garrison stationed in the city of Gaza, which resisted for two months until October 332 BCE.

It is unlikely that Alexander ever personally came to Jerusalem, notwithstanding a detailed narrative of a visit following his successful siege of Gaza.[3] This anecdote is so full of contradictions and chronological difficulties that it must be consigned to the category of myth. Amongst other inconsistencies in the tale is the involvement of Sanballat the satrap of Samaria, who, in fact, lived in the mid-to-late fifth century BCE and was a contemporary of Nehemiah.[4] Similarly, about a dozen legends concerning Alexander may be found in Rabbinic literature and one in particular recalls elements of the story of the supposed visit to Jerusalem by Alexander,[5] but it is uncorroborated by any extant non-Jewish authority. Non-Jewish sources relate that after taking Gaza, Alexander *with all his army marched on to Egypt.*[6]

Once he had entered Egypt, Alexander established a defensive garrison at Pelusium. He then sailed up the Nile to be warmly welcomed by the Persian satrap in Memphis in November 332 BCE. Close to a small Egyptian village called Rhakotis, Alexander founded a city that bore his name, and in time Alexandria became the most important centre of Greek culture in the ancient oriental world.[7] Having secured control of Egypt, Alexander returned to Tyre and then into northern Syria on his way to Mesopotamia to deal once and for all with Darius and the Persians.

Excavations in Palestine and Transjordan have revealed Greek influences in this part of the world as early as the seventh century BCE, and which became extensive during the fifth and fourth centuries BCE. The trade routes for spice and incense between the Greek states and South Arabia passed through southern Palestine, and it was the seaports that were the first to experience the impact of the new Hellenistic civilization. The material remains of Greek culture have been unearthed in places such as Eilat, Acco and even in localities in the Jerusalem area.[8] Jerusalem itself, however, was rather remote from the commercial and strategic considerations of the eastern Mediterranean world, over which the values, styles and ideas of the Greeks were slowly spreading during the fourth century BCE.

Alexander's conquest of Palestine further facilitated the extension of the process historians refer to as Hellenization. The intrusion of the self-conscious Hellenic lifestyle on the equally self-assertive Judean culture was, however, bound to cause disharmony:

> *For I have bent Judah as my bow;*
> *I have made E'phraim its arrow.*
> *I will brandish your sons, O Zion,*
> *Over your sons, O Greece,*
> *and wield you like a warrior's sword.*[9]

Nevertheless, despite Jewish disapproval, *the adoption of foreign ways*[10] seemed inevitable. Initially as the Persian administration of Palestine gave way to Greek control, it seems that the limited Judean autonomy permitted by the Persians endured. The indirect evidence for this is that the high priest in Jerusalem retained authority over domestic matters and that the Jews remained subject to their traditional Mosaic Laws. The most obvious method of communicating this dispensation to the Judeans would have been by letter sent on behalf of Alexander to the Greek satrap of Coele-Syria.[11]

With Asia Minor, Palestine and Egypt under Macedonian control, the Hellenic League army crossed the Euphrates and Tigris rivers into the Mesopotamian heartland. In October 331 BCE Alexander defeated Darius at the Battle of Gaugamela,[12] effectively ending the rule of the Achaemenid royal house of Persia. Darius fled and was then murdered by his own Persian nobles, clearing the way for Alexander to become the lawful king of Persia.

By the age of thirty Alexander had created one of the largest empires of the ancient world, stretching from Greece southwards to Egypt and eastwards to India's Indus Valley. In June 323 BCE illness resulted in his death shortly before his thirty-third birthday, and the Macedonian empire was plunged into a frenzy of chaos and bloodshed, as his surviving relatives and generals sought to consolidate their power, promote their own self-interest and secure control of the empire.

At the time of his death, Alexander's wife Roxana was pregnant and, upon hearing of Alexander's death, she is reported to have had his other two wives murdered. It was agreed that Alexander's half-brother Philip Arrhidaeus should be king, on the understanding that if the yet unborn child were male, he would rule as joint king once he became of age. In the meantime, as Arrhidaeus was not considered fit to rule, Perdiccas, one of Alexander's most senior generals was appointed regent of the Macedonian empire.[13] He led an elite cabal that supported the claim of Roxana's unborn child to the succession.

Under Perdiccas, the already established system of regional satrapies endured. They were governed by Alexander's preeminent generals who, following his death, came to be known as the *Diadochi* or Successors. Laomedon of Mitylene became the satrap of the region known as Coele-Syria,[14] which included the province of Judea. The period under the rule of Laomedon (323 to 320 BCE) was a relatively peaceful interlude for Jerusalem prior to the serious disruption of the wars between the *Diadochi*.

Perdiccas did not survive long, however, as his attempts to dominate Alexander's other former generals created dissension that resulted in his murder at the hands of mutinous officers in 321 BCE, and power then lay in the hands of the *Diadochi*. Numerous intrigues at court resulted in the murders of many including Arrhidaeus, Roxana, her child (Alexander IV) as well as Olympias, the mother of Alexander the Great.[15]

Control of Egypt had been entrusted to Ptolemy, another of Alexander's generals. Ptolemy understood very well that whoever governed the Palestinian and Phoenician ports effectively controlled the important eastern Mediterranean trade routes. He also realized that Palestine could be used as a future staging post for an invasion of Egypt. For these reasons Ptolemy *set about in earnest to become master of those regions.*[16] His offer to purchase Laomedon's satrapy was, however, declined and so instead, in 320 BCE, he used force to achieve the territorial expansion that he desired.

Another general, Antigonus (*Monophthalmus*) had been put in charge of three regions in Anatolia. Antigonus was, however, the most contentious and ambitious of the *Diadochi*. In 315 BCE, he extended his control over all of Asia Minor, Syria, Palestine, Persia, Media and Mesopotamia. Thus, in the space of eight years, three different former generals of Alexander the Great had been nominally in charge of Jerusalem through their hegemony over Palestine. In the face of Antigonus' aggression, Seleucus, satrap of Babylonia since 321 BCE, was forced to flee to the safety of Ptolemy's Egypt. Antigonus regarded himself as supreme ruler of all Alexander's heritage, demanding that others yield completely to his power.[17]

In 312 BCE Ptolemy defeated Antigonus' son at the Battle of Gaza and overran Palestine. Having important future consequence for Jerusalem, Seleucus returned to Babylonia to re-establish his rule there. Rather than contest the approaching army of Antigonus, Ptolemy withdrew from Palestine so that if he were attacked his defences would be stronger in Egypt.[18] As Antigonus was unable to secure a decisive victory over his many *Diadochi* opponents, the rivals agreed the terms of a treaty, which maintained the peace, albeit temporarily.

The *Diadochi* demonstrating absolute rule in their respective dominions began to discard the echelon of satrap in favour of the supreme authority of kingship. In 306 BCE Antigonus adopted the title of the King of Asia, and during the following year Ptolemy assumed the designation King of Egypt, while Seleucus had himself crowned in Babylonia.

In 302 BCE, the *Diadochi* formed an alliance to overthrow Antigonus. At the beginning of the war Ptolemy overran Palestine and his army reached the Phoenician city of Sidon. However, a false rumour of a victory by Antigonus and his early arrival in Syria induced Ptolemy to once again retreat to the safety of Egypt.[19] Without assistance from Ptolemy the coalition forces defeated Antigonus in 301 BCE at the Battle of Ipsus.[20] Antigonus lost his life and the remaining land that formed his kingdom.

As Ptolemy had played no part in the final battle, the Macedonian kings excluded him from any share of Antigonus' vast territory and granted tenure of Coele-Syria to Seleucus. However, when Seleucus went to Phoenicia to establish his authority, he found that Coele-Syria was once again under the control of Ptolemy.[21] The issue of who had sovereignty over Coele-Syria became the *cause célèbre* of the region for the next two hundred years and resulted in several so-called Syrian Wars.

Chapter 11

The Ptolemies

Following the death of Alexander in 323 BCE, one of his Macedonian generals, Ptolemy, *son of Lagos*, was appointed satrap of Egypt. Towards the end of the fourth century BCE, the *Diadochi* began to assume the titles of kings and Ptolemy was no exception. In 305 BCE, taking the name Ptolemy *Soter*, he founded the Egyptian Ptolemaic dynasty that was to last three hundred years until the death of Cleopatra VII in 30 CE.

One perception of the size and population of late fourth-century BCE Jerusalem together with a description of its Temple is provided by an account attributed to Hecataeus of Abdera:

> *The Jews have many fortresses and villages in different parts of the country, but only one fortified city, which has a circumference of fifty stades[1] and some 120,000 inhabitants;[2] they call it Jerusalem. Nearly in the centre of the city stands a stone wall, enclosing an area about five plethra long[3] and a hundred cubits broad,[4] approached by a pair of gates. Within this enclosure is a square altar, built of heaped up stones, unhewn and unwrought; each side is twenty cubits long and the height is ten cubits. Beside it is a great edifice, containing an altar and a lampstand, both made of gold and weighing two talents; upon these is a light which is never extinguished by night or day. There is not a single statue or votive offering, no trace of a plant, in the form of a sacred grove or the like. Here priests pass their nights and days performing certain rites of purification, and abstaining altogether from wine while in the temple.[5]*

Ptolemy I was quick to realize that if he were to have sovereignty over Palestine, the defensive capabilities of Egypt against invasion from the east would be much improved. Palestine would serve as a significant obstacle to be overcome before Egypt itself could be attacked. Additionally, as the greater part of international trade was seaborne, he was aware that having control of the eastern Mediterranean seaports in Palestine would bestow considerable economic benefits upon his kingdom. In the final quarter of the fourth century BCE therefore, the key element of his foreign policy was to secure control of Coele-Syria,[6] including Judea and its principal city of Jerusalem.

During this period Ptolemy invaded Coele-Syria on no fewer than four occasions. His initial hegemony over the region lasted five years from 320 to 315, but in both 312 and 302 BCE Ptolemy withdrew in the face of real or imagined threats from his adversary Antigonus. Not, however, before capturing Jerusalem, probably during his third invasion, when the loyalties of Jerusalem's inhabitants were more or less equally divided between Antigonus and Ptolemy.[7] A brief record of the event recalls how the *Jews, who have a strong and great city called Jerusalem, which they allowed to fall into the hands of Ptolemy by refusing to take up arms.*[8] On the fourth occasion, however, there would be no retreat and from 301 BCE Ptolemy was there to stay.

Following their victory at Ipsus in 301 BCE, the decision of the Macedonian kings to award the whole of Syria and Palestine to Seleucus, despite Ptolemy's fourth invasion of the region giving him *de facto* control, drove an irreconcilable wedge between the former comrades-in-arms. Ptolemy felt slighted that Seleucus had accepted the apportionment of lands that were already under the control of Ptolemy, and Seleucus, for his part, maintained that only those who had fought in the Battle of Ipsus should be awarded shares in what had been Antigonus' territorial empire. For the time being Seleucus accepted Ptolemy's *fait accompli*, but this was accompanied by the menacing threat that he *would consider later how best to deal with friends who chose to encroach.*[9]

The Eleutherus River formed the boundary between the rival kings, which meant that in addition to his Egyptian lands, Ptolemy ruled Palestine, most of Phoenicia (including Tyre and Sidon from c.288/9 BCE), the Bekaa Valley and the southern part of the Eleutherus Valley. Ptolemy's Coele-Syria territory, incorporating several urban centres, was much wealthier than Seleucus' undeveloped and thinly populated Syrian lands north of the Eleutherus, and this contributed to the simmering Seleucid resentment. However, not least due to the threats posed to

Ptolemy and particularly to Seleucus by various regional enemies, an uneasy peace prevailed during the rest of their lifetimes, but the seeds had been sown for a series of Syrian Wars to be fought between successive Ptolemaic and Seleucid rulers during the third century BCE and beyond.

In 274 BCE Ptolemy II (282–246 BCE), feeling threatened by Antiochus I (281–261 BCE) and his allies, went on the offensive and attacked the Seleucids in northern Syria. He was repelled, as was the Seleucid counter-attack along the coastal road through Palestine. The 1st Syrian War ended in 271 BCE with Ptolemy and Antiochus agreeing peace term and returning to the pre-war boundaries. The kings were honour bound to adhere to the peace treaty until one or the other was no longer alive.

Two years after Antiochus I died the 2nd Syrian War began in 259 BCE, with Antiochus II (261–246 BCE) attacking a Ptolemaic city in Asia Minor. The focus of the war quickly moved to Syria, when in 258 BCE Ptolemy II invaded by sea and made initial, but not lasting progress. The fighting moved back to the Aegean and when peace was agreed in 253 BCE, Ptolemy had lost some territories in the Aegean, but the Coele-Syria border remained unaltered. The terms of the armistice included the marriage of Ptolemy's daughter, Berenice to Antiochus II.

Early in 246 BCE saw the death of Ptolemy II and a few months later Antiochus II passed away. Ptolemy III (246–221 BCE) succeeded his father very rapidly, but the succession in the Seleucid court was more problematic. Both Antiochus' eldest adult son Seleucus, from his first marriage to Laodice, and his youngest infant son Antiochus, from his marriage to Berenice (the sister of Ptolemy III), were claimants to the Seleucid throne.

Ptolemy III travelled by sea to Syria to visit Berenice and his nephew, but arriving at Antioch found that they had been murdered by supporters of Laodice. Calling up reinforcements, his 'visit' turned into an occupation of Syria, Cilicia[10] and Seleucid territory as far east as the Euphrates. The 3rd Syrian War (the Laodicean War) had begun. Ptolemy abandoned most of northern Syria and returned to Egypt to direct the war in Asia Minor and the Aegean. It took Seleucus II (246–226 BCE) some years to remove the Ptolemaic presences from most of his Syrian cities and in 242 BCE he invaded Phoenicia, only to be driven out again. Ptolemy III and Seleucus II eventually agreed a peace treaty in 241 BCE.

The 4th Syrian War began when the army of Antiochus III (223–187 BCE) marched into the Bekaa Valley in 221 BCE. Resistance by Theodotus, the Ptolemaic governor of Coele-Syria, plus a revolt in Babylonia induced him to temporarily withdraw. Encouraged by a switch of allegiances by Theodotus, Antiochus resumed his invasion in 220 BCE. By the winter of 218 BCE Antiochus had conquered the Phoenician coast and parts of Palestine and Transjordan. There were no signs of any campaign in the Judean hills and probably Jerusalem was ignored.[11] In June 217 BCE the Battle of Raphia (Rafiah), near Gaza resulted in a victory for Ptolemy IV (221–205 BCE), who retook the lost territories of Coele-Syria.

Jewish mercenaries were used by both Ptolemies and Seleucids, though not necessarily for service close to their homeland. It is unlikely that Jerusalem experienced any fighting during first four Syrian Wars, although indirect consequences would have been felt. Ptolemaic taxes were increased to finance the wars, particularly during the 2nd Syrian War, and there would have been social and economic disruption as troops were billeted in the houses of Jerusalem's residents, as part of the Ptolemaic bolstering of their major cities' defences.

During the reigns of the first three Ptolemaic kings, the Jews, both in Egypt and Palestine, enjoyed a period of relative calm and also some degree of prosperity. Despite imposing heavy taxes, the Ptolemies treated their Jewish subjects reasonably well and significant numbers of Palestinian Jews relocated to Egypt, where Greek soon became their native language. Of uncertain authorship, *The Letter of Aristeas*[12] refers to the translation of the Pentateuch into Greek at Alexandria during the reign of Ptolemy II. The discourse relates how Jerusalem's high priest Eleazar (c.260–245 BCE) agreed to the request of Ptolemy II to supply seventy-two scribes to undertake the translation.[13] If this were true, it would have necessitated a significant pool of Greek speaking biblically authoritative Jews residing in Jerusalem and thus indicate a high degree of Hellenization, at least within the intellectuals of the city by the mid-third century BCE.[14] Aristeas also offers his admittedly uncertain estimate of the size of Jerusalem: *It is about forty stades in circumference, as far as one could conjecture.*[15]

The Ptolemaic approach towards the Jews began to change after the victory of Ptolemy IV, *Philopator*, at the Battle of Raphia. Generally considered to be non-canonical, the apocryphal *III Maccabees* relates Ptolemy's failed attempt to enter the forbidden inner sanctuary of the temple in Jerusalem, his subsequent hatred of the Jews and the persecution and murder of Jews in Alexandria. The historical basis of this is flimsy, but under the rule of Ptolemy IV, life did become more difficult for the Jews living in Egypt. Tolerance was replaced with enmity and maltreatment and discontent with Ptolemaic rule began to spread throughout Palestine. This change in attitude would prove be an important factor in the outcome of the 5th Syrian War.

When Ptolemy IV died in 205 BCE his son, the future Ptolemy V, was only five years old. A series of regents was appointed as chaos descended upon the royal court in Alexandria and a serious revolution occurred in southern Egypt. In the spring of 202 BCE Antiochus III launched an inland invasion of Coele-Syria and with a surprise attack captured Damascus. He went unhindered through Palestine securing a number of cities, eventually seizing Gaza in 201 BCE.[16] Seleucid control of Gaza was a serious hindrance to any potential Egyptian reinforcements entering Palestine, thus providing Antiochus with the opportunity to eliminate large numbers of Ptolemaic Palestinian strongholds. Additional assistance came as the Satrap of Coele-Syria defected to Antiochus, indicating either an appraisal of the likely victor and/or the scope of discontent with the rule of the Ptolemies.

Nevertheless, a surprise Ptolemaic counter attack occurred in the winter of 201 BCE, when the Seleucid army had mainly either been withdrawn and/or confined to winter quarters. In the second half of 200 BCE the rival armies fought the Battle of Panion, south-east of Damascus. The result was a decisive victory for Antiochus, who recovered the rest of Palestine and then took his army to blockade the Ptolemaic mercenary forces that had fled to Sidon.

The first four Syrian Wars had little direct impact upon Jerusalem, but the 5th Syrian War was devastating for the city as Ptolemaic control was lost to the Seleucids, regained by the Egyptian forces and then recaptured by Antiochus, all within the space of three brutally vicious years. It was in the course of Antiochus' spring 202 BCE invasion that Jerusalem was wrenched from its 100-year long period under Ptolemaic sovereignty. During the 201 BCE counter offensive the Egyptian military retook the city, but following Antiochus success at the Battle of Panion,[17] the garrison of Ptolemaic soldiers was driven out and Jerusalem succumbed to Seleucid rule.[18]

Sidon and Joppa fell to Antiochus III in 199 BCE, and by early 198 BCE the Coele-Syria campaign was over. Antiochus had finally taken control of the Coele-Syria territories that had been awarded to the very first

Seleucid king more than one hundred years earlier. The 5th Syrian War continued to be fought in the Aegean, but eventually the terms of a peace treaty were agreed in 195 BCE.

Antiochus' ten-year-old daughter, Cleopatra, was betrothed to Ptolemy V and they were duly married in 193 BCE. Possibly repeating a fabrication originating in the Ptolemaic capital city of Alexandria, various ancient sources[19] suggested that the dowry for the marriage was the lands of Coele-Syria or the revenues thereof. Modern historians tend to the view that bearing in mind Antiochus had fought two wars in order to reclaim land, which he felt had been illegally occupied for more than a century, it is almost impossible to regard this assertion as being creditable,[20] or at best it was a pledge that was never honoured.[21]

Chapter 12

The Seleucids

Seleucus had been appointed Satrap of Babylonia in 321 BCE, but between 315 and 312 BCE he had been in exile in Egypt, as rival *Diadochos* Antigonus extended his control over much of Asia Minor, Syria, Palestine and Mesopotamia. The success of Ptolemy I at the Battle of Gaza in 312 BCE afforded Seleucus the opportunity to reclaim his domain and in 305 BCE he assumed the regal title of Seleucus, *Nicator*. He founded the Seleucid Empire, a dynasty that endured for around two hundred years (see figure 11).

In 281 BCE both Seleucus and Ptolemy Keraunos (Ptolemy II's half-brother) harboured ambitions to become king of Macedon. Keraunos won the competition by the prevailing traditional method of murdering his rival and Antiochus succeeded his father as the new Seleucid king. After ruling for twenty years, Antiochus died in Babylon in June 261 BCE to be succeeded by his second son, Antiochus II, as his first son had previously committed a violation so heinous that he had been executed. Upon the death of Antiochus II in the summer of 246 BCE, his eldest son, Seleucus II, inherited the throne despite some opposition. Seleucus II failed to survive a riding accident and his eldest son Alexander came to the throne, also using the regnal name of Seleucus. Seleucus III was murdered in 223 BCE by two of his own officers, leading to the accession of his younger brother, Antiochus III, who later came to be known as Antiochus the Great.

At the beginning of the second century BCE, Jerusalem along with the rest of Palestine and Phoenicia became part of the Seleucid Empire. The 5th Syrian War had taken its toll on the inhabitants and structure of Jerusalem, but the change in suzerainty did not give rise to cultural change, at least not immediately.[1] Out of gratitude for the support of the Jews in his confrontations with the Ptolemies, Antiochus III allegedly issued a decree proposing to rebuild Jerusalem and establishing the rights and privileges of the Jews under the Seleucid monarchy. In this purported *Letter to Ptolemy*,[2] Antiochus declares:

> King Antiochus to Ptolemy, greetings. Insomuch as the Jews, from the very moment when we entered their country, showed their eagerness to serve us and, when we came to their city, they gave us a splendid reception and met us with their senate[3] and furnished an abundance of provisions to our soldiers and elephants, and also helped us to expel the Egyptian garrison in the citadel, we have seen fit on our part to requite them for these acts and to restore their city which has been destroyed by the hazards of war and to repopulate it by bringing back to it those who have been dispersed abroad. In the first place we have decided, on account of their piety, to furnish them for their sacrifices an allowance of sacrificial animals, wine and oil and frankincense to the value of 20,000 pieces of silver, and sacred *artabae*[4] of fine flour in accordance with their native law, and 1,460 *medimni*[5] of wheat and 375 *medimni* of salt. And it is my will that these things be made over to them as I have ordered, and that the work on the temple be completed, including the porticoes and any other part that may be necessary to build. The timber, moreover, shall be brought from Judaea itself and from other nations and Lebanon, without the imposition of a toll-charge. The like shall be done with the other materials needed for making the restoration of the Temple more splendid. And all the members of the nation shall have a form of government in accordance with the laws of their country, and the senate, the priests, the scribes of the temple and the temple-singers shall be relieved from the poll tax and the crown-tax, and the salt-tax which they pay. And, in order that the city may the more quickly be inhabited, I grant both to the present inhabitants and to those who may return before the month of Hyperberetaios[6] exemption from taxes for three years. We shall also relieve them in future from the third part of their tribute, so that their losses may

be made good. And as for those who were carried off from the city and are slaves, we herewith set them free, both them and the children born to them, and order their property to be restored to them.[7]

It is clear from Antiochus' proclamation that not only was Jerusalem's temple badly damaged during the 5th Syrian War, but that the residents had suffered greatly, including some being driven out of the city and others carried off into slavery. In recognition of the support of Jerusalem's inhabitants against Ptolemy's armed forces, Antiochus sets the scene for the restoration of the Temple, the alleviation of taxes, the repatriation of exiles and slaves and most importantly the right of the Jews to live under their traditional laws and customs.

Armed conflict between the Romans and the Seleucids culminated in the defeat of Antiochus III at the Battle of Magnesia[8] in 190 BCE. The subsequent Treaty of Apamea in 188 BCE formalized Rome's indirect influence in the East and Antiochus' empire was reduced to Cilicia (the southern coast of Asia Minor), Syria, Palestine, Mesopotamia and western Persia. Antiochus was obliged to relinquish his territories in Europe and Asia Minor west of the Taurus. He was also forced to yield up hostages that included his third son Antiochus, later to become Antiochus IV, *Epiphanes* and hand over his ships and war elephants. Of significant economic consequence were the huge annual indemnities that the Seleucids had to pay.[9]

In 187 BCE Antiochus III was assassinated and succeeded by his second son, Seleucus IV. The Romans demanded that the new king's son Demetrius act as surety, and he took the hostage place of his uncle Antiochus, who was duly released from his detention. Seleucus IV alleviated the burden of the Roman indemnity payments by imposing draconian taxes upon his subjects, including the Jews of Palestine. The multifarious court intrigue that followed the 175 BCE murder of Seleucus IV ended when his younger brother was recognized as the new monarch, Antiochus IV.[10] Although the traditional lifestyle of Jerusalem's Jewish inhabitants persisted after the city had transferred to Seleucid rule in 200 BCE, external influences soon began to have an impact; more than ever following the accession of Antiochus IV to the throne in 175 BCE, as Hellenic art and architecture continued to spread throughout the Near East generally.

There were differences in the theological approaches of Jerusalem's Pharisees and Sadducees, both of which were rooted in antiquity.[11] The most outstanding characteristic of the Pharisees was their unique doctrine of the Oral Law, which they considered as binding as the written Torah. The Sadducees held that although the Torah had to be followed rigorously, anything not expressly forbidden was permissible and this made it easier for them to embrace non-Jewish customs. Essentially the Sadducees comprised the affluent and aristocratic Jewish priestly families, who found the Greek (Hellenistic) way of life especially appealing. They embraced the wishes of Antiochus IV to such an extent that they opened the door to Hellenism not only in social life, but also within religious worship.[12] The Sadducees began to display an undisguised disdain for conventional Jewish behaviour and, encouraged by Antiochus IV, effectively converted Jerusalem into a Greek city.

The status and authority of Jerusalem's scribes, the interpreters of law and justice, had been elevated by the 198 BCE declaration of Antiochus III.[13] This scribal class, especially those belonging to the very devout sect known as the Hasidim, were also traditionalists opposed to the emerging Greek lifestyle. The struggle between the opposing ideologies would soon lead to civil war, immense destruction in Jerusalem and the so-called Maccabean Revolt striving for religious and political freedom from Judea's Seleucid rulers.

Antiochus IV's roots of were, of course, Greek and it was reasonable for him to support the aspirations of his empire's major cities towards Hellenization. Nevertheless, one of his principal domestic policies was raising cash to finance his sprawling kingdom, and also to pay the tribute owed to Rome, that his predecessor had allowed to fall into arrears.[14] Within a year of ascending the throne, Antiochus IV took advantage of the Jewish factionalism and sold the position of high priest of Jerusalem to the highest bidder. The incumbent, Onias III, was opposed to the Hellenization of the city, but in 174 BCE Antiochus caused outrage in the city by accepting a bribe that secured the high priesthood for Onias' Hellenistically inclined brother Jason. Further payments were made, which allowed Jason to extend the process of Hellenization, including the building of a gymnasium,[15] a partially open roofed structure with a floor of polished flagstones, from which it took its name of *Xystus*. Here young men exercised naked in flagrant contravention of Jewish religious practice.

Jason's promotion of Greek culture accelerated the process of Hellenization and led to the elevation of Jerusalem's status to that of a *polis*, a Greek city, with all the accompanying constitutional rights and privileges for those who attained citizenship. Normally qualifying by virtue of property ownership or standing in the community, an eastern *polis* had a restricted number of citizens, while the remaining inhabitants were regarded as foreigners, notwithstanding being born in the city and being permanent residents. Despite heavy Seleucid taxes, the population of Jerusalem had expanded as the city had become more prosperous and an estimated 3,000[16] adult males were formally enrolled as citizens of the new *polis*, with their male children accordingly qualifying for education in the *Xystus*.

Jerusalem's elevated status of *polis* did nothing to alleviate the very volatile nature of the city's internal politics and in fact, may have added to the tensions. Amongst the rival factions of the priesthood, the situation virtually amounted to civil war. The Hellenistically inclined Jason met his match in an even more radical Hellenistic cabal of wealthy Jewish aristocrats, who probably as the result of an even larger bribe being offered to Antiochus IV in 171 BCE, usurped the high priesthood for their preferred choice, Menelaus. Jason had to flee and the dispute spread to broader sections of the population, as Menelaus incurred widespread displeasure by pilfering the Temple treasure and orchestrating the murder of Onias III. The astute Menelaus was, however, able to cling on to his position as high priest,[17] although nine years later he was to meet with a very unpleasant death.[18]

In Egypt, Ptolemy VI was approaching adulthood, but his shared triple monarchy with his younger siblings Cleopatra II and Ptolemy VIII remained under the control of regents, who were preparing for war to regain Coele-Syria. Similarly, Antiochus IV was readying his army to defend his territory. In 170 BCE hostilities broke out and although Antiochus occupied Egypt, he subsequently returned to Syria after agreeing terms with his nephew Ptolemy VI.[19]

A series of events conspired to induce Antiochus to repeat his invasion of Egypt in the spring of 168 BCE. The ruling council in Alexandria had repudiated the peace terms that had been agreed between Ptolemy VI and Antiochus IV, Greek mercenaries were being hired and the Ptolemaic Cypriot navy had become a threat. Antiochus occupied Memphis and much of the Egyptian Delta and initiated a half-hearted attack upon

Alexandria. However, both sides were aware that the powerful Roman Republic could not allow the Seleucids to gain control of Egypt by capturing Alexandria. There was relief all round when the expected Roman delegation arrived to prevent the downfall of one regional power and the aggrandizement of the other.[20] Certainly, the Ptolemies preferred the obligations that would accompany Roman protection as an alternative to Seleucid subjugation and by now Antiochus, knowing the war to be unwinnable, was seeking a way to withdraw without losing face.

In the Alexandrian suburb of Eleusis,[21] the Roman consul Popilius drew a circle in the earth around Antiochus using a vine stick, and stipulated that he remain inside the circle until he gave an answer to Rome's demand that he withdraw from Egypt.[22] Antiochus, was humiliated and forced to accede, but his consolations were future safety from attack from Egypt during his reign and recognition from Rome and the Ptolemies that Coele-Syria belonged to his family. Chastened, but wealthier due to the looting he had carried out, Antiochus duly returned to Syria.[23]

Havoc and devastation were inflicted upon Jerusalem during and immediately after the 6th Syrian War, but this was not due directly to the Ptolemaic-Seleucid conflict. During one or other of his campaigns in Egypt, a false rumour that Antiochus had been killed spread to Palestine and induced Jason to return and try to take Jerusalem by force. A bloody civil war ensued and Jason either fled before the return of Antiochus or was driven out by the Seleucids who came to restore order.

1 Maccabees details two separate Seleucid assaults upon Jerusalem. The first of these took place in 169 BCE when Antiochus, returning from Egypt on his way back to Syria, desecrated and looted the city temple.[24] The second incident occurred when a Seleucid tax collector arrived *two years later ... plundered the city, burned it with fire, and tore down its houses and surrounding walls. And they took captive the women and children and seized the cattle.*[25]

2 Maccabees places the rumour of Antiochus' death and the civil war initiated by Jason during Antiochus second invasion of Egypt. Concluding that Judea was in a state of rebellion, Antiochus attacked Jerusalem with such ferocity that over a three-day period, 40,000 men, women and children were massacred and a further 40,000 sold into slavery. The Temple was profaned and looted before Antiochus departed, leaving behind a Seleucid administrator, Philip, to rule alongside the high

priest Menelaus. Perhaps the situation in Jerusalem remained disorderly as a further Seleucid force was dispatched resulting in even more deaths in the city.[26]

The Jews were savagely persecuted as a determined and thorough attempt was made to eliminate their religion. Holy books of the law were destroyed, circumcision of infants was criminalized and the celebration of Greek religious rites became compulsory. Jerusalem's Temple was utterly defiled and renamed after the Olympian god Zeus.[27] Only seven years after being elevated to the illustrious status of *polis*, Jerusalem was degraded to the lowest and most humiliating rank of military colony.

It was fairly standard practice for the Seleucids to construct fortresses on the outskirts of their cities for the dual purpose of maintaining internal order and as protection from external enemies. In 168 BCE, the potential for disorder and rebellion in Jerusalem was such that a Seleucid citadel, known as the *Akra*, was established within the city and manned by a garrison of foreign troops, who were most likely Syrian/Aramaean recruits or mercenaries overseen by Greek Seleucid officers.[28]

The site of the *Akra* is not known, despite 1 Maccabees' repetitious allusions to it being in the City of David,[29] giving rise to the opinion that *it lay on the southern slope of the eastern hill, therefore to the south of the temple rock.*[30] One of the uncertainties in this respect is that as 1 Maccabees had been written no earlier than the late second century BCE, it is possible that the author had not correctly identified the site of the City of David.[31] If the *Akra* were situated on the Ophel, the question then arises as to whether the citadel encompassed the whole or just part of the ancient City of David.[32]

Josephus places the *Akra* in the Lower City situated south of the Temple Mount. However, he also maintains that *it was high enough to overlook the temple,*[33] which seems improbable on the grounds of topography. Even Josephus' claim that when the *Akra* was eventually taken by siege, the hill on which it stood was levelled off *in order that the temple might be higher,*[34] is not really a convincing justification that suggests he has the correct original location. Of the many theories put forward, the contention that the *Akra* was on the western ridge seems *to make better topographical sense.*[35] The twenty-first-century discovery of a pre-Hasmonean wall under the Givati parking lot in the ancient City of David is also unconvincing as the site of the *Akra* on the grounds that it is too low on the hill to have overlooked the Temple Mount.

Walls and houses were demolished to provide some of the building materials for the construction of the *Akra*, which was used not only to house the troops and those Jews allied to the Seleucids, but also served as a storage centre for weapons, food and valuables plundered from the Temple and domestic dwellings. It may also have functioned to incarcerate hostages to help ensure the maintenance of good order.[36] The *Akra* residents enjoyed economic independence from the rest of Jerusalem and its very presence, the militia within it, their prostitutes and their way of life was a constant source of outrage and resentment to the Jewish inhabitants of Jerusalem. There were attempts to disrupt and/or blockade the *Akra*,[37] but, nevertheless, the fortification was strong enough to survive for more than a quarter of a century.

Chapter 13

The Maccabean Revolt

The Maccabean Revolt was an extraordinary struggle in the history of Jerusalem, its environs and Coele-Syria.[1] It was a war, or rather a series of wars, that lasted ten years and the major sources for the events that took place are 1 Maccabees and 2 Maccabees.[2] More independent information, which is less biased towards the Maccabees, is provided by Josephus, but this is fairly limited in scope. The accounts in 1 Maccabees and 2 Maccabees are from time to time at variance, partly because they were written from contrasting perspectives, but also no doubt due to the fact that on occasion they used different sources.

Both books date events according to the Seleucid era, but for each the year began at a different point in time. For the author of 2 Maccabees, the first day of the year was in the autumn and for the author of 1 Maccabees, the year began in the spring, and understandably this leads to occasional chronological disparities.[3]

2 Maccabees offers a version whereby the struggle between the Hellenistic and Traditional Jews leads to civil war, but that the observance of Yahweh's requirements will ultimately lead to deliverance.

1 Maccabees lays the responsibility for the conflict more on the anti-Jewish actions of Antiochus IV and the heroic efforts of the Hasmonean family to ensure the survival of Judaism. Both have valid arguments for the outbreak of the rebellion, but while 2 Maccabees must still be taken into account, 1 Maccabees does allow for a more orderly presentation of the conflict.

In addition to destroying much of Jerusalem, Palestine's Seleucid overlord, Antiochus IV, had pronounced the Judaic religion illegal. In 166 BCE, functionaries who had been dispatched around the countryside to enforce the adoption of state approved pagan sacrificial rites reached the village of Modein, seventeen miles north-west of Jerusalem. An elderly Jewish priest, Mattathias Asamonaeus, refused to take part in the ritual, whereupon a Jew of the village agreed to undertake the pagan sacrifice. However, before he could do so, he was slain by Mattathias, who also despatched the presiding Seleucid dignitary, before fleeing with his five sons to the mountains of the Judean wilderness.[4]

Although the exact beginning of the Maccabean Revolt is a contentious issue, the diminution in Seleucid prestige following the Romans' humiliation of Antiochus IV, at the so-called Day of Eleusis, almost certainly incentivised the rebels in pursuit of their cause. The brawl in the village of Modein instigates the rebellion according to 1 Maccabees, whereas 2 Maccabees does not mention Mattathias, and sees Judas Maccabee as the initiator.[5] Another view is that the sect known as the Hasidim had begun the insurgency a year earlier, and that Judas added the dimension of allowing the Jews to fight on the Sabbath when he became the movement's leader.[6] Whatever was the initial spark the Maccabean Revolt had begun and although Mattathias died shortly after, his sons commanded a powerful guerrilla militia, led by Judas Maccabee (see figure 12).

Ostensibly, the Maccabees did not belong to either of the religious groupings known as Pharisees and Sadducees. However, their eagerness to preserve the religion of their fathers allied them with the Hasidim, who were participating in the armed struggle. This in turn resulted in a leaning towards the Pharisees, who as strict observers of the Jewish laws essentially shared the same theology as the Hasidim.

The insurgents raided towns and villages, murdering Antiochus' officials, destroying non-Jewish altars and killing pro-Greek Jews that were worshipping pagan gods. Despite often being heavily outnumbered the rebels were successful in a number of battles against various militia groups representing the Seleucid government.

Antiochus IV's primary concern was the problems in the eastern reaches of his empire and after a sumptuous celebration to commemorate his earlier perceived victory in Egypt, he left Antioch in the spring of 165 BCE for a venture that would take him to distant lands including Babylonia, Bactria[7] and Persia. Before he left, Antiochus IV appointed his eight-year-old son as joint king, with the high-ranking nobleman Lysias acting as regent. Lysias was entrusted with combating the problem in Judea, but even heading a huge contingent of Seleucid infantry and cavalry, he was unable to prevent the rebels entering Jerusalem.

The pro-Greek factions in Jerusalem were repressed and ousted from government and although Menelaus retained the position of high priest, he was no longer able to exercise the functions of his office. Judas prevented any interference by the Seleucid militia occupying the Akra, while his followers restored, cleansed and purified the damaged and defiled Temple. In December 164 BCE, three years to the day after the Temple had been desecrated, a service was held for its rededication and this was followed by an ostentatious eight-day celebration.[8]

Judas now controlled both the city of Jerusalem and Judea, the territory of the ancient Kingdom of Judah. He strengthened the defences of the former and enhanced national security by fortifying the town of Beth-zur on the southern border with Idumaea.[9] To protect external traditional Jews and to consolidate their power, Judas and his brothers then began to raid the neighbouring regions of Idumaea, Ammon, Gilead, Galilee and territory belonging to the Philistines.

Antiochus IV's eastern venture ended with an illness and his subsequent death in Persia in late 164 BCE, while in Jerusalem the *Akra* remained a threat to Jewish authority in the city. In 162 BCE Judas decided that he was now powerful enough to put an end to this nuisance and instigated a siege of the hated foreign-occupied citadel. Escapees from the *Akra* were joined by Hellenistic Jews in requesting assistance from the authorities in Antioch, prompting a further incursion into Judea by Lysias and the young king, Antiochus V, *Eupator*. They arrived with a large army of Seleucid forces supported by mercenaries from a number of countries and initially laid siege to Beth-zur,[10] in the Judean hill country. Judas had to abandon the siege of the *Akra* and march south to meet the Seleucid forces south-west of Jerusalem at Beth-zechariah.

A ferocious battle was fought during which Eleazar Avaran, one of the Judas' brothers, suspected that a particularly tall elephant was carrying the Seleucid king. Eleazar stabbed the beast from below and perished when the elephant collapsed on top of him.[11] On this occasion the rebels were beaten and had to retreat to Jerusalem. Lacking provisions and facing either starvation or surrender to the besieging Seleucid army, the outlook for Judas and his followers appeared bleak.

Lysias, however, had problems of his own as his food supplies were diminishing and he realized that securing victory against those in the Jerusalem stronghold presented an arduous challenge. News of an attempted coup d'état in Antioch motivated Lysias to propose a peace settlement. Hoping to have his position as high priest reaffirmed, Menelaus had joined up with Antiochus V and Lysias. The latter realized that the price of peace with the Jews would include the sacrifice of Menelaus and he persuaded Antiochus to send the high priest to Beroea[12] for execution.[13] Lysias and the rebels reached agreement that in return for the Jews being allowed the freedom to worship their God, they would remain politically loyal to the Seleucid Empire. With this, Lysias and Antiochus V, together with their army departed, after dismantling the strong walls that the rebels had constructed around the Temple.[14]

When disease took the life of Antiochus IV, the rightful heir to the Seleucid throne was Demetrius, *Soter*, the son of Seleucus IV. However, as he had been detained as a hostage in Rome since 188 BCE, the young Antiochus V had been crowned as the new Seleucid king. The Roman Senate twice refused Demetrius' pleas to be granted his freedom, but, nevertheless, influential figures in Rome managed to engineer his escape.[15] He returned to Antioch in 162 BCE to claim his throne, happily allowing his supporters to put to death both Antiochus V and his regent Lysias.[16]

Jerusalem remained a city vehemently divided between the pro-Greek faction and the traditional Jews, who held the reins of power under the leadership of Judas Maccabee. At the head of the Hellenistic Jews was an individual named Alcimus, whom the Seleucids had possibly appointed high priest after the death of Menelaus.[17] They were persistent in their endeavours to reassert dominance and the latest change of Seleucid sovereign allowed them an opportunity too good to forego. Alcimus and his followers encouraged Demetrius I to resume the war, which he did by dispatching the ruthless high ranking general Bacchides with a substantial army to Judea.

Once Bacchides had established himself in Jerusalem, Alcimus was ratified as high priest and even though he was not in direct line of succession, he was accepted as such by the Hasidim scribes on the basis that he had ancient priestly ancestry.[18] This marked a rift in the alliance between the Hasidim, who were not concerned with political freedom, and the rebels led by Judas Maccabee, for whom the desire for political independence had grown and now stood alongside the aim of religious freedom. The distrust felt by the rebels was vindicated when Alcimus subsequently caused consternation amongst the people of the city by reneging on his promise not to harm the scribes by slaughtering sixty of them *in one day*.[19] Bacchides felt confident that his task had been fulfilled and, leaving a contingent of troops for support, he returned to Antioch leaving Alcimus *in charge of the country*.[20] Judas Maccabee and his supporters left Jerusalem and the next stage of the revolt began. The resumed guerrilla war was successful to such a formidable extent that Alcimus was obliged once more to go and plead for assistance from Demetrius.

Yet another military force arrived to resolve the Judean problem, this time under the leadership of Seleucid general Nicanor. This detachment was no more successful than its predecessors and following a reversal in a confrontation with the rebels north-west of Jerusalem, Nicanor threatened the priests that he would burn down the temple *unless Judas and his army are delivered into my hands*.[21] Reinforcements joined Nicanor, but to no avail when the opposing sides met in a decisive encounter at Adasa.[22] In 161 BCE the Seleucid army was routed by Judas's militia and Nicanor was slain *on the thirteenth day of the month of Adar*.[23]

Although Judas was again in command of the local situation, he realized that ultimately, he was no match for the military might of the Seleucids and that he needed a more powerful ally. Emissaries to Rome were despatched and a treaty of friendship and mutual aid was secured as well as a forceful warning letter being sent to Demetrius by the Roman senate. For Judas, however, all of this was too late as before the emissaries returned and the letter had been delivered to the Seleucid monarch, Demetrius had sent Bacchides and Alcimus to Judea for the second time. A savage battle ensued that began near Jerusalem, but ended near Ashdod on the Mediterranean coast. Judas Maccabee was killed and the leadership of the rebels passed to his brother Jonathan in the autumn of 161 BCE.

This phase of the Maccabean Revolt ended with another retreat into the Judean wilderness, during which John Gaddi became the third of the brothers to perish when he was murdered by a band of Amorite bandits. Jonathan and Simon, the surviving Maccabee brothers, exacted a bloody revenge upon the robbers,[24] before encountering Bacchides at the river Jordan. This confrontation proved inconclusive and Bacchides returned to Jerusalem in order to consolidate his position in Judea. In May 160 BCE the high priest Alcimus suffered a stroke and died. Soon after this Bacchides, believing that the garrisons he had built provided the necessary security for Seleucid control of Judea, returned to Antioch and *the land of Judah had rest for two years*.[25]

In 158 BCE, the pro-Greek Jewish faction persuaded Bacchides to return to Judea for a third time, with an army supposedly strong enough to eliminate the now flourishing Maccabean party and its supporters. Nevertheless, Jonathan and Simon headed separate contingents of rebels, which proved too difficult for Bacchides to conquer. Bacchides finally realized the futility of continuing to expend precious resources sustaining the Hellenistic Jews, who by themselves were not able hold on to power for any length of time.[26] He therefore resolved the dilemma by making peace with Jonathan. A release of prisoners of war was negotiated and Bacchides departed promising that he would never again mount military action in Judea. It had been almost ten years since the beginning of the Maccabean Revolt, but the traditional Jews had finally triumphed over their Hellenistic kinsmen and they were now well on their way to securing independence from their Seleucid overlords.

Jonathan was effectively in charge of Judea, but initially he did not reside in Jerusalem, where presumably the pro-Greek faction still held sway, at least for the time being. He set himself up seven miles north-east of Jerusalem in the town of Michmash.[27] It was from here that *Jonathan began to judge the people, and he destroyed the ungodly out of Israel.*[28]

Chapter 14

Independence

From 158 BCE onwards, Jonathan's influence in Judea increased considerably. Without Seleucid support, the authority of Hellenistic Jews diminished as the people returned to their spiritual roots, and were increasingly attracted by the Maccabean concept of political as well as religious freedom.[1]

Neither his own subjects, nor other heads of state, found the new Seleucid king, Demetrius, *Soter* very much to their liking.[2] A pretender to the throne named Alexander Balas was backed by the kingdoms of Pergamum and Cappadocia and most importantly by Egypt's Ptolemy, *Philometor* VI. The sponsors secured the Roman Senate's concurrence to the dubious assertion that Antiochus IV was the father of Balas and his sister, Laodice, and that Balas was therefore the rightful Seleucid king[3] (see figure 13). Ptolemy VI had the financial muscle to resource a war against Demetrius and in 153 BCE Balas and large mercenary army arrived in a fleet of ships at the Palestinian port of Ptolemais.[4]

The Seleucid civil war that began served to strengthen the position of Jonathan, as Demetrius could ill afford the Maccabees joining with his enemies. He wrote to Jonathan requesting an alliance, giving him the authority to recruit troops and ordered the release of the hostages held in the *Akra*. A triumphant Jonathan then occupied Jerusalem and instigated the rebuilding of its defensive walls.[5]

Both Seleucid factions viewed the Judeans as potential allies and, to this end, in 152 BCE Balas sent Jonathan a purple robe and a golden crown to signify his acceptance of Jonathan's elevated status. He also appointed Jonathan *to be the high priest of your nation.*[6]

Disapproval of Jonathan's acceptance of the high priesthood is likely to have acted as the catalyst for many of the religious community known as the Essenes to leave Jerusalem and move to the caves at Qumran in the desert near the Dead Sea. The Essenes accepted an austere dietary regime and a commitment to celibacy, other than for procreation. All property was communally held and as they disdained animal sacrifice, the Essenes were prohibited from entering the Temple precinct in Jerusalem. The studious and peaceful majority of Essenes who remained in Jerusalem rejected the concept of bodily resurrection and postulated a purely spiritual afterlife. Generally, their rituals and practices set them apart from the mainstream Judaean Jewish way of life.[7] More than 2,000 years later, the so-called *Dead Sea Scrolls* were discovered in the Qumran caves. These manuscripts modified and added to scholastic understanding of the Hebrew Bible, Judaism and early Christianity in addition to Essene theology.

1 Maccabees relates that Demetrius countered the overtures from Balas with a series of extravagant promises and concessions.[8] Undoubtedly, Demetrius offered more than he intended to deliver, but equally it is likely that the list of indulgences was itself exaggerated by the author of 1 Maccabees. In the event, Jonathan declined to accept Demetrius' latest pledges, doubting that they would be honoured and also sensing that Demetrius would end up being the loser in the civil war.

Alexander Balas, *Epiphanes* became the undisputed Seleucid monarch when he defeated Demetrius I in 150 BCE. Demetrius died during the battle and his eldest son was killed during the subsequent purge. Of later consequence was Demetrius' decision before the final battle to remove from Syria his other two sons, who subsequently were to rule the Seleucid Empire as Demetrius II and Antiochus VII.

Jonathan's princely status was further reinforced at the splendid ceremony in Ptolemais to mark the marriage of Balas to Ptolemy VI's daughter, Cleopatra Thea. The pro-Greek Jews present were snubbed while Jonathan was seated next to Balas, clothed in royal purple. Jonathan was already the effective ruler of an anti-Hellenistic Jewish state, but at this meeting of royal personages he was formally endowed with the titles of military and civil governor of Judea.[9] Nevertheless, the Jerusalem that Jonathan returned to was still not yet free from the despised foreign garrison known as the *Akra*. Judea remained nominally subject to Seleucid sovereignty, but Balas' empire itself was beginning to take on the appearance of an Egyptian client state as Ptolemy VI expanded his sphere of influence. The aim of the latter was once again to regain control of Coele-Syria.

When the eleven-year-old Demetrius was sent from Syria by his father of the same name, he left with a great deal of gold and an experienced entourage. For the next three years the groundwork was undertaken, both outside and inside Syria, for Demetrius to return *to the land of his fathers*[10] with a mercenary army in 147 BCE. Amongst numerous intrigues and changing of sides, Jonathan initially stayed loyal to Balas, although the notoriously lazy and inefficient incumbent monarch generally lacked support. On behalf of Balas, Jonathan and his brother Simon secured victories at the towns of Joppa and Azotus,[11] following which they burned and pillaged the surrounding towns before returning to Jerusalem with their plunder.

Ptolemy VI arrived in southern Palestine with a huge army and fleet of ships ostensibly in support of his son-in-law, Balas. Ptolemy worked his way up the coastal towns, pointedly leaving a garrison in each. Jonathan joined him at Joppa, but once they reached the Eleutherus River, the historic Ptolemaic/Seleucid border, Jonathan departed for Jerusalem. Ptolemy had no doubt shown his displeasure over Jonathan's earlier destruction of towns that Ptolemy now considered to be his territory. Ptolemy controlled the Coele-Syrian coast and whether or not he had originally arrived to support his son-in-law, he now felt that maintaining his position in Coele-Syria was better served by supporting Demetrius rather than Balas. Not only did he switch his allegiance, he also repudiated the marriage of his daughter to Balas, and thus in 145 BCE Cleopatra Thea became the wife of the sixteen-year-old Demetrius.

The army of Alexander Balas engaged the combined forces of Ptolemy and Demetrius by the Orontes River just north of Antioch. Ptolemy was seriously injured, but Balas lost the battle and fled. Balas was then murdered either by the Arab chief,[12] with whom he sought sanctuary, or by his own officers.[13] Within days Ptolemy succumbed to his wounds and also died, leaving the new Seleucid king, Demetrius II both victorious and free from the overbearing intrigues of Ptolemy VI. Nevertheless, the unquestioned supremacy exercised by Seleucid monarchs until recently had been undermined, as *none of the kings of Syria was henceforth sure of his throne*.[14]

In Jerusalem, Jonathan began to manoeuvre for greater Judean political freedom, initially by instigating a siege of the *Akra*. He was summoned to Ptolemais to explain his aggressive action, but the weakness of Demetrius' position became evident as Jonathan extracted a number of concessions in return for ending the siege. Jonathan's titles, including that of high priest, were confirmed and territories belonging to Samaria were ceded to Judea, which was hereafter exempted from Seleucid taxation.[15]

Before the dissolution of Cleopatra Thea's union with Alexander Balas and her subsequent marriage to Demetrius II, she had given birth to Balas' son, who as pretender to the Seleucid throne was known as Antiochus VI (*Dionysus*). Of course, in 145 BCE, he was still an infant and his entitlement to the throne was being championed by one of Balas' former generals named Diodotus Tryphon.[16] Demetrius' position was already precarious and because his own troops had deserted, he needed Jonathan's military strength to subdue an insurrection in Antioch. To secure Jonathan's vital intervention, Demetrius pledged to remove the foreign militiamen from the reviled *Akra*. In the event Demetrius failed to keep this promise and thus temporarily lost the support of the Jewish people. He was forced to abandon Antioch, as Tryphon seized the traditional Seleucid western capital city on behalf of the infant Antiochus VI. The new Seleucid regime endorsed Jonathan as Jerusalem's high priest, and confirmed his territorial possessions as *one of the friends of the king.*[17]

Jonathan pursued friendly international relationships with Rome and Sparta and he and his brother Simon undertook a number of successful military operations in support of Antiochus VI. In Jerusalem, they continued with the reinforcement of the defensive walls and a barrier was erected that effectively placed the *Akra* into quarantine.[18] Judea's political and military potency had increased to such an extent that full independence from the Seleucid Empire now appeared possible and prompted Tryphon into action to forestall any move towards Jewish self-determination.

Tricked by Tryphon into entering Ptolemais with an insufficient protective force, Jonathan was taken prisoner[19] and Simon became the new Jewish leader. Between unsuccessful attempts to invade Judea from the north-west and the south, Tryphon claimed Jonathan was only being held prisoner because he had not paid for the titles that had been conferred upon him. Money and Jonathan's sons as hostages were sent to the duplicitous Tryphon, but nevertheless, in 143 BCE, Tryphon had Jonathan put to death.[20] Simon arranged for Jonathan to be buried in Modein, in a tomb below a majestic monument commemorating the Maccabean brothers and their parents.

Having arranged for the young Antiochus VI to be murdered, Tryphon declared himself to be the new Seleucid king.[21] Simon's response was to press ahead with the defensive installations in Jerusalem and other Judean cities and to once again open a dialogue with Demetrius, whose negotiating position was frail. He confirmed Simon's rightful possession of all strongholds that had been constructed and freed the Judeans from all arrears and future tributes and taxes. Thus in 142 BCE Judea's political independence was recognized as *the yoke of the Gentiles was removed from Israel.*[22]

Demetrius, however, did not control southern Syria, let alone Palestine, and it was up to Simon to convert Demetrius' rather hollow declaration into actuality. Simon besieged and then captured the strategically important town of Gazara, which dominated the passes through the mountains from Jerusalem to the Mediterranean coast. Then, as the political and religious freedom in Jerusalem remained incomplete and frustrated by the foreign occupation of the *Akra*, Simon blockaded the citadel until famine forced its surrender in early June 141 BCE. The replacement occupants of the fortified *Akra* were Jews.[23] An alternative version of events describes how Simon took the citadel by siege, razed it to the ground and levelled the hill on which it stood, *in order that the temple might be higher than this.*[24]

The energies of the Seleucids were consumed by their internal conflicts and civil war and for a period of time the people of Jerusalem enjoyed the independence of Judea. *They tilled their land in peace ... Old men sat in the streets ... No one was left in the land to fight them.*[25] The contributions that Simon and his late brothers had made in bringing about this situation was formally acknowledged in September 140 BCE by a declaration that Simon was to be the leader and high priest *for ever, until a trustworthy prophet should arise.*[26] The terms of this affirmation were inscribed on bronze tablets, which were to be prominently displayed inside the Temple compound. Simon and his future descendants were henceforth to hold the titles of high priest, military commander and head of the nation of the Jewish people until Yahweh decreed otherwise. The hereditary aspect of the proclamation effectively created the Jerusalem-based Judean Hasmonean dynasty.

Before the formal legitimization of Simon's rule by the people and the priests in Jerusalem, a delegation had been despatched to Rome hoping to reaffirm the understanding that Jonathan had established with the Roman Senate. The envoys returned in 139 BCE bearing copies of letters confirming the support of the Romans and instructing various kings and countries to respect Judean integrity.[27] One of the intended recipients of Rome's instructions was Demetrius II,[28] thereby confirming the ending of Seleucid hegemony over Judea, at least in the eyes of the most authoritative Mediterranean super-power.

The Seleucid Empire was no longer under the control of a single individual and to make matters worse, the Parthian king Mithradates I invaded Babylonia, prompting declarations of independence by minor south-eastern kingdoms[29] within the Seleucid Empire. More concerned with the potential disintegration of the eastern reaches of his empire than the stalemate with Tryphon in Syria, Demetrius II marched to the east to confront the Parthians. In the summer of 139 BCE, however, he was captured and spent the next ten years as their prisoner.

Before embarking for Syria to take his elder brother's place, Antiochus believing that he would need Jewish assistance to overcome Tryphon, wrote to Simon confirming the sovereign rights of the Judean state.[30] In the event, Antiochus proved to be a more proficient soldier than Demetrius and he was able to drive Tryphon from Antioch. While the latter was besieged in the coastal town of Dor, Simon sent troops, money and military equipment to augment the demise of Tryphon. However, now that Antiochus had gained control of Syria, he affected a complete *volte-face*, refused the offerings and reneged upon his earlier undertakings to Simon.

With the collapse of Tryphon's authority, Antiochus VII *Sidetes* was now the undisputed Seleucid monarch. He demanded that the Jews return the cities of Joppa and Gazara to Seleucid control, as well as the *Akra* fortress within Jerusalem, which previously had been occupied by pro-Seleucid forces for around twenty-five years until 141 BCE. The alternative was a payment of a hugely disproportionate sum of one thousand talents. Refusing to hand over any territory, Simon sent the Seleucid negotiator back to Antioch with an offer to pay no more than one hundred talents,[31] setting the scene for renewed armed conflict between the Judeans and the Seleucids.

While Antiochus VII pursued Tryphon,[32] who had managed to escape from Dor, a Seleucid commander-in-chief was sent to wage war upon

Judea. It had been thirty years since the Maccabeans had originally taken up arms and Simon was now quite elderly. His sons, Judas and John, led the Judean army against the Seleucid cavalry and infantry in the plain outside Modein, the village where the Maccabean rebellion had originally begun. Although Judas was wounded, John led a successful campaign and pursued the Seleucids almost to the Mediterranean coast before safely returning to Jerusalem.[33]

Chapter 15

The Hasmoneans

None of the five sons of Mattathias Asamonaeus managed to avoid a violent death and Simon's came in 134 BCE. History recalls little about Ptolemy, the son of Abubus, other than he was governor of the region of Jericho and had married one of Simon's daughters. At a banquet in the fortress of Dok near Jericho, Simon and two of his sons, Mattathias and Judas, were enjoying the celebrations a little too much and when they were too drunk to mount any serious resistance, Ptolemy ordered his men to assassinate his father-in-law and brothers-in-law.[1] Ptolemy's intention to secure the leadership of Judea for himself was thwarted when another of Simon's sons, John Hyrcanus, the Governor of Gazara, circumvented an attempt on his life by Ptolemy's assassins and reached Jerusalem before Ptolemy.[2] Six years earlier the people and priests of Jerusalem had given Simon the titles of leader and high priest in perpetuity and accordingly John Hyrcanus legally inherited the titles held by his late father (see figure 14).

Unable to gain entrance to Jerusalem, Ptolemy took refuge in the Dok fortress, where he was besieged by John Hyrcanus. The assault on the fortress stalled as John Hyrcanus hesitated to press the fight when his mother, held prisoner by Ptolemy, was threatened with being hurled from the ramparts.[3] The advent of a Jewish Sabbatical Year[4] then intervened, placing a religious obligation on the Jews to abandon the siege altogether. Ptolemy seized the opportunity to flee, but not before killing John Hyrcanus' mother.

A few years earlier Simon had replied to demands made by Antiochus VII with a token gesture and subsequently the Judean army inflicted a humiliating defeat upon the Seleucid forces. By 134 BCE, however, Antiochus' internal affairs were in better shape and with a more powerful army he invaded Judea, wreaking havoc throughout the country before laying siege to Jerusalem. The strength of the defensive walls prevented a swift resolution and the Seleucids settled in for a protracted encounter by surrounding the city with ditches and towers. John Hyrcanus' forces assailed the aggressors at every opportunity, but as time passed, the blockade created food shortages in the city and he ejected those of the population who could not contribute to the war effort. As Antiochus would not allow the refugees to pass, they were trapped, hungry and exhausted in a no-man's land between the city walls and the Seleucid installations.[5]

The outcasts were rescued when those remaining in the city allowed them to return for the seven-day Feast of the Tabernacles. Antiochus agreed to a truce and even provided contributions to the Temple sacrifice. A peace settlement ensued with the Judeans willing to agree to all Antiochus' demands except one. John Hyrcanus accepted that the Jews would have to surrender their weapons and pay tribute for a number of disputed cities, but with memories of the *Akra* still fresh in Hasmonean minds, he could not agree to the reintroduction of a Seleucid garrison in Jerusalem. Instead Antiochus accepted an offer of hostages including the last remaining brother of John Hyrcanus and five hundred talents of silver.[6] The money to pay off Antiochus was part of the three thousand talents that John Hyrcanus took from the tomb of King David.[7]

The siege was lifted in 132 BCE and several sources report that before Antiochus departed, he demolished the walls that encircled Jerusalem.[8] How extensive and effective was the dismantling of the walls is a moot point and perhaps it was only the battlements that were destroyed. Whatever the extent of the damage, however, before the end of Hyrcanus' reign the walls had been rebuilt.

In 130/29 BCE John Hyrcanus joined Antiochus VII in a war against the Parthians. Antiochus was killed in battle facilitating the return as Seleucid king of his brother Demetrius II, who had been released from his decade long captivity by the Parthians. Seleucid influence dwindled as multiple claimants contested control of what was left of the Seleucid realm in an almost unending series of civil wars. Jewish independence could at last be deemed absolute and after the death of Antiochus VII, no further tributes were ever paid to Seleucid kings.[9]

John Hyrcanus was now completely free to embark upon campaigns to extend the territory of Judea. In Transjordan, he captured Medeba and in the north, he seized Shechem and Mount Gerizim and destroyed the rival Samaritan temple. He then took his army to the south and in c.127 BCE subdued Idumaea, allowing its people to remain only if they converted to Judaism.[10] Future rulers of Jerusalem would include the Jewish Idumaeans Antipater and his son Herod the Great, who married Mariamne, a direct descendant of John Hyrcanus.

The Samaritans were long standing enemies of Jerusalem and in around 108/7 BCE John Hyrcanus attacked the city of Samaria, placing his sons Antigonus and Aristobulus in charge of a vigorous siege. In response to appeals for help, Seleucid and Egyptian militia attempted to assist the Samaritans, but their efforts were unsuccessful and eventually the Hasmoneans overpowered and completely destroyed the city.[11]

Spiritually the Maccabeans had leaned, albeit loosely, towards the Pharisees since the beginning of the revolt in 166 BCE. This alignment had survived the rift with the Hasidim in 162 BCE, but came to an end during the rule of John Hyrcanus. The reputed incident giving rise to the schism, the questioning of Hyrcanus' right to the high priesthood because his mother had been held captive during the reign of Antiochus IV,[12] is perhaps a mythological explanation for what in reality was a natural progression. As the political ambitions of the Hasmoneans assumed greater significance to the detriment of their traditional religious ideology, a change in allegiance to the worldlier Hellenistic Sadducee party became inevitable.[13] The Greek names of the future Hasmonean rulers bear witness to this transformation. Salome Alexandra, the wife of Hyrcanus' eldest son Aristobulus, was also the sister of Rabbi Shimon ben Shetach, who as a prominent Pharisee was obliged to go into hiding during the period of Hyrcanus' persecution of this faction of Judaism.

John Hyrcanus died in 104 BCE after a reign of thirty-one years that had seen a Jewish nation finally break free from Seleucid interference and also the aggrandisement of Judea through conquest in every direction. Unsurprisingly his tenure as Jerusalem's high priest and leader of Judea was regarded as a great success.[14]

The legacy of John Hyrcanus was an unsuccessful attempt to separate religious and secular power in Jerusalem. In 104 BCE, Aristobulus I succeeded as Jerusalem's high priest, but Hyrcanus' will named his wife as his replacement head of state.[15] Aristobulus, however, was having none of this and responded by imprisoning three of his four brothers and his widowed mother, who was starved to death. Apparently Aristobulus was close to Antigonus, the next eldest of his siblings, but it was not long before Aristobulus also became suspicious of Antigonus' ambitions and the latter was duly assassinated.

Just as John Hyrcanus had enforced conversion to Judaism to the south in Idumaea, Aristobulus extended this strategic policy northwards, where he attacked and seized a section of the territory under Ituraean[16] control. Conversion to Judaism was compulsory for those inhabitants who wished to remain in the annexed area.[17] Aristobulus succumbed to a painful illness and died in 103 BCE. Either during his short reign or alternatively during the longer reign of his successor, Alexander Janneus, the Hasmonean rulers assumed the royal title *basileus*.[18]

Salome Alexandra, the widow of Aristobulus, released the three brothers that he had imprisoned a year earlier and appointed Alexander Janneus as the new king.[19] As the union with Aristobulus had been childless, Salome Alexandra married his brother Alexander Janneus in accordance with traditional Jewish protocol. Alexander Janneus allowed his brother Absalom to live, but put to death a more ambitious brother, whose name is unrecorded. The Hasmonean hereditary position of Jerusalem's high priest also devolved upon Alexander Janneus.

The very combatant Alexander Janneus instigated a series of external wars that commenced with a siege of the Palestinian coastal city of Ptolemais, prompting the arrival of a military force led by Ptolemy Lathyrus.[20] After bouts of political and military manoeuvring Lathyrus inflicted a crushing defeat on the army of Alexander Janneus, whose authority in Palestine was salvaged only by the intervention of Lathyrus' mother, Cleopatra III, the current ruler of Egypt. Alexander Janneus then began to attack cities in Transjordan and Philistia, culminating in the sacking of Gaza in 96 BCE.[21]

At home in Jerusalem, Alexander Janneus lacked popular support and the influential Pharisees were becoming increasingly alienated, especially with his role as high priest. About to offer sacrifice at the altar, Alexander Janneus' authority was seriously challenged on one occasion when he was pelted with the lemons, which were traditionally carried along with palm-branches during the Feast of the Tabernacles. His mercenaries intervened leading to the massacre of six thousand Jews.[22]

A number of further external campaigns almost cost Alexander Janneus his life, but he survived an ambush and managed to return to Jerusalem. He was already very unpopular and as his authority was now in a precarious state, his opponents launched an open rebellion. The ensuing civil war fought between the foreign mercenaries of Alexander Janneus and the Jewish people lasted six years during which 50,000 Jews were killed. In 88 BCE, he sued for peace, but the Pharisees' intransigent demand was that he forfeit his life. One of the last of the Seleucid rulers, Demetrius III, agreed to a request to assist the Pharisees and their supporters to depose the unpopular Hasmonean monarch. Near Shechem a combined militia of Demetrius III's army and the Jewish rebels defeated the army of Alexander Janneus causing the king/high priest to flee to the mountains.[23] However, for a significant number of the Jews, it seems that the idea of relinquishing an independent Jewish state and returning to Seleucid rule was so loathsome[24] that six thousand of them switched sides and left Demetrius III to join up with Alexander Janneus.

Demetrius left Judea and the civil war raged on until eventually Alexander Janneus was victorious. His celebration in Jerusalem included crucifying 800 prisoners of war while their wives and children were brought before them and butchered. Such fear was generated by the atrocity that eight thousand Jews who opposed Alexander Janneus fled Judea and those who remained no longer dared to voice any dissent.[25]

Although Jerusalem was now peaceful, parts of Judea and its surrounding territories continued to experience armed conflicts, some of which resulted from the civil wars in the disintegrating Seleucid Empire and others that arose with the emergence of a powerful Nabataean kingdom in northern Arabia and the southern Levant. Between 80 and 83 BCE, the ever-warlike Alexander Janneus conducted successful military campaigns in Transjordan to receive a hero's welcome upon his return to Jerusalem.[26] By 79 BCE Alexander Janneus' excessive alcohol consumption had begun to affect his health and although he continued to play the part of a belligerent campaigning warrior, the combination of the exertion that this required together with his illness brought about his death at the age of forty-nine in 76 BCE.

Alexander Janneus vastly expanded the territory of Judea, which he protected by constructing a number of sturdy fortresses, including Alexandrium on a mountain near the confluence of the Jordan and Jabbok rivers. More often than not, the cities that he conquered faced the choice between being laid to waste or accepting Judaism, thereby significantly suppressing the Hellenistic culture that had previously permeated much of the region. Fifteen or so years would pass before the Romans such as Pompey would reintroduce foreign cultures and ideologies to these Palestine cities.[27]

The Seleucid empire had collapsed into almost unending civil war after the death of Antiochus VII in 129 BCE. Consequently, the lack of any significant foreign interference in the affairs of Judea enabled a transformation to take place during the reigns of John Hyrcanus and Alexander Janneus. Strong defensive walls around Jerusalem was a very desirable geopolitical expedient, afforded further incentive as the area of the city expanded to accommodate a surge in the population.

The earlier actions of Jonathan and Simon to strengthen the city walls[28] had been reversed to a greater or lesser extent during the siege of 134–132 BCE. Subsequently, Jerusalem was once again enclosed by a sturdy wall, probably completed before the death of John Hyrcanus.[29] Despite the fact that there were earlier fortifications, the description of the wall in the work of Josephus has ensured its classification as the *Ancient Wall* or *First Wall* (see figure 15).[30] It extended eastwards from the north-west corner of the Upper City, to the public speaking and exercise area known as the *Xystus* and then on to the western portico of the temple compound. From the north-west corner, the wall also continued in a southerly direction, defining the western limits of the Upper City. Above the Valley of Hinnom the wall once again turned eastwards, forming the southern boundary of the city. In the region of the Pool of Siloam, it continued in a northerly direction to the south-eastern corner of the Temple precinct, above the Valley of Kidron and delineating the eastern boundary of the Lower City.[31]

The Upper City provided a cool, airy environment for the aristocratic Hellenized Jews, with the north-eastern section in particular being a prominent residential quarter housing important public buildings. A luxurious palace was constructed in this region of the Upper City and within its confines were all the usual accoutrements of a royal household, including ministers, bureaucrats, courtiers and bodyguards. Splendid tombs on the outskirts of the city further demonstrated Jerusalem's increasing wealth.

A bridge was built over the Tyropoeon Valley to link the Temple with the *Xystus* and the Hasmonean Palace. Either just inside the temple precinct, or adjacent to the south-west side, stood the Council Chamber, where the Sanhedrin usually met to interpret civil and religious laws and to judge the priests.[32] The bridge epitomized the developing gulf between the rich and powerful in the Upper City and the less well-off community in the commercial area of the Lower City. The Lower City and the old sections of the town south of Temple Mount housed the poorer classes, interspersing the tangled bazaars of traders such as coppersmiths and cloth merchants.

To increase the defensive attributes of the growing city of Jerusalem, the Hasmoneans built a fortified citadel at the north-west corner of the Temple compound. The primary purpose of the so-called *baris*[33] was to directly guard the compound and thereby afford indirect protection to the Temple itself.

Although the sizeable increase in the population of Jerusalem and its burgeoning suburbs was one of the motivations for the construction of the *First Wall*, the very existence of this enclosure attracted more and more people to come and settle in Jerusalem. The number of people that lived in the city following its rapid expansion, during the reigns of John Hyrcanus and Alexander Janneus, can only be guessed at, with 30,000 being a common approximation.[34] Other unconvincing estimates of Jerusalem's population during this period vary from much lower figures that lack credibility to substantially higher numbers that are equally dubious and improbable.[35]

What is significant, however, is that the growth in the population contributed to the need for an extension of Jerusalem's wall further to the north. The Hasmoneans were conscious that although the enlarged Jerusalem was protected on three sides by steep valleys as well the *First Wall*, on its northern perimeter there was only the wall, which itself offered limited security to the city inside the ramparts and none at all to the newer residential dwellings that had developed outside. To help protect this more vulnerable flank, a so-called *Second Wall* was also constructed from the *baris* westwards, and possibly northwards, from the north-west corner of the Temple precinct. The *Second Wall* eventually joined the northern line of the *First Wall* and it was evidently built by the Hasmoneans, as it was in place before the siege and capture of Jerusalem by Herod the Great in 37 BCE.[36]

Josephus' numbering of the walls continued with the phrase: *The second wall started from the gate in the first wall, which they called Gennath,*[37] but the position of this gate is not known and neither is the extent to which the wall extended to the north. Archaeological excavations have provided clues, but the interpretations of the results lack unanimity of acceptance.[38] In all probability the *Second Wall* was erected during the reign of Alexander Janneus to provide security for the rapidly expanding population. Feasible alternative proposals for the boundary of the *second wall* are illustrated in figure 16. A first-century BCE calculation of Jerusalem's circumference asserted that *the city has a circuit of twenty-seven furlongs*,[39] equivalent to around 5,400 metres.

Of course, the additional residents placed greater demand upon the city's water supply and during the Hasmonean and Roman periods two aqueducts were constructed to augment the existing resources. The workmanship of the later Upper Aqueduct was unmistakably Roman whereas the Lower Aqueduct was more rudimentary, suggesting that it may have been constructed earlier.[40] It began twelve miles south of Jerusalem, but meandered for around forty-two miles before terminating in the Temple compound. The Hasmonean kings had built an aqueduct to their Jericho palace and therefore had the necessary expertise as well as the wealth and incentive to construct Jerusalem's Lower Aqueduct.[41]

Notwithstanding the declaration made only sixty-four years earlier that Simon and his future descendants were henceforth to hold the titles of high priest, military commander and head of the nation of the Jewish people until Yahweh decreed otherwise, Alexander Janneus, who had two sons, bequeathed his royal title to his widow Queen Salome Alexandra.[42] She was accepted as the head of state because not only did she make peace with the Pharisees, but crucially she conceded the power to govern Jerusalem and Judea to them. Keeping faith with the 140 BCE declaration, Salome Alexandra appointed her elder son as high priest, but with the weak-willed Hyrcanus in this role, the sway of the Pharisees was effectively enhanced.[43]

The transfer of power to the Pharisees corresponded with the Jewish Council of Elders admitting an increasingly large number of scribes. In due course this reformed Council, now comprising Pharisiac scribes as well as both Sadducean secular and priestly nobility, became the organization known as *the Great Sanhedrin of Jerusalem*. The influence now exercised by the Pharisees was illustrated by the revengeful assassinations of those thought to be responsible for advising Alexander Janneus to crucify eight hundred opponents some ten years earlier. Despite a deputation that included her son Aristobulus asking Queen Salome Alexandra to intervene, her authority in the matter was clearly limited.[44]

Nevertheless, Salome Alexandra prudently protected her sovereign status by recruiting a hefty contingent of mercenaries to augment her own substantial army.[45] Unlike her late husband, Salome Alexandra rarely used her military forces against neighbouring states, although in around 70 BCE she sent an expedition led by Aristobulus II in an attempt to provide assistance to Damascus, which was being menaced by Ptolemy the son of Mennaeus.[46] The following year, Judea was under threat of invasion by Tigranes II, the king of Armenia, but a combination of gifts sent to him by Salome Alexandra and the intervention of Roman troops in Armenia forestalled the danger.

The rapprochement between Salome Alexandra and the Pharisees brought about a period of peace and prosperity in Jerusalem during which the foundations for the emergence of the Pharisees as the leaders of rabbinical Judaism were laid. Salome Alexandra's brother, Shimon ben Shetach now headed the Pharisee dominated *Sanhedrin*, and he was instrumental in introducing an educational system for all children to learn the Torah.

However, the potency of the Sadducees had only been weakened rather than destroyed and their leader was none other than Salome Alexandra's younger son, Aristobulus II. In 67 BCE, the seventy-three-year-old Queen Salome Alexandra fell gravely ill and rather than see his elder brother Hyrcanus II succeed to the throne, Aristobulus began a campaign of seizing Judea's fortresses as a prelude to outright rebellion. A fearful Hyrcanus together with the Jewish elders approached the Queen and were granted permission to take whatever action they felt was necessary.[47] Although the astute Salome Alexandra must have known what was about to take place, her subsequent death precluded her from witnessing the spectacle of a civil war fought between her two sons.

Chapter 16

The Romans

The 5th Syrian War between the Ptolemies and the Seleucids officially ended with the signing of a peace treaty in 195 BCE. The Egyptian garrison had been driven from Jerusalem five years earlier and the Seleucid king, Antiochus III, had controlled all Palestine since 198 BCE. Primary factors in Egypt's defeat were anarchic internal discord and a lack of support from the Roman Republic.[1] In 192 BCE, however, war broke out between the Romans and the Seleucids and, with assistance from Philip V of Macedon, the Romans defeated Antiochus III at the Battle of Magnesia[2] in 190 BCE.

Rome's authority in the East was firmly established by the victory at Magnesia and the subsequent Treaty of Apamea in 188 BCE. Its influence was exercised through embassies, arbitration to resolve disputes, and alliances with friendly states. An infamous example of Rome's prestige and stature was the 168 BCE humiliation of Antiochus IV by the Roman envoy, Popilius Laenus, who successfully insisted that the Seleucid king withdraw from Egypt when he was close to capturing Alexandria.[3] Relations with the Greek states had long been fractious and in the middle of the second century the Romans undertook military action which concluded with the sacking of Corinth and the annexation of Macedonia in 146 BCE.

Roman anxieties in the East included the burgeoning of the Parthian Empire and also an increase in piracy, which was disrupting the Eastern Mediterranean trade routes. However, it was the unfolding events further north in Anatolia that finally prompted Rome to engage directly in the Middle East. In 112 BCE Mithridates VI, the ruler of the relatively small kingdom of Pontus on the south-east coast of the Black Sea, began to expand his domain, culminating in a vast state extending from the Crimea across the Caucasus to the Aegean Sea. On occasions this involved armed conflict against Roman troops, who eventually achieved an element of re-conquest and restored peace for a period.

Armenia, ruled by the son-in-law of Mithridates VI, had observed neutrality during the Roman/Pontus wars and had coincidentally occupied Syria, with Roman acquiescence since 83 BCE. Hostilities between Rome and Pontus resumed in 74 BCE and eventually Mithridates was forced to flee to Armenia. However, in 69 BCE the Armenian troops withdrew from Syria, leaving Mithridates in charge and in effect engineering a Pontic counter offensive. This very greatly escalated the problem as the Romans could not allow Syria, with its access to the Mediterranean Sea, to be controlled by Mithridates.[4]

There followed a period of relative success for the Romans led by the consul Lucius Licinius Lucullus. The Romans reinstated the Seleucids in Syria by appointing Antiochus XIII[5] as puppet ruler of Syria under Roman hegemony. During the following two years Lucullus' army fought various battles against Armenian troops, until 67 BCE, when internal rivalries and disputes amongst the Romans provided sufficient distraction for Mithridates and his son-law Tigranes II to reoccupy Pontus and Armenia.

The long-standing problem of piracy in the Eastern Mediterranean was finally eradicated by the great Roman statesman and general Pompey, who pursued the sea-bandits as far as their land bases. He had safeguarded Rome's essential grain supplies and elevated his status in the capital to *primus inter pares*.[6] Pompey was then nominated to succeed Lucullus as commander of the Roman forces in the East, with the mission *(imperium)* of restoring Roman authority in the area.

In Jerusalem, Queen Salome died in 67 BCE leaving her two sons vying for power. Hyrcanus II had been the high priest since 76 BCE and now legally inherited Judea's crown. However, the younger Aristobulus II was ambitious and a stronger character, who had already made preparations to seize the throne. The respective armies of the rival brothers fought near Jericho and Hyrcanus II was forced to flee to Jerusalem following the desertion and change of allegiance of sections of his militia. The power struggle appeared to have ended with an agreement that Hyrcanus would *live without taking part in public affairs*[7] and that the younger brother should rule.

A close adviser to Hyrcanus was the Idumaean nobleman, Antipater, whose father had been appointed governor of Idumaea by the late Alexander Janneus. It is likely that Antipater succeeded as governor of Idumaea during the reign of Queen Salome Alexander.[8] Using his position and wealth Antipater had *attached to himself persons of influence in every quarter.*[9] Antipater began a verbal campaign against Aristobulus in favour of the elder brother, Hyrcanus, who was eventually persuaded that his life was in danger and he accompanied Antipater to Petra, to seek assistance from the Nabataean king, Aretas III.[10] Assured by promises of the return of cities taken from the Nabataeans by Alexander Janneus during the external expansion of his reign, Aretas marched against Aristobulus with an army of 50,000 cavalry and infantry.[11]

Aristobulus was duly defeated and on this occasion, it was many of his troops that switched sides. With the support of the Sadducean priests, Aristobulus took refuge in Jerusalem's Temple, where he was besieged by Aretas and Hyrcanus. It is reported at this time that an act of God resulted in an unusually ferocious wind that decimated the crops and caused hyperinflation in wheat prices.[12] This may have been connected to *the greatest earthquake ever experienced* in Asia.[13]

While Pompey was conducting a very successful military campaign in Asia,[14] his military tribune, Aemilius Scaurus was appointed to oversee affairs in Syria. In around 65 BCE the reports of the hostilities in Jerusalem induced Scaurus to travel from Damascus to the besieged city, whereupon he was immediately assailed by envoys from both sides offering him money in return for his assistance. Scaurus put an end to the siege by accepting payment from Aristobulus and with the authority of Rome, he ordered Aretas to withdraw. Scaurus' return to Damascus provided Aristobulus with the opportunity to march against the retreating Aretas and Hyrcanus and inflict a substantial defeat upon them. Those slain numbered around 6,000, including Antipater's brother, Phallion.[15]

In Damascus in the spring of 63 BCE, Pompey listened to the rival claims of Aristobulus and Hyrcanus and also representatives of the Jews who rejected the claims of both to be king with the assertion that they should be led by a high priest rather than a monarch.[16] Pompey instructed the rivals to keep the peace until he came to Judea to reveal his decision after he had first dealt with the Nabataeans.[17] Rather than wait for a decision and while feigning obedience to Pompey, Aristobulus nevertheless made preparations for war. Pompey was forced to postpone his planned military excursion against the Nabataeans and use the troops to march against Aristobulus, who initially took refuge in the Hasmonean fortress of Alexandrium.

Compelled into surrendering the stronghold to Pompey, Aristobulus left immediately for Jerusalem to better prepare for a war that now seemed inevitable. Pompey followed and after setting-up camp near Jericho, he then set out for Jerusalem. The courage of the would-be king of Jerusalem failed at this point and he left the city to meet the Roman general and sue for peace. The promise of money and the submission of Jerusalem to the Romans came to nothing when Aristobulus' supporters refused to allow Pompey's envoy Gabinius to enter the city. With Aristobulus under arrest, Pompey's response was to march against Jerusalem. The supporters of Hyrcanus II were willing to allow the Romans into the city and as they were in the majority, their wishes prevailed. Aristobulus' partisans, however, would not surrender and established themselves in the stronghold formed by the Temple compound. Their ability to resist was heightened by destroying the bridge connecting their sanctuary to the Upper City.[18]

With the rebels barricaded inside, Pompey set up his camp to the north of the Temple precinct and gave instructions for the construction of earthworks to facilitate siege engines, battering rams and catapults. The Hasmonean *Second Wall* was not a formidable defensive structure, but the walls of the Temple compound and the towers of the *baris* fortress were not easily breached. Notwithstanding that the Romans had complete freedom of action once a week on the Jewish Sabbath, it took three months, until the Autumn of 63 BCE, before they overran the Jewish rebel fortifications.[19] The destruction inflicted on the *Second Wall* and the locality of the Temple was so great that it was at least fifteen years before repairs were effected.[20]

Following the eventual success of the Roman army, reputedly twelve thousand of those that supported the cause of Aristobulus II were massacred, some by the Roman soldiers and others by Jews on the side of Hyrcanus II.[21] In violation of the Jewish law that forbade the presence of anyone other than the high priest in the Temple's inner sanctuary, Pompey entered the holy shrine,[22] but avoided giving further offence by declining to appropriate the Temple treasure as booty.[23]

The surviving leaders of Aristobulus' partisans were beheaded and, as punishment for the dissidence, Jerusalem was declared to be a Roman tributary, as indeed was Judea with its territory greatly reduced. Pompey rewarded the assistance that Hyrcanus had afforded the Romans by reinstating him as Jerusalem's high priest, but he was not permitted to assume a royal title. The denial of a royal title to Hyrcanus met with the approbation of the Pharisees, who not only disputed the Hasmonean royal lineage, but also disapproved of the duality of the combined roles of high priest and king. Judea had lost its independence as it now fell within the jurisdiction of Aemilius Scaurus, the governor of the recently created Roman province of Syria. Antipater shrewdly took advantage of the situation to move from his Idumaean capital of Marisa to Jerusalem, where his influence continued to escalate.[24]

Pompey set off for Rome via Cilicia, taking with him a number of prisoners including Aristobulus II, his two daughters and his sons Alexander and Antigonus. Before setting sail for Rome, they spent the winter of 63–62 BCE in Asia Minor and at some stage of the journey Alexander managed to escape.[25] He thus avoided the ignominy imposed upon his father who was paraded as one of Pompey's many prestigious captives in Rome in 61 BCE.[26] A few years on, Alexander reignited the civil war that had been fought between his now imprisoned father and his uncle, Hyrcanus. Alexander began to carrying out raids in Judea and his harassment of Hyrcanus II even extended to an attempt to repair the damage caused during Pompey's siege of the Temple precinct.[27]

In 57 BCE Gabinius was appointed governor of Syria[28] and he used his army, led by a young general called Mark Antony and augmented by a contingent of Jewish soldiers, to defeat Alexander, who had increased his forces to 10,000 infantry and 1,500 cavalry. After a battle outside Jerusalem and subsequent retreat to the Alexandrium, one of the well-built fortresses constructed by his grandfather, Alexander, was compelled to accept defeat and departed in exchange for handing over the three fortresses he had been using as strongholds. Gabinius subsequently destroyed the Hasmonean fortresses at the suggestion of Alexander's mother, whose motive was to promote the cause of her husband Aristobulus II and her other children, who at that point in time were still being held captive in Rome.[29]

The political authority of Hyrcanus II was further diminished as Gabinius reconstituted Judea's civil administration into five regions, each with its own council. Jerusalem was but one of these new administrative districts and Hyrcanus' role was restricted to that of Temple custodian.[30] In the meantime, his brother and rival Aristobulus II, escaped from Rome together with his younger son, Antigonus. In a similar vein to the recently failed campaign of Alexander, the latest rebellion centred on the old Hasmonean fortresses, which had been destroyed by Gabinius.

Once again Mark Antony was involved in supressing the insurgency and, following much bloodshed, Aristobulus and Antigonus were captured and sent back to Rome in 56 BCE. Feeling that he owed a debt to Alexander's mother for her earlier collaboration, Gabinius arranged for her children to go free, although Aristobulus was once again incarcerated.[31]

Notwithstanding the bitter rivalry between Aristobulus II and Hyrcanus II, Alexander, the elder son of the former, married his cousin Alexandra, the daughter of the latter. The couple had three children who were, of course, the grandchildren of both Aristobulus II and Hyrcanus II. These were: the future wife of Herod the Great, Mariamne I, born c.53 BCE; Aristobulus III, born c.52 BCE; and an unnamed daughter, born c.50 BCE, the future wife of Herod the Great's brother Pheroras.[32]

In 55 BCE at the behest of Pompey, Gabinius went to Egypt to reinstate Ptolemy Auletes to the throne following a popular uprising. Significant resources were committed to this campaign by both Hyrcanus II and Antipater, illustrating the Idumaean's continued prominence in the affairs of Judea. While Gabinius was in Egypt, Aristobulus II's son Alexander once again mounted an offensive to take Judea by force. The Governor of Syria made a hasty return from Egypt and gave Antipater a mission to persuade potential rebellious Jews to abandon their support for Alexander. Despite some success on the part of Antipater, Alexander retained an army of 30,000 men, which was, however, eventually defeated by Gabinius at Mount Tabor, some sixty-five miles north of Jerusalem at the eastern end of the Jezreel Valley. Following his victory, Gabinius travelled to Jerusalem to instigate changes to the laws of the city required by Antipater, in a further strengthening of the latter's authority.[33]

Gabinius was replaced as the Roman governor of Syria by M. Licinius Crassus in the spring of 54 BCE, and seemingly impervious to Jewish sensibilities, he stripped Jerusalem's Temple of all its treasure, including the two thousand talents that Pompey had declined to loot nine years earlier. The gold was used to finance a disastrous expedition against Parthia, which resulted in the slaughter of Crassus and his army in the spring of the following year. Crassus' legate, C. Cassius Longinus, managed to escape the carnage and subsequently became the replacement governor of Syria. During his tenure, there was yet another attempted Judean rebellion by supporters of the Roman detainee, Aristobulus. Once the insurgency had been supressed, its leader Peitholaus was executed by Cassius on the recommendation of Antipater.[34]

By the middle of the first century BCE, Pompey and Julius Caesar were on opposite sides of an internecine Roman conflict. Pompey and the Senate had been forced to flee as Caesar seized control of Rome in 49 BCE. Hoping that the Hasmonean would be able to bring Judea and Syria to his side, Caesar released Aristobulus II with two legions of troops. Caesar's plan was, however, thwarted by Pompey's friends and allies, who arranged for Aristobulus to be poisoned before his departure from Rome. In Antioch, Aristobulus' elder son Alexander was beheaded by Pompey's father-in-law, Metellus Scipio, the new governor of Syria. Aristobulus' three remaining children, Antigonus Mattathias, Alexandra III and another daughter were taken from their mother's care in Ascalon[35] to Chalcis by the Ituraean prince Philippion. Alexandra III initially married the prince, who was then murdered by his father, Ptolemy son of Mennaeus in order that he could marry Alexandra.[36] Subsequently, Ptolemy became an active supporter in the attempts by Antigonus Mattathias to promote himself as the lawful king of Judea.

In August 48 BCE, Pompey was defeated by Julius Caesar at the battle of Pharsalus in central Greece and subsequently took flight. Caesar followed Pompey to Egypt, where the latter was assassinated and Caesar became embroiled in a war against king Ptolemy XIII.[37] In the spring of 47 BCE, Hyrcanus II and particularly Antipater, proved very useful in assisting Caesar's struggle for victory in Egypt.[38] They were duly rewarded for their efforts when Caesar came to Syria in the summer, granting Roman citizenship and exemption of taxes to Antipater. Antipater was also appointed viceroy or procurator of Judea, while Hyrcanus was confirmed as high priest and Ethnarch[39] with both titles being hereditary. They were given permission to repair the damage that Pompey had inflicted on the walls of Jerusalem and Caesar also exempted Judea from being used by Roman troops for winter quarters and money being demanded of the Jews. The complaints of Aristobulus' surviving son Antigonus Mattathias, that the rule of Hyrcanus II and Antipater was illegal, failed to have any impact upon Caesar.[40]

Regional Roman authority was exercised by Sextus Iulius Caesar, the governor of Syria and a relative of Julius Caesar. Jerusalem and Judea had Hyrcanus as a local figure-head, but in reality, it was Antipater that was in command. He appointed his elder son, Phasael, as governor of the region of Jerusalem and his younger son, Herod, was assigned to govern the region of Galilee, where he captured and killed a gang of marauding bandits. Resentment against the growing popularity of Antipater and his sons surfaced amongst Jerusalem's leading Jews, and Hyrcanus was persuaded to summon Herod to Jerusalem to be tried for manslaughter by the *Sanhedrin* for executing the bandits without the due process of Jewish law. The trial was somewhat farcical as a far from repentant Herod turned up with fear-inspiring bodyguards and Sextus sent Hyrcanus a letter warning against finding Herod guilty. Despite a strong condemnation of Herod by a Pharisee called Samaias, Hyrcanus either ordered an acquittal or postponement of the trial and Herod left to join Sextus in Damascus, where he was granted further responsibility as governor of Coele-Syria and Damascus. Herod was only dissuaded from a revenge attack on Jerusalem by the pleas of Antipater and Phasael.[41]

The ferocious struggle for leadership of the Roman world did not end with the death of Pompey and the violence included wars aimed at securing the domination of Syria. Sextus Caesar had been murdered in 46 BCE and after a succession of short-lived governorships, Gaius Cassius Longinus took charge of the region in 44 BCE, following the assassination in Rome of Julius Caesar.[42] As always, keen to support whoever seemed to be winning, Antipater and Herod were enthusiastic in their collection of the tax of 700 talents imposed upon Judea to help finance Cassius' large army. Herod's standing amongst the Roman hierarchy was enhanced further as Cassius supplied him with an army and, echoing the designation made a few years earlier by Sextus, also appointed him governor of Coele-Syria. Additionally, Cassius promised Herod the throne of Judea once the war was ended. Malichus, a Jewish nobleman at the court of Hyrcanus II and also involved in the collection of the levy on Judea, sought to gain greater influence by eliminating Antipater, whom he arranged to have poisoned in 43 BCE. The politics of the day precluded immediate retribution, but eventually Herod, with the authority of Cassius, avenged his father's death by having Malichus slain.[43]

Cassius left Syria early in 42 BCE and the situation in Judea became even more chaotic. Phasael was obliged to put down a Jewish revolt in Jerusalem and Antigonus Mattathias, the surviving son of Aristobulus II once again invaded the country, supported by local potentates.[44] Herod defeated Antigonus and subsequently arrived back in Jerusalem to a hero's welcome.[45] He may well have been accompanied by Alexandra II and her children, including the twelve-year-old Mariamne, who was now betrothed to marry Herod.[46] The role that Alexandra II played in the marriage agreement in unclear, but her husband had been executed seven years earlier, she had three young children and was herself the daughter of Hyrcanus II, a virtual puppet of the Herodian dynasty in Jerusalem. Additionally, she had witnessed her sister-in-law, Alexandra III, being forcibly taken from Ascalon and married to Philippion and then Ptolemy of Chalcis. Subsequently, Alexandra's dislike of Herod became clear, but for the time being she was unlikely to have been in a position to oppose the engagement of her young daughter to the increasingly powerful Herod.

In October 42 BCE, the forces of Cassius and Marcus Brutus were defeated at the eastern Macedonian city of Philippi by the military alliance known as the Second Roman Triumvirate, comprising Octavian, Mark Antony and Marcus Lepidus. Octavian then returned to Rome while Mark Antony assumed the role of supreme Roman overlord in the East. To finance his extravagant lifestyle, he imposed onerous taxes upon all the provinces under his supervision, including Judea.[47]

Jewish delegations who were unhappy with the power wielded by Herod and Phasael twice petitioned Mark Antony to alter the status quo. The first approach was denied when Herod bribed him and the second when Hyrcanus voiced his support for the brothers, whom Mark Antony appointed tetrarchs responsible for the administration of Judea. Hyrcanus II, as high priest and ethnarch, remained the head of Judea, but in name only. The Jewish opponents of the new tetrarchs continued to agitate, resulting in many of them being slain by Mark Antony's troops near the city of Tyre.[48]

Antigonus Mattathias, the nephew of Hyrcanus II, had failed in his previous attempts to seize Judea in 56 and 42 BCE, but Parthian territorial expansion into Syria provided him with yet another opportunity to promote himself as the rightful heir to the Judean throne. Probably while Mark Antony was distracted by events in Rome and/or his affair with Cleopatra VII of Egypt, the Parthians had moved into northern Syria. In 40 BCE, Antigonus Mattathias or his nephew Lysanias[49] bribed the Parthians to advance his cause and invade Judea.

While the Parthians divided their forces between an interior and a coastal invasion of Judea, Antigonus Mattathias was joined by large numbers of disaffected Jews, who after a skirmish with their opponents, entered Jerusalem and besieged the palace. They were then driven into the temple compound as the city endured a violent and bloody civil war at a time when it was overcrowded with visitors who had arrived for the Feast of Pentecost. The Parthians arrived at the city walls, which were being defended by Phasael and despite Herod's forebodings, Phasael and Hyrcanus II were persuaded to leave the safety of Jerusalem and journey to the Parthian army headquarters, ostensibly to negotiate a settlement. The deception ended with Phasael and Hyrcanus II being placed in chains as Parthian prisoners.[50]

When the news reached Herod, he and his family left Jerusalem under the cover of darkness. Battling against pursuing Parthians and Jews, Herod's party endured a tortuous journey that included Masada,[51] Idumaea, Petra, Pelusium, Alexandria and Rhodes, before Herod eventually reached Rome.[52] In the meantime, the Parthians looted Jerusalem and ravaged much of the country as a prelude to installing Antigonus Mattathias in Jerusalem as the last Hasmonean king of Judea, whom modern historians refer to as Antigonus II.[53] The coinage that began to be issued in 40 BCE, indicated that as well as the Judean crown, Antigonus also assumed the title of high priest.

The Parthians captives, Hyrcanus II and Phasael, were taken to Jerusalem to be tortured by Antigonus. Phasael, however, forestalled his probable treatment by dashing his own head on a rock and either died as a direct result or subsequently at the hands of the physicians treating him. Antigonus mutilated the ears of Hyrcanus, as a permanent physical defect would henceforth disqualify him from holding the office of high priest. Perhaps a glimmer of family affection dissuaded Antigonus from having his uncle killed, as Hyrcanus was then returned to the Parthians as their prisoner.[54] For the next four years Hyrcanus lived amongst the Jewish diaspora of Babylon, who treated him with great respect.

Chapter 17

Herod the Great

Herod's escape from Jerusalem and subsequent odyssey finally ended in Rome late in 40 BCE, where he was ratified as king of Judea. This was despite a somewhat dubious assertion that Herod's arrival was to claim the throne on behalf of Aristobulus III, *his* [intended] *wife's brother.*[1] Octavian and Mark Antony both owed debts of gratitude to Herod's late father, Antipater, and they persuaded the Senate that Herod would be most suited to serving Rome's interests in opposing their Parthian enemies, who had appointed Antigonus II as the king in Jerusalem.

The situation in Judea was chaotic. Herod's brother Joseph was conducting a guerrilla war against Antigonus, who was besieging Herod's relatives in Masada. In 39 BCE, Mark Antony's legate, Ventidius, drove the Parthians out of Syria, but took no action against Antigonus, other than extorting money from him. Ventidius withdrew from Jerusalem leaving a contingent of troops under his subordinate, Silo, who effected the same tactic of extorting money from Antigonus.[2]

Having set sail from Italy, Herod disembarked at the northern Palestinian port of Ptolemais. His army, comprising Jewish supporters and mercenaries, increased in strength as campaigns were conducted in Galilee, Joppa and Idumaea, where he rescued his relatives who had taken refuge in Masada. Although Herod's army reached Jerusalem together with Silo's contingent of Roman troops, no further progress could be made as, triggered by the corruption of Silo, the Romans began to voice dissent concerning their lack of provisions. Herod undertook strenuous efforts to resolve the problem, but in the end the Roman troops had to be dismissed to their winter quarters.

In the spring of 38 BCE, the Parthians renewed their invasion of Syria, but by June they had been defeated by the Roman general Ventidius, who then besieged the Parthian sympathizer, Antiochus of Commagene, in the city of Samosata.[3] Unhappy with the corruption and lack of support from the Roman generals in the region, Herod set off to consult Mark Antony, who had joined the siege of Samosata. He received an enthusiastic welcome and before long the Roman attack was successful. Mark Antony left for Egypt, but instructed Sosius[4] to send military aid to Judea to assist Herod. In the meantime, however, Herod's brother Joseph, supported only by five cohorts of inexperienced Roman recruits, had been killed in battle near Jericho. This victory spurred support for Antigonus, who celebrated by having Joseph's head removed from his body and the savage civil war was reignited throughout Judea.[5]

Initially delayed by the onset of winter storms, Herod reached Jerusalem in the spring of 37 BCE. He camped in the north outside the Temple compound and more vulnerable Hasmonean *Second Wall*, intending a repetition of Pompey's successful attack on the city twenty-six years earlier. While his officers were supervising the construction of earthworks and towers for the impending siege, the hubristic Herod took temporary leave and journeyed to Samaria to marry the Hasmonean princess Mariamne. Possibly soon after he was appointed governor of Galilee in 47 BCE, Herod had married his first wife, Doris,[6] with whom he had a son Antipater II, named after his grandfather. Doris was dismissed so that Herod could wed Mariamne and Antipater was only allowed to visit Jerusalem on festival dates.[7] By marrying the granddaughter of both Hyrcanus II and Aristobulus II, in the eyes of some, Herod had legitimized his role as king of Judea.[8]

Herod re-joined his camp and Jerusalem was now faced with an assault by a huge army comprising the Roman forces under Sosius and Herod's own army of Jews and mercenaries. Nevertheless, the inhabitants of the city exhibited brave resistance until the northern walls succumbed and the armies of Herod and Sosius overran the city and began to slaughter the inhabitants. *Masses were butchered in the alleyways ... No quarter was given to infancy, to age, or to helpless womanhood.*[9] Ultimately, Herod was forced to restrain the Romans from further violence, as well as defiling the Temple and plundering the city. This was achieved partly by force, but also by bribery.[10]

The ancient sources present some inconsistencies concerning both the date and duration of the siege, but a reasonable reconstruction of events is the erection of the earthworks beginning in February, the bombardment of the city commencing in May and Jerusalem being overrun in July 37 BCE.[11] Antigonus II was taken in chains to Antioch where he was executed by Mark Antony,[12] and three years after the Roman senate had declared Herod king of Judea, he at last had control of his capital city.

Borne more out of necessity than choice, Herod's initial actions in Jerusalem caused resentment amongst the Jewish population that already harboured doubts about the validity of his kingship. Because he had needed support to take Jerusalem from Antigonus II, Herod was obligated to make substantial payments by way of rewards and bribes to the Roman legions and his overlord, Mark Antony. Many of Antigonus' chief lieutenants were killed and had their property looted to help to facilitate these payments.[13] Once in control of the city, Herod appointed the high-ranking Idumaean Costobar to prevent the escape of those who had opposed him and also those who were considered to be in debt.[14]

The prominent families with their roots in Hasmonean society were decimated and the new ruling class that emerged during Herod's reign were *primarily Idumaeans, which had supported Herod during the war with Antigonus*.[15] The Idumaeans had been coerced into accepting Judaism by the Sadducee-influenced John Hyrcanus nearly one hundred years earlier, but the now more dominant Pharisees rejected the legitimacy of forcible conversion and the contention that the Idumaeans were Jewish was not readily conceded. A king with a Hellenistic lifestyle was always likely to cause offence to Jerusalem's stricter Jewish community, but nevertheless a working relationship with the Pharisees owed much to the latter's preference for a king that was not overtly foreign, especially Roman, and one that did not demand the title high priest for himself.

Herod's brother Joseph II had been killed before the siege, but after the fall of Jerusalem, Herod took responsibility for Joseph's unattached daughter and married her in 37 BCE. He was to repeat this procedure in 34 BCE with the unmarried daughter from the first marriage of his uncle Joseph I (see figure 17). Thus, one of Herod's wives was his niece and another was his cousin. Neither had their names recorded in the ancient sources and neither had any children.[16]

The capture and subsequent execution of Antigonus in 37 BCE had left the position of high priest unoccupied. As an Idumaean, Herod could not assume the title and to avoid appointing a high priest from amongst the Hasmoneans, Herod arranged for Hananel, a priest from the Jewish *diaspora* in Babylon, to take up the position in Jerusalem.[17] Antigonus II's previous mutilation of Hyrcanus II's ears precluded his reappointment as high priest, but nevertheless, in what was little more than a public relations exercise, Herod persuaded Hyrcanus to leave Babylon and return to Jerusalem in 36 BCE. Herod allowed Hyrcanus *the most honoured seat at the banquet-table and called him Father,*[18] but it is an indication of Herod's insincerity, that six years later he executed the aged Hyrcanus.

At the same time that Herod was consolidating his position in Jerusalem with the appointment of a high priest and the return of Hyrcanus, Mark Antony was accommodating the territorial demands of his paramour, the Ptolemaic queen Cleopatra VII. In 37/36 BCE, Antony gifted various realms to Cleopatra and again further lands in 34 BCE, which included the balsam woods of Jericho, which Herod then had to lease back from her.[19]

Even before he had been required to relinquish the balsam woods, Cleopatra's friendship with his mother-in-law, the Hasmonean princess Alexandra II, had caused difficulties for Herod. Alexandra, inconsolable that her son, Aristobulus III, had not been appointed high priest, wrote to Cleopatra asking her to intercede. The subsequent involvement of Mark Antony resulted in Herod taking the politically expedient step of appointing the seventeen-year-old Aristobulus as high priest in place of Hananel early in 35 BCE. As a consequence of this plot, Alexandra was prohibited from leaving the palace and was kept under constant surveillance. Further correspondence with Cleopatra led to a scheme for Alexandra and Aristobulus to attempt an escape from Jerusalem, but the intrigue failed when a spy reported it to Herod. Only fear of further alienating Cleopatra constrained Herod's immediate response to one of forgiveness.[20]

Nevertheless, the tenure of Aristobulus III as high priest was short, as late in 35 BCE, after the Feast of Tabernacles, Herod contrived an accident to have Aristobulus III murdered and Hananel once again occupied the office of Jerusalem's high priest.[21] Following a further written plea from Alexandra II, Cleopatra persuaded Mark Antony to call for Herod to explain the death of Aristobulus. Herod left his uncle Joseph I, who was also the husband of his sister Salome I, in command while he was away responding to Antony's summons. Herod's bribery and eloquence persuaded Antony to acquit him, following which Herod returned to Jerusalem and executed Joseph on suspicion of having had an affair with his wife Mariamne I.[22]

At some stage during Herod's first five or six years in charge of Jerusalem, when he was closely attached to Antony, he transformed the Hasmonean fortification known as the *baris* at the north-western corner of the temple compound. The rebuilt palatial fortress, designed to protect both Jerusalem's northern defence line and the temple, was designated *Fortress Antonia* to honour Mark Antony.[23] As war loomed against Octavian in 32 BCE, Herod prepared his army to support Antony, but instead was redirected by his Roman overlord to go war against the Nabataeans, who had ceased to pay tribute. This war was bloody and protracted, not the least due to the treachery of one of Cleopatra's generals, and was interrupted in the spring of 31 BCE as Judea endured a massive earthquake, which caused substantial damage to property and much loss of life. Nevertheless, Herod was eventually successful when the Nabataeans conceded defeat late in 31 BCE.[24]

In the meantime, however, on 2 September 31 BCE, Octavian had defeated Antony and Cleopatra in the waters of Actium. When this news reached Jerusalem, Herod, insecure and fearful that the legitimacy of his kingship could be denied in favour of the Hasmoneans, had the aged Hyrcanus II put to death. Hyrcanus' alleged crime was that of treasonable conspiracy with the Nabataean king Malchus I, but the veracity of the accusation is open to question.[25]

Herod had to act expediently to secure his position and in the spring of 30 BCE, he journeyed to Rhodes to declare his transfer of allegiance. Octavian, the now undisputed leader of the Roman world, was won over by Herod and was also under the impression that the Judean king had already rendered service by helping to overcome a force of pro-Antony gladiators.[26] Octavian reconfirmed Herod as king of Judea and an almost immediate opportunity arose for Herod to demonstrate his loyalty by provisioning Octavian's army as it marched through Judea on its way to Egypt. Herod's bribery and largesse reaped early rewards when Octavian returned the Judean land that Antony had given to Cleopatra, and awarded Herod several additional territories plus Cleopatra's personal bodyguard.[27]

There was a great deal of family tension in Herod's household, as his mother Cyprus I and sister Salome I clearly did not get on with his wife Mariamne I and her mother Alexandra II. Mariamne *openly jeered at both his mother and sister for their low birth*.[28] Late in 30 BCE, after escorting Octavian to Antioch, Herod returned to Jerusalem, where the intrigue and scheming at court led to further suspicion that Mariamne had been unfaithful and was also plotting to poison him. After a trial of sorts,

Herod ordered the execution of Mariamne I towards the end of 29 BCE, following which he endured a period of severely debilitating depression.[29] The ever conspiratorial and manipulative Alexandra II sought to take advantage of Herod's illness, but her seditious manoeuvring was reported to the king and in 28 BCE she too was executed, as were a number of suspected disloyal friends and enemies of Herod during 27 BCE.[30]

In the meantime, in the north-west of Jerusalem's Upper City, work had already begun on a new royal palace for Herod,[31] who had married for a fifth time. Confusingly, this wife had the same name as his recently executed spouse and is therefore referred to as Mariamne II. She was the daughter of the priest, Simon Boethus and according to one source, in order to ascribe an acceptable level of social standing to the family, Herod removed the existing high priest and replaced him with Mariamne II's father, following which the wedding took place.[32] However, Simon Boethus did not become high priest until sometime later and an alternative view is that the marriage took place commensurate with work starting on the new palace building.[33]

Two further marriages were contracted by Herod during the period 28/27 BCE. One to a woman referred to as Malthace *the Samaritan* and the next to Cleopatra *of Jerusalem*,[34] but apart from these nomenclatures, nothing is known of their origins.

In 27 BCE, Octavian, now known as Augustus (*Sebastos* in Greek), took the first steps in the process of becoming the first Roman emperor. Herod seeking to enhance the security of Judea, and its capital city of Jerusalem, decided to construct a northern buffer on the site of the ancient city of Samaria. This site was chosen partly because the distance of thirty-five miles between Samaria and Jerusalem could be traversed by an army in the course of one day. A temple was raised and six thousand colonists were resettled within the new fortified high walls that surrounding the city, which Herod renamed Sebaste in honour of the Roman emperor.[35]

Although Herod made no attempt to force Hellenism upon the Jews, the introduction of contests, held both in and just outside Jerusalem, was offensive to the traditional Jewish way of life. Games were held every four years throughout the Roman world in honour of Emperor Augustus and Herod could not exclude Jerusalem from such ceremonies, even if he had wanted to. He *built a theatre in Jerusalem, and after that a very large amphitheatre in the plain*.[36] Despite attempts to uncover archaeological evidence, both of the existence and shape,[37] of the Herodian structures used for the contests, most likely they were made of wood that did not endure, rather than the stone constructions more commonly used much later on by the Romans.[38]

The contests that Herod oversaw were quite eclectic. They comprised artistic activities such as gymnastics, music, and acting, whereas more spirited displays took the form of chariot competitions and horse-racing. There were also blood-thirsty spectacles such as wild animals pitted against condemned prisoners or fighting other animals. As disturbing as the traditional Jews found these pursuits, most of all it was the display of trophies surrounded by weapons that occasioned the strongest denunciation against what was perceived as the worship of images and idols.[39] The Dead Sea Scrolls *Commentary on Habakkuk* refers to the *Kittim* (i.e. Roman) practice of sacrifice to their emblems and worship of their weapons.[40]

To pacify the Jews, Herod removed the surrounding ornamentation to show that the bare wooden trophies were not images of men, but nevertheless, a Jewish conspiracy was hatched to kill Herod for his perceived sacrilege. Herod's effective organization of spies uncovered the intrigue and resulted in the members of the cabal being *put to death after enduring every torment.* When subsequently, Herod's informant was killed, retribution was meted out not only to the murderers, but also their families.[41]

A regional drought caused severe crop failures followed by famine and plague. Herod's treasury had already been severely depleted by his many building projects and successive crop failures resulted in a drastic reduction in his tax revenues. To alleviate the widespread suffering, Herod utilized gold and silver ornaments from his palace to purchase grain from his friend Petronius, the Roman Prefect of Egypt.[42] The distribution of the grain to his own Judean people and also inhabitants of Syria went some way to redressing the hostility previously directed towards him by many of his Jewish subjects.[43] However, in the long run Herod's innate insensitivity to Jewish traditions would define him as a tyrant, as evidenced by his introduction of a law condemning burglars to deportation and slavery. To be enslaved to non-Jewish foreigners was considered by the Jews to be a religious defilement.[44]

Herod maintained order in Jerusalem through his network of spies, his regular use of torture and a militia, which incorporated a significant number of mercenaries. His character was undoubtedly complex and arbitrary incidents may be used to demonstrate his brutality, just as there are examples of his benevolence towards his subjects. Pharisees who refused to take an oath of loyalty to Herod were initially treated leniently, but upon hearing that they had *corrupted some of the people at court*, Herod not only killed the seditious Pharisees, but *also killed all those of his household who approved of what the Pharisee said*.[45] Conversely, in addition to averting the dire consequences of the c.24 BCE drought and subsequent crop failures, Herod refunded one third of his subjects' taxes in 20 BCE, and six years later he made a similar gesture and reimbursed a quarter of the previous year's taxes.[46]

One of Herod's greatest building projects outside Jerusalem was the construction of a major city and seaport on the site of the town called Strato's Tower. Work commenced in c.23 BCE and it took ten to twelve years to complete the many new structures, which included a temple, a palace, civic halls, a theatre, an amphitheatre, sewers and circular harbour walls. Once again to honour the Roman emperor, the city was renamed Caesarea.[47]

The beginning of the Strato's Tower/Caesarea endeavour coincided with the conclusion of work on Herod's new palatial residence. Magnificent banquet halls and hundreds of luxuriously furnished bedrooms were complemented by open courtyards filled with exotic trees, bronze statues and water features. The compound of buildings and gardens was enclosed by high walls interspersed with ornamental turrets, and protecting the northern aspect of the palace, three imposing towers were incorporated into the wall that had been built by the Hasmoneans. The towers were named Hippicus, Phasael and Mariamne and were *for magnitude, beauty and strength without their equal in the world*.[48] Together, the palace and the towers afforded a solid defensive shield on the city's vulnerable north-western boundary.

23 BCE was also the probable date that Simon Boethus replaced Jesus son of Phiabi[49] as Jerusalem's high priest, although the linking of this appointment with the marriage of Herod and Mariamne II is contentious and discussed earlier in this chapter.[50] Before the era of Herod the Great, the position of high priest had been a lifetime appointment. Herod's arbitrary appointment and dismissal of Jerusalem's high priests, which had begun with Hananel in 37 BCE and now culminated in the appointment of his father-in-law, devalued the role from one of genuine authority to one of being little more than a puppet of the king.[51]

Herod's passion for building was witnessed throughout Judea with the creation of new cities, often named after relatives, and the construction of fortresses as well as the rebuilding of those that had suffered war damage. Furthermore, porticos, temples, civic halls, theatres, aqueducts and public baths etc., were erected at his expense in several cities outside Judea.[52] Arguably however, Herod's greatest architectural feat was the rebuilding of Jerusalem's temple.

The royal palace that had been constructed for Herod was far more sumptuous than the existing temple and whether it was to prove his zeal for Judaism, or simply the hubris of a Hellenistic benefactor on a grand scale, or indeed any other reason, in 20/19 BCE[53] Herod announced that he would renovate Zerubbabel's Temple to give it the splendour and opulence that it lacked. Herod began the reconstruction of the Temple of God on Mount Moriah at his own expense, after convincing the sceptical population that he had the means to complete the project.[54]

The builders enlarged the temple precinct,[55] and raised it to a more imposing height. The drop from the portico at the south-east corner of the temple compound to the floor of the Kidron Valley was so steep that *vision would be unable to reach the end of so measureless a depth.*[56] This, *the pinnacle of the temple*, is traditionally considered to be the site of the temptation of Christ.[57] Although the number of ten thousand[58] skilled artisans set to work on the venture is probably an exaggeration, clearly the project provided long-term employment for huge numbers of Jerusalem's residents.

Various sources[59] describe the revitalized temple, its inner sanctums, its surrounding courts, porticos and gates. The details are not always consistent, but the following quotations provide admirably succinct summaries of what was achieved: *The expenditure devoted to this work was incalculable, its magnificence never surpassed,*[60] and *in the centre was the temple itself, beautiful beyond all possible description.*[61] Despite rabbinical advice against plating the temple with gold,[62] the vast amount used in the renovation is indicated by the devaluation of the precious metal ninety years later after the temple was looted by the Romans after the 66–70 CE Jewish/Roman War.[63]

Although it took eight years to finish the porticos and the outer courts, some eighteen months after work began, a celebration was held in the summer of 18 BCE (see figure 18) to mark the completion of the temple's inner sanctuary.[64] References to the completion of the project long after

Herod's death[65] are likely to pertain to the entire temple mount complex as well as additional ornamentation and/or maintenance work on the temple.

The 17 BCE return to Jerusalem of Alexander and Aristobulus IV,[66] the two elder sons of Herod and Mariamne I, presaged a decade of family feuding that led ultimately to the execution of them both. The same perception of a greater nobility due to their royal Hasmonean lineage, which had brought about the downfall of their mother and grandmother, created enemies amongst many of Herod's other relatives, who eventually succeeded in poisoning Herod's mind against the pair.[67] When Alexander and Aristobulus were finally charged with plotting to kill their father, Emperor Augustus conceded that Herod could deal with them as he saw fit, but suggested that he first take the advice of the eminent men of the region. In c.8 BCE, a trial was convened in Berytus, where Alexander and Aristobulus IV were pronounced guilty and subsequently taken to Sebaste for execution.[68]

During the period of conflict between the king and his Hasmonean sons, Herod's eldest son Antipater II had been recalled to the court in Jerusalem, followed not long after by his mother, Doris. Antipater became Herod's favoured son and was named as the king's successor, but further family intrigue resulted in Antipater and his mother being implicated in the assassination of Herod's brother, Pheroras and a plot to murder Herod himself. Mariamne II (Herod's fifth wife) was also accused of having known about the conspiracy. She was punished by Herod divorcing her, removing their son, Herod-Philip[69] from his will and dismissing her father from the post of high priest. Doris was once again sent away from Jerusalem and in 6 BCE, Antipater II was imprisoned for his alleged crimes.[70]

As the now aged king lay ill, a mob was incited to remove the great golden eagle that he had placed above the temple gate. Herod demonstrated that even towards the end of his life, he remained merciless and ruthless by having the ringleaders burned alive.[71] At last a missive arrived from the Roman Emperor Augustus concerning the fate of Herod's imprisoned son Antipater II. Herod was granted the choice of sending Antipater into exile or executing him. Herod chose the latter and five days later in 4 BCE, Herod himself passed away.[72]

Chapter 18

Herod's Legacy

Herod's son by Doris and his three sons by Mariamne I had all predeceased him, and his only son by Mariamne II had been disinherited. Five other sons survived, as did a number of wills that Herod had composed before he died in 4 BCE. There were three principal claimants to the substantial territories ruled by Herod and these were Malthace's sons, Archelaus and Antipas,[1] and Cleopatra's son Philip. Cleopatra's other son, Herod IV,[2] seems not to have been involved in the family power struggle and Pallas' son, Phasael III, was only about 11 years old at the time (see figure 19). Herod's royal title existed only by Roman appointment and sufferance and was not hereditary. Accordingly, the appointment of any successor named in the king of Judea's will needed the sanction of the Roman emperor Augustus, who also had the authority to refuse or vary the terms of the bequests and even the status of any territories involved.[3]

Archelaus expected to be confirmed as the new king and was eager to leave for Rome to receive his official sanction. Seven days mourning were observed, followed by an address to Jerusalem's populace during which Archelaus agreed to various demands including a reduction in taxes. He was delayed, however, by an increasingly violent demonstration by the supporters of the priests that Herod had burned alive for removing the great golden eagle above the temple gate shortly before his death. When appeasement and reasoning both failed and with the Passover festival imminent, Archelaus attempted to use soldiers to disperse the protesters in the Temple. Outnumbered and under attack by the stone-throwing mob, the soldiers were forced to retreat, following which Archelaus called out his entire army and cavalry. Around three thousand rioters were killed before those remaining gave up and fled.[4]

With an entourage of friends and relatives, Archelaus went to Caesarea in readiness to sail to Rome for Augustus' adjudication of Herod's wills. He was met firstly by the Syrian procurator Sabinus, who was intent upon

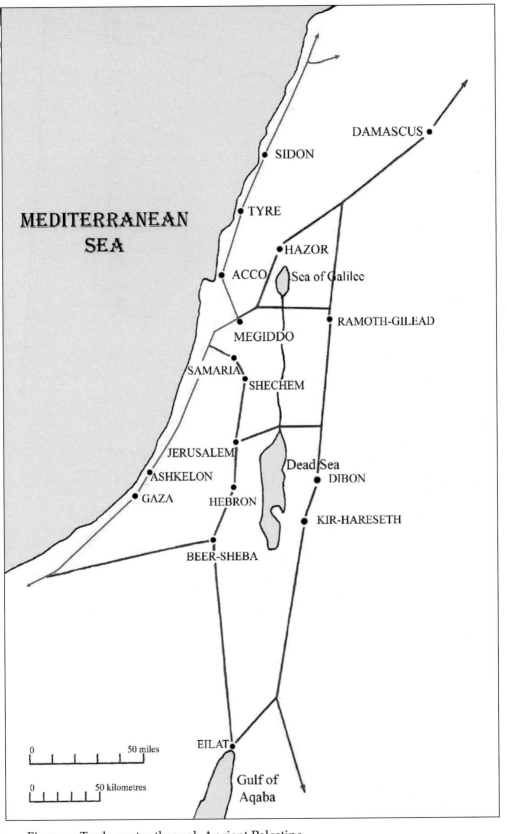

Figure 1: Trade routes through Ancient Palestine.

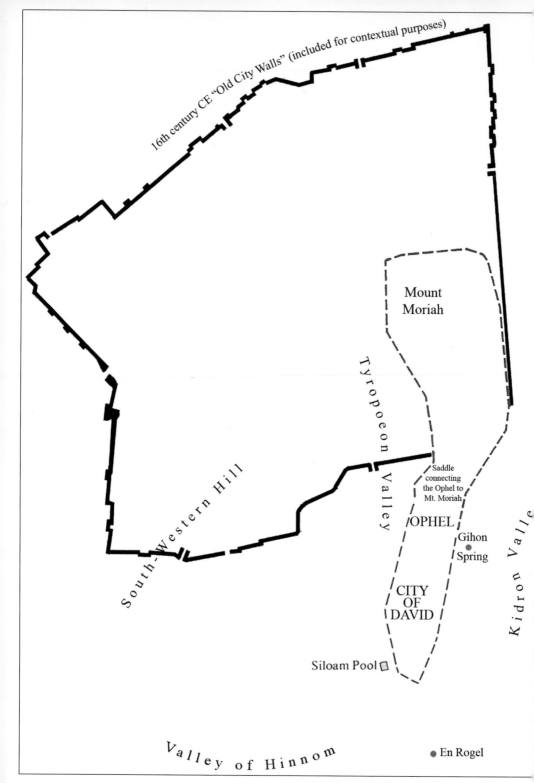

Figure 2: The City of David on the Ophel.

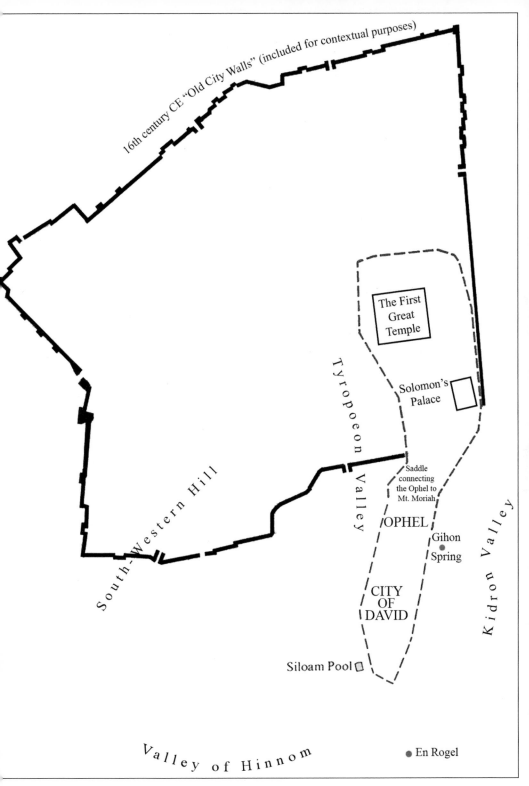

Figure 3: Extension of the city onto Mt Moriah.

Figure 4: Palestine's Separate Kingdoms (late tenth century BCE).

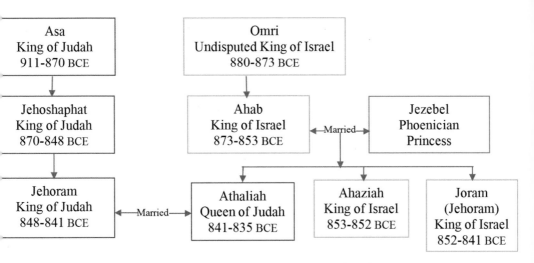

Figure 5: Kings of Judah and Israel during the early and mid-ninth century BCE.

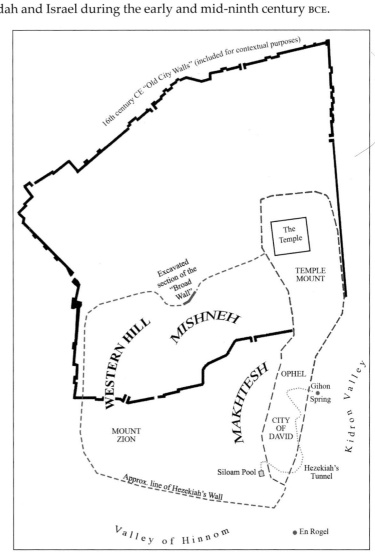

Figure 6: Hezekiah's late eighth century BCE expansion onto Jerusalem's Western Hill.

Figure 7: Palestine c.701 BCE.

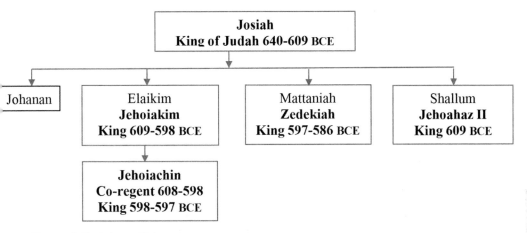

Figure 8: Josiah and his successors.

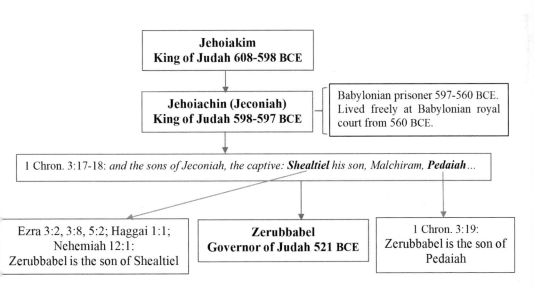

Figure 9: Zerubbabel's Davidic lineage.

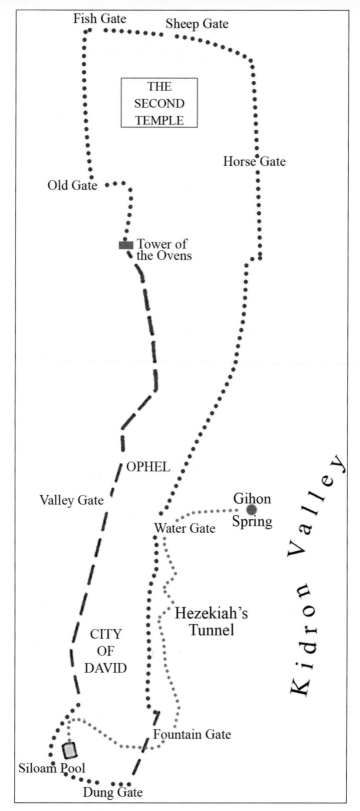

Figure 10: Nehemiah's reconstruction of the walls of Jerusalem (mid-fifth century BCE).

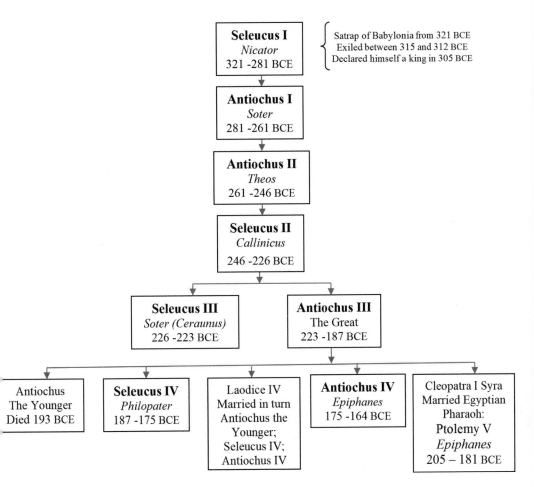

Figure 11: The Seleucid Kings 321–164 BCE.

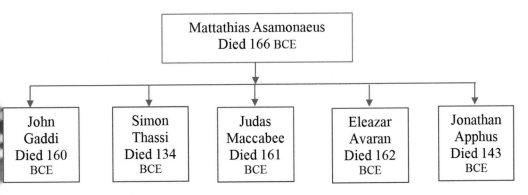

Figure 12: The Sons of Mattathias Asamonaeus.

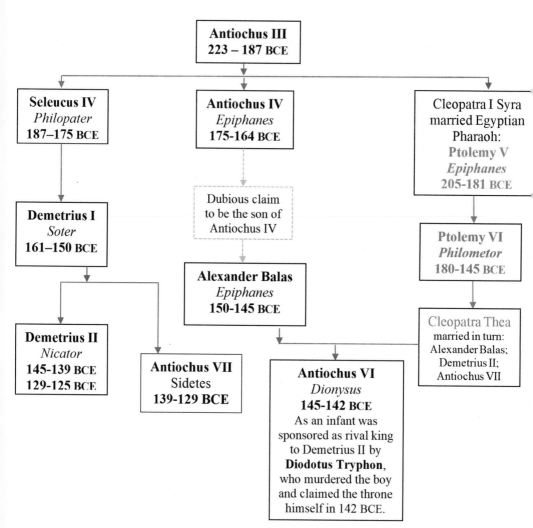

Figure 13: The Seleucid Kings 223–125 BCE.

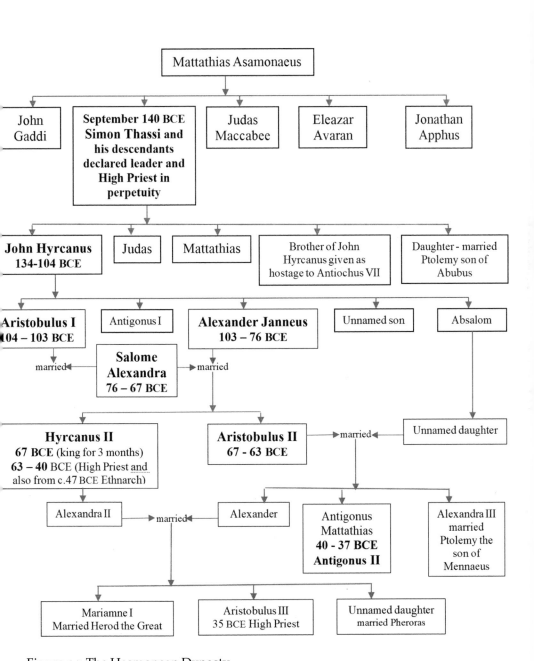

Figure 14: The Hasmonean Dynasty.

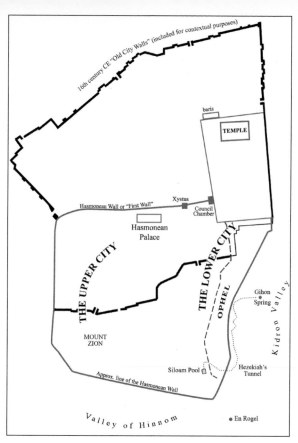

Figure 15: *The First Wall.*

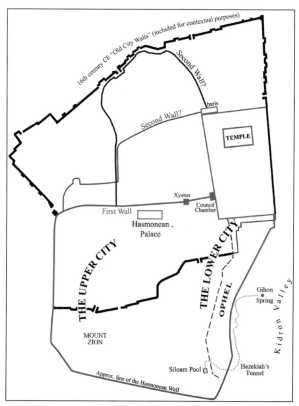

Figure 16: *The Second Wall.*

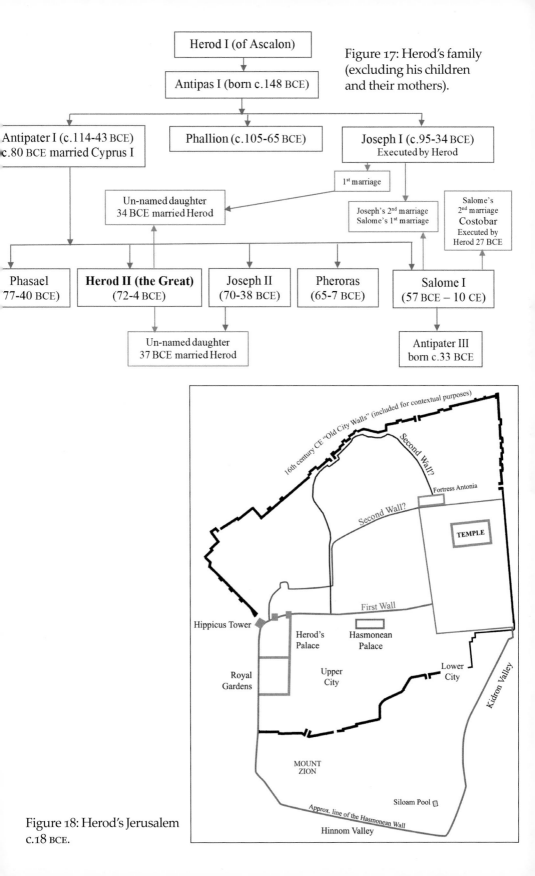

Figure 17: Herod's family (excluding his children and their mothers).

Figure 18: Herod's Jerusalem c.18 BCE.

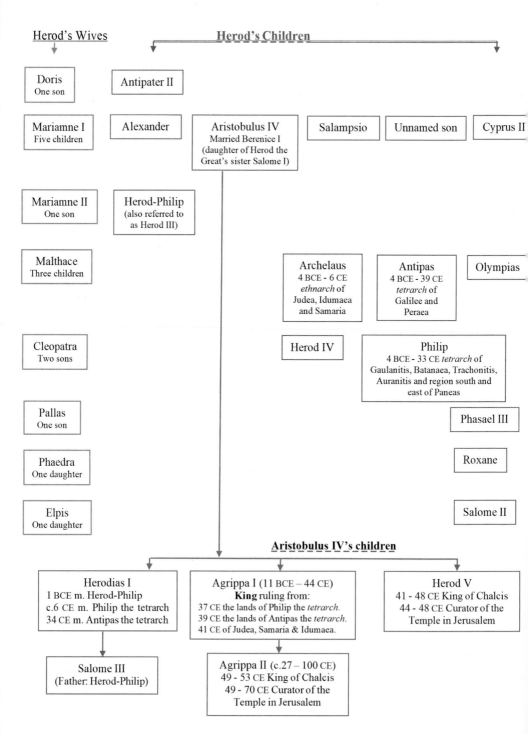

Figure 19: Herod II (the Great) 72–4 BCE; children, their mothers and selected offspring.

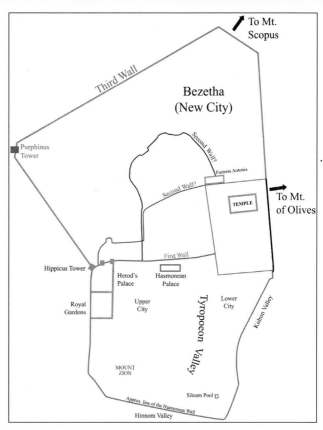

Figure 20: Jerusalem c.70 BCE.

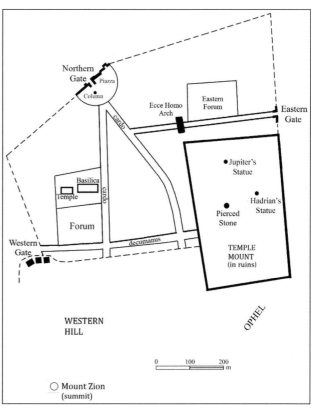

Figure 21: Aelia Capitolina.

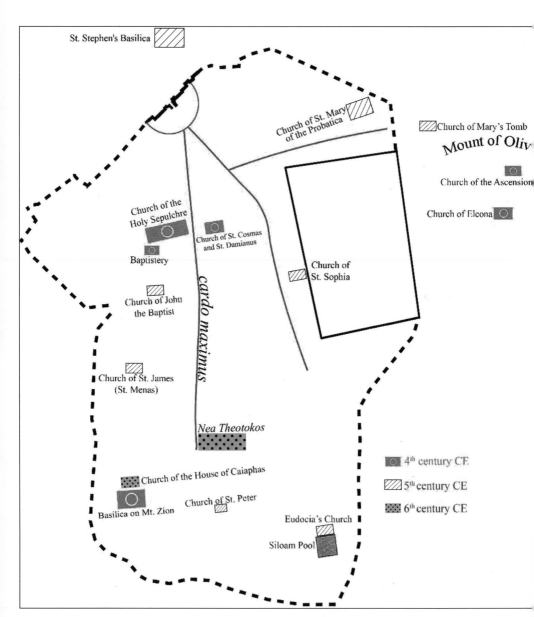

Figure 22: Jerusalem's Byzantine churches.

helping himself to at least some of Herod's great fortune. Sabinus was temporarily thwarted by the arrival of the more senior Syrian governor Varus. It was agreed that Sabinus would take no action pending the Roman emperor's decision, but as soon as Archelaus set sail for Rome and Varus returned to Antioch, Sabinus resumed his mercenary quest. He took possession of the royal palace in Jerusalem and although the treasury officials stalled his demands, a rebellion in the city necessitated the return of Varus to restore order. Upon the subsequent departure of Varus, Sabinus goaded the Jews even more and the arrival of tens of thousands of Jews for the Pentecost festival in Jerusalem at the end of May, was as much to punish Sabinus as for religious observance. Serious conflict ensued, followed by looting by Sabinus and his Roman troops. Disturbances broke out across Judea and once again Varus had to step in to put down a number of uprisings.

In the meantime, Emperor Augustus and a council of advisers had begun to consider the claims of the various factions in Rome. Antipas had arrived to contend that Herod's earlier will naming him as successor had greater validity than the later codicil in favour of Archelaus. Antipater III, the son of Salome I, spoke against Archelaus and advocated the cause of Antipas. The main proponent supporting Archelaus was Herod's official court historian, Nicholas of Damascus. Philip was also in Rome to request a share of royal power because Varus had told him that partition of Herod's territories was possible. Additionally, Varus had sanctioned the attendance of a delegation of fifty Jews to plead for Judea to be joined to the Roman province of Syria rather than a continuation of the Herodian dynasty. Their petition was championed by eight thousand Jewish residents of Rome.[5]

The extensive lands ruled by Herod the Great were partitioned by Emperor Augustus, who detached the cities of Gaza, Gadara and Hippus from the kingdom and added them to Syria. Philip, with the title of *tetrarch*, was to rule the region to the south and east of Paneas and the territories on the north-eastern side of the river Jordan. Antipas also received the title of *tetrarch* and was allocated Galilee and Peraea, a more southerly region east of the river Jordan.[6]

Archelaus was to rule the more traditional Judean regions of Judea itself, Idumaea and Samaria, together with the cities of Caesarea, Sebaste, Joppa and Jerusalem. He was not given the title of king, but a lesser title of *ethnarch* with the promise of the royal title should he prove worthy.[7] Previously, Hyrcanus II had been honoured by Julius Caesar with title *ethnarch* as protector of the Jews living outside, as well as inside Judea. On this occasion, Emperor Augustus bestowed the title upon Archelaus with a much more territorial bias rather than an ethnic functioning.[8]

The return of Archelaus to Jerusalem was far from happy. His second wife, Glaphyra, had previously given birth to two sons during her marriage to Archelaus' half-brother Alexander. Her subsequent marriage to Archelaus caused offence,[9] though not long after arriving in Jerusalem, Glaphyra died.[10] The *Ethnarch* undoubtedly upset a local village by diverting half of their irrigation water to his rebuilt Jericho palace, and in Jerusalem he continued the irreverent custom begun by his father of replacing living high priests.[11]

The greatest distress, however, was caused by his brutal and relentless campaign of revenge against those who had rebelled both before he had left for Rome, and particularly while he was in Rome presenting his petition. Archelaus' treatment of both his Judean and Samaritan subjects was so harsh that after nine years of misery, the leaders of both communities approached the Roman emperor and denounced him. Augustus duly summoned Archelaus to Rome in 6 CE, and after hearing from both sides, stripped him of his titles, confiscated his property and sent him into exile.[12]

The territories of Judea, Idumaea and Samaria[13] formerly comprising the *ethnarchy* ruled by Archelaus became an extension of the province of Syria, but with its own governor or Prefect appointed by the Roman emperor. Additionally, a census of Syria was carried out for the purpose of Roman tax computations. The gathering of this information met with resentment and resistance, led in particular by a rebel referred to as Judas of Galilee. Although the protest was short lived, Judas is credited with forming the sect known as The Zealots, who became increasingly influential sixty years later in the build-up to the 66–70 CE Jewish/Roman war.[14]

The Roman Prefects of Judaea were based in Caesarea and normally only stayed in Jerusalem to oversee security measures on occasions such as major Jewish religious ceremonies during which huge numbers of visitors would descend upon the city. Local political control was vested in the Prefects, who were, however, subordinate to the governors of Syria in certain circumstances. The Jews were no longer allowed to appoint

Jerusalem's high priest, as this fell within the remit of the Roman governor of Syria or the Prefect of Judaea. Nevertheless, the Roman officials were generally heedful of Jewish sensitivities, particularly in their choices of high priest, who tended to be drawn from the old-established priestly families.[15]

The Prefects would exercise their judicial prerogative where political crimes were involved and in extraordinary instances. Otherwise the application of civil and criminal law was administered by the local Jewish courts. After the demise of Herod and Archelaus, *the constitution became an aristocracy, and the high priests were entrusted with the leadership of the nation.*[16] The high priest was also the president of the aristocratic *Sanhedrin*, which became the governing institution responsible for internal Jewish affairs. The Roman Prefect was mainly concerned with political, military and security matters, while concurrently sustaining the preeminent authority of the Roman emperor.

The first three Roman Prefects[17] were assigned by the elderly Emperor Augustus, who died in 14 CE and was succeeded by his adopted son Tiberius. Valerius Gratus became the fourth Prefect of Judaea in 15 CE and he dismissed and appointed a series of high priests[18] over a relatively short period, before settling upon Joseph Caiaphas, who held the position of Jerusalem's high priest from 18–36 CE.

Tiberius appointed Pontius Pilate as the Roman Prefect of Judaea in 26 CE. The initial impression made by Pilate was poor as, when transferring his army to its winter quarters in Jerusalem, his troops carried standards bearing images of Tiberius, thereby subverting Jewish law. The strength of protest, even in the face of threatened deadly reprisal, eventually persuaded Pilate to remove the offending image bearing standards.[19] More dissidence was to follow when he used Jerusalem's sacred treasure, the *Corbonas*, to fund the construction of an aqueduct. Pilate arranged for soldiers in plain clothes to mingle with those protesting against the misuse of the Temple funds and as the demonstration became increasingly vocal, the troops drew clubs and many Jews were beaten to death and others trampled underfoot during the mêlée.[20]

During the later years of Pilate's Prefecture, bitter tensions arose between the orthodox Jews in Jerusalem and the new Christian cult, not the least of which was the trial and crucifixion of Jesus. The trial and stoning to death of the Stephen,[21] and the anti-Christian activities of Saul before his conversion as Paul,[22] may lack historical corroboration, but, nevertheless, are symbolic of the religious divide during the years 30 to 36 CE, when Joseph Caiaphas was Jerusalem's high priest and supported by his father-in-law Ananus.[23]

Pilate's role in Palestine ended ignominiously in 36 CE after a petition was made to the governor of Syria that Pilate had unjustly ordered the deaths of some supposedly revolutionary Samaritans. Vitellius, the Syrian governor installed Marcellus as Prefect and ordered Pilate to return to Rome and account to the emperor for his actions.[24] At the time of the Feast of Passover (end-March) 36 CE, Vitellius visited Jerusalem and, to popular acclaim, remitted the sales taxes on agricultural products and restored custody of the high priest's robe to the temple.[25] Vitellius was also in Jerusalem one year later when the news broke that there was a new emperor in Rome. Before Pilate had reached Rome, Tiberius had died in 37 CE and had been succeeded by Caligula, who possibly compelled Pilate to commit suicide.[26] Ironically, as history would reveal, Jerusalem's Jewish population became the first in the Syrian region to declare their loyalty to the new emperor Caligula.[27]

The crowning of Caligula was very good news for one of Herod the Great's grandchildren, Agrippa I, the son of Aristobulus IV. Agrippa had been named after Marcus Vipsanius Agrippa, the son-in-law of the Roman emperor Augustus, and as a child and young adult he lived in Rome amongst the highest echelons of society. Consistent with the consanguineous nature of Herodian dynasty marriages, he wed his cousin Cyprus III.[28] Aged around 43 years and having lived beyond his means, the penniless and debt-laden Agrippa eventually left Rome for Idumaea in around 32 CE. Agrippa's uncle Philip, who had ruled as *tetrarch* of part of Ituraea and various regions on the north-eastern side of the river Jordan for thirty-seven years, died in 33 CE without an heir and his territories were added, albeit temporarily, to the Roman province of Syria.[29] The following year, Agrippa's sister, Philip's widow, Herodias I,[30] married his half-brother Antipas, the *tetrarch* of Galilee and Peraea. A year or two later in response to a plea for help from his wife, Herodias I and her new husband, Antipas, engaged Agrippa as *agoranomos*[31] in Tiberias to provide him with an income.[32] This employment did not endure and neither did a brief sojourn in Antioch, but by borrowing whenever and wherever he could, Agrippa made his way back to Rome to become a guest of the emperor Tiberius.[33] However, an overly close friendship with Tiberius' adopted son Caligula and a loose tongue landed Agrippa in prison in October 36 CE.[34]

Six months later, the new emperor Caligula released a greatly relieved Agrippa, who was then appointed king over the territories that until 33 CE had made up the *tetrarchy* of his uncle Philip.[35] Further regions were added to Agrippa's domain in 39 CE when Antipas the *tetrarch* fell out of favour with Caligula. Antipas was sent into exile and Galilee and Peraea were added to the kingdom of Agrippa I.[36] In the meantime, anxious to please Caligula, who had become convinced of his own divinity,[37] the Greeks in the Egyptian city of Alexandria began to rail against the Jews, whose religious convictions would not allow them to accept Caligula as a god. The visit of king Agrippa I to Alexandria acted as a catalyst for tensions to boil over, triggering a deadly anti-Jewish pogrom during the autumn of 38 CE.[38] Rival Greek and Jewish deputations from Alexandria went to Rome in 40 CE, to petition Caligula,[39] but before the Jews had been contemptuously dismissed for failing to recognize Caligula as a deity,[40] further religious conflict erupted in the Judean coastal town of Jamnia. Upon hearing that the Jews had destroyed a pagan altar, Caligula decreed that a statue of himself should be erected in Jerusalem's temple.[41] Such an undertaking would have resulted in a massive Jewish uprising and war in Judea, had not representations from Agrippa I and Petronius, who had replaced Vitellius as the governor of Syria, finally persuaded Caligula to abandon the project.[42]

Caligula was murdered in January 41 CE, following which both Agrippa and his brother Herod V assisted Claudius to become the new Roman emperor. Claudius rewarded Agrippa by adding to his kingdom the rest of the territory earlier ruled by his grandfather, namely Judea, Samaria and Idumaea. The kingdom of Agrippa I now matched or exceeded that formerly ruled by Herod the Great. Claudius also rewarded Herod V with the kingdom of Chalcis.[43]

Notwithstanding some fairly obvious Greco-Roman pagan activities abroad,[44] within the confines of his kingdom and sometimes even externally,[45] Agrippa championed Judaism. Once ensconced as king in Jerusalem, Agrippa consistently and enthusiastically performed all the expected temple rituals.[46] The gold chain given to him by Claudius upon his release from prison was donated to the temple and Agrippa extended charity to help the poor to make their temple offerings.[47] Despite his 'foreign' links, the Pharisaic hierarchy esteemed Agrippa[48] and his generosity made him a popular leader in Jerusalem.[49] Upholding pious Judaism in Jerusalem, however, possibly also brought Agrippa into conflict with the growing cult of Christianity.[50]

The 'kings' of the region were, of course, client-kings by sufferance of the Roman emperor, and when on occasions Agrippa acted in a way that might be considered an attempt to exercise a degree of independence, the Romans immediately became suspicious. Agrippa's meeting in Galilee, in the city of Tiberias, with five other client kings aroused misgivings and the Romans duly put an end to the proceedings.[51]

Another cause for concern for the Romans was Agrippa's decision to build a new wall on the north side of Jerusalem. Following the designation of the Hasmonean walls as the *First* and *Second Walls*, Agrippa's northern wall is referred to as the *Third Wall*, a detailed description of which was provided by Josephus.[52] The exact line of the wall became the subject of much debate and controversy amongst archaeologists, until it was positively identified with the remains of a wall approximately one-fifth of a mile further north than the present wall of the Old City of Jerusalem.[53] The motive for the mooted construction may have been to protect the inhabitants of the Bezetha Hill north of the temple compound, as well as the more sparsely populated area even further to the north,[54] by enclosing them within the walled city, or to improve Jerusalem's defences, but it was probably a combination of the two.

According to Josephus, the wall was not completed during the reign of Agrippa I for three varying and conflicting reasons, which were that Emperor Claudius sent a letter demanding the Judaean king desist, that Agrippa desisted of his own accord after laying the foundations because he feared Claudius would become suspicious, and finally that the work ceased because Agrippa died.[55] It has been mooted that the wall was, in fact, hurriedly completed more than twenty years later by the insurgent Jews during the 66–70 CE Jewish/Roman War, but this is somewhat contradicted by the modern excavation of large ashlars with margins dressed in the Herodian manner.[56] Logically the cost and time needed for such a vast project would suggest that Agrippa's reign of 41–44 CE was too short for the undertaking to have been fully completed, and indeed final touches may have been necessary during the war,[57] but equally the evidence would allow for work on the wall to have been carried out after Agrippa's death and before hostilities began.

In the summer of 44 CE, while attending a festival in Caesarea, severe illness brought about a painful end to the colourful life of Agrippa I.[58] Not only had this grandson of Herod the Great briefly ruled a Judaean kingdom with borders as wide-ranging as they had ever been, but he was also responsible for the concept and original implementation of the wall that bounded the greatest ever northerly expansion of the ancient city of Jerusalem.

Chapter 19

Roman Procurators and Temple Curators

Notwithstanding that during the previous century, his grandfather, Herod the Great, had rebuilt Caesarea (Strato's Tower) and Sebaste (Samaria), the inhabitants of both cities celebrated the death of Agrippa I in 44 CE.[1] Both towns formed part of the region of Samaria, whose rapport with Jerusalem had been fragile and often hostile during the past one thousand years.

The Roman emperor Claudius, angry at the reaction of the Samaritans, was initially inclined to appoint Agrippa's seventeen-year-old son Agrippa II, as the successor king of Judaea. Advisers to the emperor, perhaps with the suspicion that the Judaeans were beginning to prepare for independence from Rome, persuaded Claudius that the responsibility would be too much for the youth and a Roman procurator was appointed to oversee the kingdom.[2]

The emperor did, however, accede to the request by Herod, the king of Chalcis and brother of the late Agrippa I, to be appointed as curator in charge of Jerusalem's temple and holy vessels, with the authority to dismiss and appoint Jerusalem's high priests. Herod of Chalcis discharged the incumbent Elionaeus ben Cantheras and replaced him with Joseph ben Camei as Jerusalem's new high priest. Three years later in 47 CE, Herod once again exercised his prerogative as Temple curator to discard Joseph and assign the high priesthood to Ananias ben Nedebaeus, who held the position for the next twelve years.[3]

As with earlier series of the Roman Prefects, the procurators from 44 to 70 CE, exercised local control, but were subordinate to the Roman governors of Syria. The first of the Roman procurators of Judaea, Cuspius Fadus (44–46 CE) undertook action to reduce the region's endemic banditry, but also contentiously resolved to reverse the action taken eight years earlier by Syrian governor Vitellius, who had restored custody of the high priest's sacred robe to Jerusalem's temple authorities. A Jewish delegation petitioned Claudius and was successful due to a favourable intercession by the youthful Agrippa II, who at that time was in residence at the court of Claudius.[4]

Apart from the crucifixion of rebels, the subsequent procurator, Tiberius Alexander (46–48 CE) appears to have been relatively uncontroversial. During his time in office, however, a famine that had begun earlier reached crisis proportions and thus required relief programmes for Jerusalem and the region of Judaea.[5]

In 48 CE Ventidius Cumanus became the third procurator of Judaea (48–52 CE) and as 48 CE drew to a close, Herod of Chalcis died. As his children were too young to succeed Herod, Claudius appointed Agrippa II as king of Chalcis and curator of the temple in Jerusalem, although opinion is divided as to whether or not there was an interregnum between Herod's death and Agrippa's succession.[6] Authority over the Temple by Herod of Chalcis and subsequently Agrippa II was despite neither actually residing in Jerusalem on a permanent basis. Jerusalem's temple was, however, so central to Jewish religious and social interactions that as curator, Agrippa was able to exercise considerable influence over Judaean affairs.

During Cumanus' time as procurator, an important meeting of the nascent Judeo-Christian movement took place in Jerusalem in around 49 CE.[7] The outcome was the decision that Gentile converts to Christianity were not obliged to adhere to most traditional Jewish laws, including circumcision. This so-called *Council of Jerusalem* may be considered as a precursor to later Ecumenical Councils convened to decide matters of Church doctrine and practice.

Discord between the Romans and the Jews erupted during the Passover festival in Jerusalem when a crude insulting gesture by a Roman sentry caused outrage and demands upon procurator Cumanus to punish the offender. As matters got out of hand, Cumanus called out the guard, causing the Jewish protestors to stampede through the narrow streets and resulting in a large number of fatalities.[8] During a subsequent dispute just outside the city, a Roman soldier destroyed a copy of the Jewish sacred laws, but on this occasion Cumanus defused the situation by yielding to Jewish demands for the offender to be put to death.[9]

Violence broke out between the Jews of Galilee and Jerusalem and their traditional enemies, the Samaritans. As the disorder escalated, one of those who became involved in the ferocious fighting was a particularly infamous Jewish brigand originally called Eleazar, who had operated for several years from his mountain retreat. The endeavours by the first Roman procurator Fadus to eliminate the rampant banditry were negated as, *from that time the whole of Judaea was infested with bands of brigands*.[10] Eleazar became known by the pseudonym 'Son of the Murderer' and so many unlawful killings took place that the Temple authorities in Jerusalem decided to discontinue the sacrifice of atonement for unknown murderers.[11]

It was either ineptitude or dishonesty in dealing with the turmoil that caused the eventual downfall of Cumanus. Ummidius Quadratus, the governor of Syria, sent the leaders of the Samaritans and the Jews as well as Cumanus to Rome, as the facts concerning the fighting and capital punishments that had been meted out were put before Emperor Claudius in 52 CE. Agrippa II once again used his influence to support the Jewish version of events with the result that Cumanus was sent into exile.[12] Included amongst the Jewish representatives were the high priest Ananias ben Nedebaeus and the *sagan*[13] Ananus, as well as the former high priest Jonathan ben Ananus. Although he would have cause for future regret, Jonathan requested that the emperor appoint Marcus Antonius Felix as the new procurator of Judaea.[14]

Duly appointed by Claudius, Felix became the fourth procurator of Judaea (52–60 CE). Originally, he and his brother Pallas had been slaves before becoming 'freedmen' and Pallas, in particular, had risen to a position of power in Rome as secretary to Claudius and later in the same role to Emperor Nero for a brief period. Felix' marriages may also have added to his political connections. His first wife was a granddaughter of Mark Antony, who was also the grandfather of Emperor Claudius. Second, he wed Drusilla, the sister of Agrippa II, whom Felix persuaded to leave her husband and marry him in defiance of Jewish law forbidding marriage to a non-Jew.[15] His character and actions were not reported favourably with the assertion that Felix *practised every kind of cruelty and lust, wielding the power of king with all the instincts of a slave*.[16]

At the behest of Emperor Claudius in 53 CE, Agrippa II relinquished the throne of Chalcis in favour of taking over a more expansive territory in the region north-east of the river Jordan. In October 54 CE Claudius died and early actions of the new Roman Emperor Nero included presenting Agrippa II with additional cities and territory in Peraea and Galilee and confirming the position of Felix as procurator of Judaea.[17] Felix pursued the country's brigands ruthlessly, crucifying huge numbers of those he suspected of complicity with the outlaws. A false promise duped Eleazar into surrendering and he was then sent to Rome as a prisoner.[18]

Just as the rural outlaws were being aggressively and effectively dealt with, a new breed appeared in Jerusalem. Assassins began committing murders, often in broad daylight during festivals throughout the city, including the Temple compound. These so-called *sicarii* used daggers concealed under their outer-clothes to despatch their enemies and others that they were simply paid to slaughter. Reportedly, the first killing was that of the former high priest Jonathan, who had voiced too many complaints about the behaviour of Felix. Furthermore, having been bribed by Felix to commit the crime, which then went unpunished, the *sicarii* were left with the impression that they could persist in their murderous exploits with virtual impunity.[19]

Jerusalem became a hub for anti-Roman sentiments of all kinds and it was often difficult to distinguish the fine lines dividing criminals, charlatans, religious fanatics and political revolutionaries. Whatever the motives of the various antagonists, Felix responded with extreme violence and repression throughout Judaea.[20]

In 59 CE, Agrippa II had exercised his authority as curator of the Temple in Jerusalem to appoint Ishmael ben Phabi as the new high priest. The families from which the high priests were drawn were currently perceived as abusing their power and civil disturbances occurred between the aristocratic clique of the high priests and lower ranking priests, who had popular support. Distracted by the need to constrain the anti-Roman elements, Felix appears to have ignored the disorder caused by the ecclesiastical dispute in Jerusalem.[21]

On several occasions towards the end of his time as procurator, Felix met and conversed with Saul, now known as Paul after his conversion from Christian oppressor to Apostle. Paul failed to provide the bribes that Felix had hoped for and was incarcerated in Caesarea.[22] A dispute over civil rights between the Jews and the Hellenized Syrians of Caesarea escalated into violent conflict, culminating in Felix using his troops against the Jewish faction which had refused to disperse. Eventually, Felix sent representatives of both sides to argue their respective causes before Emperor Nero in Rome.[23] This was pretty much the last significant action by Felix in his role as procurator because in 60 CE, he was replaced by Porcius Festus (60–62 CE).[24] There was disappointment for the Jewish community in Caesarea as their claim for equal civil status was rejected and frustration for the leaders of Jerusalem's Jews who wanted Festus to hand Paul over to them, which almost certainly would have resulted in his death. After some deliberation, Festus sent Paul to Rome where he continued to preach.[25]

Just as Felix had to deal anti-Roman factions of various denominations, Festus experienced problems with the *sicarii* and other extremists during his short time as procurator.[26] He also became involved in a dispute between Agrippa II and Jerusalem's temple priests. Despite Agrippa II having his capital at Neronias,[27] he also spent some time residing in Jerusalem in the former Hasmonean palace, close to the temple precinct and the bridge over the old Tyropoeon Valley. Agrippa took pleasure in observing all that was happening in Jerusalem including witnessing the temple ceremonies. To facilitate this pastime, he had a higher tower built at the palace to give himself a better view of the city. The temple priests felt that it was highly inappropriate for the hallowed sacrifices to be spied upon in this way and a wall was erected to block Agrippa's view. Perhaps coincidently, the new wall also blocked the view of the Roman supervisory guards tasked with maintaining public order.[28]

Both Agrippa II and the procurator were outraged and although the priests were commanded to demolish the wall, they persuaded Festus to have the matter referred to Emperor Nero and a deputation was duly dispatched to Rome. Poppaea, the emperor's wife, who harboured Jewish leanings, swayed Nero into siding with the priests and allowing the wall to remain. However, Poppaea insisted that the high priest, Ishmael ben Phabi, remain behind in her household and subsequently, Agrippa chose Joseph Kabi as Ishmael's replacement.[29]

Following the death in office of Festus early in 62 CE, Agrippa II removed Joseph Kabi and assigned the high priesthood to Ananus ben Ananus. Encouraged by the hiatus of there being no procurator *in situ*, and emboldened by the fact that his father and his four brothers had all previously served as high priest, Ananus swiftly began to misuse his authority. Without proper sanction, he convened the *Sanhedrin* judges to pass death sentences on a number of alleged transgressors, including James (*the Just*), regarded by Christians as the brother of Jesus and the first bishop of Jerusalem.[30] Lucceius Albinus, the replacement procurator (62–64 CE) was on his way from Alexandria and upon hearing of the chaos in Jerusalem wrote to Ananus threatening retribution. However, prior to Albinus' arrival in the summer, Agrippa II had replaced Ananus with a new high priest named Jesus ben Damnaeus.[31]

Work on Herod the Great's magnificent temple rebuilding project is reported to have finally concluded with the result that significant numbers were left without jobs and hence with no income. The hardships caused by the loss of employment was at least partially alleviated as Agrippa II sanctioned the paving of Jerusalem's streets with white stone.[32] Agrippa's sense of responsibility as temple curator may be illustrated by his undertaking when some of the foundations of the sanctuary began to subside. Strong wooden beams were required to underpin sections of the temple building and accordingly, *King Agrippa had, at immense labour and expense, brought down from Mount Libanus the materials for that purpose, beams that for straightness and size were a sight to see.*[33]

Agrippa's principal loyalty was to Rome, where he had been brought up, and this precluded him from ever being viewed appreciatively by the Jews. His contributions to the magnificence of Jerusalem at that point in history were positive, if minor in comparison with the achievements of his great-grandfather. The grand palaces and public buildings fashioned by Herod the Great were augmented with paved colonnaded streets and supplied with water from aqueducts and cisterns. The re-built temple attracted thousands of tourists to the city[34] and accolades to the spectacle presented by Jerusalem were abundant in Christian and rabbinic literature. Some thirty years earlier an awestruck disciple of Jesus had been moved to remark: *Look, Teacher, what wonderful stones and what wonderful buildings!*[35] Talmudic passages exclaim: *Ten measures of beauty descended from the heavens – nine were taken by Jerusalem and one by the rest of the world,* and: *Whoever has not seen Jerusalem in its splendour has never seen a fine city.*[36]

Chapter 20

Insurrection

Judaea was ruled variously by people, some of whom were cruel and evil and others who acted reasonably in the context of the first century CE. With the benefit of hindsight, it seems, however, that the Jewish Judaean population desired nothing less than full religious and political autonomy. In a world ruled by the Romans, this was simply not going to happen and examination can be made of the events and people that acted as catalysts, but one is drawn to the conclusion that war was inevitable.

The Jews patently resented their Roman masters, but there were also other causes of tension and dissatisfaction. These included cultural/religious issues with Greeks and Samaritans, and in particular with a development from Hellenistic Judaism, the rise of Christianity. The conflicts that arose were complex and more often than not comprised several inter-related issues.

In addition to the frustrated political aspirations of the Judaeans, their religious struggles and their sociological dilemmas, dissatisfaction also came about for quite diverse financial reasons. Looting by roaming bands of murderous brigands added to life's difficulties, but activities such as wheat farming and the cultivation of vines, olives, balsam, papyrus and various fruits together with livestock husbandry were ostensibly capable of creating prosperity for the general Judaean region. The established system of land tenure, however, created inequalities because upon the death of a Jewish landowner, the property was divided between all of his sons, with the eldest having a share twice that of the others. This fragmentation often resulted in attempts to farm uneconomically small plots, the owners of which subsequently fell into debt. Frequently this was followed the loss of the land and forced servitude, the threat of which epitomised a sense of social injustice.[1]

Additional causes of economic hardship were the onerous taxes imposed by Judaea's Roman overlords. The Roman levies included a head tax, a tribute assessed on cultivated land, shipping charges and various other tolls. The prevailing Jewish opinion of the Romans was characterized by the words of Rabbi Simeon b. Yohai when replying to a comment of how great were the deeds of the Romans: *Yeah, but whatever they set up, they set up only for their own convenience. Sure they organize markets, but that is for places for their whores. Bathhouses? To preen themselves in them. Bridges? To collect tolls.*[2]

The whole ethos of Jewish law and its interpretation promoted exclusivity and an inability to compromise with other cultures. The Romans respected local laws and traditions, placing the Jews in a privileged position, even if they may not have thought so. The Torah was recognized as law and it followed that the Jews were exempted from military service to avoid contact with impure army pagans. Additionally, many significant Roman celebrations and customs were forbidden in Jerusalem and this special treatment caused resentment on the part of the local Roman administrators and in turn led the Romans to provoke the Jews.[3]

The new procurator Albinus arrived in Jerusalem in the summer of 62 CE and initially appears to have set about eliminating the creed of assassins known as the *sicarii*.[4] Notwithstanding this, Albinus' prime objective was to elicit money from whoever and wherever he could. Despite his twelve-year tenure as Jerusalem's high priest having ended in 59 CE, Ananias b. Nedebaeus ingratiated himself with Albinus by way of a steady stream of gifts in an effort to preserve his influential position in the city. The assassins' creed enjoyed a revival after they kidnapped Ananias' son and forced him into cajoling Albinus to release ten *sicarii* prisoners. Additional abductions then led to the freedom of more detainees and the *sicarii* movement resumed its expansion.[5]

The relatives of convicted offenders paid bribes to Albinus to have their criminal kin released from prison *and the only persons left in goal as malefactors were those who failed to pay the price*.[6] The chaotic mob rule engendered by those freed was underpinned by the unjust actions of the people supposed to be in authority, including Albinus, Ananias b. Nedebaeus and relatives of Agrippa II. The procurator misused his authority to impose extraordinary taxes and even to steal from private households to such an extent that the residents of Jerusalem *owing to their fear of the Romans, they did not want to have any money that was kept on deposit*.[7] Ananias orchestrated the violent theft of priestly tithes,[8] while Costobar and Saul, who were members of the royal family, led gangs that robbed vulnerable residents.[9]

In 64 CE, Gessius Florus took over as the Roman procurator of Judaea and he turned out to be far more avaricious, cruel and unprincipled than any of his predecessors. Criminal gangs acted with impunity in return for handing Florus a share of their plunderous exploits and many Jews simply fled the country.[10] The visit to Jerusalem of Cestius Gallus, the Governor of Syria, at the time of the Passover festival in early spring 65 CE, afforded the beleaguered Jews the opportunity to complain of the procurators' crimes and the assembled populace *loudly denounced Florus as the ruin of the country.* Although Florus derided the criticism, Gallus promised the crowd that Florus would show greater restraint going forward. Provoking war, however, was now Florus' only feasible alternative to the eventual denunciation of his misconduct to the Roman Emperor Nero and the consequences that would ensue.[11]

Some years earlier, arbitration by Nero had placed the municipal authority of Caesarea firmly in Greek hands, but this had not resolved the endemic mutual antipathy of the Jewish and Greek residents of the city, which stood seventy miles north-west of Jerusalem. In 66 CE, a dispute over a plot of land next to a Caesarean synagogue led to violence between the Greeks and the Jews. Subsequently, a Jewish bribe to Florus for assistance proved futile and a deputation sent to protest over his failure to keep his promise was simply arrested. Florus, *as if he had contracted to fan the flames of war*, then proceeded to demand a tax payment of seventeen talents from the temple in Jerusalem, where he was ridiculed by the people begging satirically for small coins to present to the *destitute* procurator.[12]

Incensed by this insult, Florus marched towards Jerusalem with a Roman cohort[13] and used cavalrymen to summarily disperse a Jewish delegation that had left the city seeking to appease him. The procurator spent the night in Jerusalem and the following day demanded that the city leaders hand over those who had insulted him. Having been informed that this was impracticable, Florus with the dual motives of further enrichment and provoking war, ordered his troops to sack the Upper City district. Murder and pillage spread throughout the city, following which residents were randomly whipped and crucified, including unprecedentedly, Jews who were also Roman citizens. Queen Berenice, the sister of Agrippa II, endangered herself by making an unsuccessful plea to Florus to put an end to the carnage, which cost the lives of an estimated 3,600 men, women and children.[14]

On the ensuing day, the Jewish leaders temporarily calmed a vocal protest against Florus, but subsequently the procurator manipulated events to ensure further bloodshed between additional Roman soldiers approaching Jerusalem and a Jewish delegation sent to greet them. Jewish rebels then prevented an attempt by Florus and his troops to reach Fortress Antonia, from which he would be able to gain access to the Temple, and to ensure that no second attempt succeeded, the insurgents destroyed the porticoes that connected the two buildings. A grudging suspension of hostilities was agreed with Florus returning to Caesarea with most of his forces, leaving the Jewish leaders a Roman cohort to maintain order, but by arrangement not those troops who had perpetrated the previous day's massacre.[15]

The turmoil in Jerusalem was duly reported to Cestius Gallus, the Governor of Syria, but the disparate versions of events described by Florus, the Jewish leaders and Queen Berenice were, of course, biased by their contrasting interests. To ascertain the truth, Gallus despatched Neapolitanus, a Roman tribune, who before proceeding was joined by Agrippa II near the Mediterranean coast. Jerusalem's prominent citizens, followed by anguished grieving relatives of those slain by Florus also came to meet Neapolitanus. Once inside Jerusalem, the Roman tribune was shown the devastation wrought by Florus' troops and he then left to make his report to Gallus.[16]

Despite calls for Florus to be denounced to the Roman Emperor Nero, Agrippa, who had remained in Jerusalem, made a loquacious attempt to avoid further conflict. His long and emotional speech on the utter futility of war against the might of Rome persuaded the Jews to rebuild the porticoes connecting Fortress Antonia to the Temple and to pay their outstanding taxes. Agrippa's entreaties to obey Florus until such time that he would be replaced were, however, so opprobrious to the Jews that he was insulted and pelted with stones. Agrippa II was then officially expelled from Jerusalem.[17]

The summer of 66 CE saw Jewish insurgents overrun a Roman fortress at Masada, close to the Dead Sea, while militant Temple officials[18] in Jerusalem banned gifts and sacrifices from foreigners, despite opposition from many of the senior priests. As the prohibition included offerings made on behalf of Rome, it was in effect a declaration of war.[19] Those opposed to the rebels asked both Florus and Agrippa II to help quell what was now an open revolt, but pleased by the prospect of war against the Jews, Florus neglected to respond, whereas Agrippa sent 2,000 cavalrymen. A week of fierce combat then ensued between the insurgents occupying the Temple and Lower City, and Agrippa's soldiers and the pro-Roman Jews ensconced in the Upper City.[20]

The rebels, assisted by the *sicarii*, forced their way into the Temple and subsequently took control of the Upper city, obliging the peace party to take refuge in Herod the Great's former palace on Jerusalem's western extremity. The insurgents exacted revenge on their opponents by setting fire to their dwellings, including the house of former high priest Ananias b. Nedebaeus[21] and the extensions to the old Hasmonean Palace used by Agrippa II and his sister Berenice. Symbolically, the repository of official documents was set ablaze, destroying proof of the debts of the poorer Jews to the wealthy.[22]

Fortress Antonia fell into the hands of the revolutionaries, who then besieged Herod's palace. Eventually, led by the *Zealot* Menahem[23] and armed with weapons confiscated from the Roman fortress of Masada, the assailants overcame the resolve of the defenders, who appealed to be allowed a peaceful evacuation of the palace. The request was granted, but applied only to Jews and Agrippa's troops, while the despairing Roman soldiers in the palace took refuge in the almost impregnable Hippicus, Phasael and Mariamne towers on the northern perimeter of the palace compound.[24] The subsequent murder of Ananias b. Nedebaeus by the *Zealots*, led to a violent rebel backlash against Menahem and although a number of *Zealots* escaped to Masada, Menahem and some of his deputies were tortured and killed.[25] The Roman troops trapped in the towers of the palace eventually capitulated, but were massacred, after accepting an insincere promise that they would not be harmed if they surrendered their weapons, and with this act in the late summer of 66 CE, the last vestige of hope for the avoidance of a Jewish/Roman war was lost.[26]

Jerusalem's uprising was the catalyst for the eruption of merciless civil wars between Jews and non-Jews throughout the Middle East. Extending from Caesarea in the west, to Damascus in the north, Philadelphia[27] in the east and as far south as Alexandria in Egypt.[28] Although the actual date is uncertain, the prospect of war looming brought about a 'revelation' for the Christians of Jerusalem, who began an exodus from the city to resettle in the city of Pella, south of the Sea of Galilee in the valley of the River Jordan.[29]

Spurred into action, the Roman governor of Syria, Cestius Gallus left Antioch with a vast army of Roman troops and cavalry. He was accompanied by Agrippa II and auxiliary troops supplied by various Roman client-kings. They marched southwards along the coast of the eastern Mediterranean, subduing a number of Jewish towns and villages. A strong force entered the heartland of Galilee, where they successfully rid the territory of Jewish rebels. An attack by land and sea overwhelmed the coastal town of Joppa and the army then followed the established route from Joppa to Jerusalem to set up camp five miles north-west of the city. The Jews attacked with great ferocity and after inflicting heavy casualties on the Romans, kept watch on the camp from the safety of the surrounding high ground. The rebels would not allow any peace negotiations with emissaries sent by Agrippa and perceiving indications of dissention in Jerusalem, Cestius attacked with his whole army. He routed the rebel forces and set-up a new camp on Mount Scopus, less than one mile north-east of the city walls.[30]

It was now November 66 CE and Cestius waited three days for a surrender that was not forthcoming. He ordered an attack and the Roman army overcame the Jewish defences to occupy the area between Jerusalem's two defensive northern walls.[31] The Romans set fire to the north-eastern suburb of Bezetha and in the north-west they penetrated as far as Herod the Great's former royal palace. Possibly Cestius now possessed a decisive advantage, but the opportunity was lost when his generals persuaded him against pressing on immediately. The rebels were able to recover and defend the wall and the north side of the Temple against repeated attacks that lasted several days. Not realizing that the Jewish resolve was weakening, the governor of Syria then inexplicably abandoned his attempt to capture Jerusalem and departed. Cestius was pursued mercilessly by the Jewish insurgents, who as well as procuring useful military equipment for future use in the war, inflicted huge numbers of casualties on the retreating Romans.[32]

A number of eminent pro-Roman Jews abandoned the city as others, not necessarily by choice, joined the insurgents and effectively Rome had now lost the support of the Jewish aristocracy. A Jewish war council was held in the Temple and decided that Joseph b. Gorion and former high priest Ananus b. Ananus would lead the war effort, and local commanders were appointed to every province of Judaea.[33] One of these was John the Essene, indicating that at least some of the normally pacifist and isolationist Essene religious community were involved in the uprising and subsequent war. These participants may have included some from the Essene cave settlement at Qumran near the Dead Sea, influenced by the prophecy *that the sons of Light would go to battle against the sons of Darkness.*[34] During the winter of 66/67 CE, attention was paid to preparing weapons and armour, providing military training and strengthening the walls.[35] This was almost certainly the period when efforts were made to complete the so-called *Third Wall* begun by Agrippa I, approximately twenty-five years earlier.

Emperor Nero appointed the well-proven general Vespasian to take charge of the Roman armies in the East,[36] and the campaign to reassert Roman domination of Judaea began in Galilee in the spring of 67 CE. Once he had been joined by his son Titus, Vespasian's army numbered over 60,000 men, comprising three legions, additional squadrons of infantrymen and cavalry, and auxiliaries supplied by four client-kings, including Agrippa II.[37] Although the war in Galilee was hard fought, the potency of Vespasian and Titus' war machine eventually overran all of the rebel fortifications and by the end of the year, the Romans were in total control of northern Judaea.[38]

A catalyst for further disorder in Jerusalem was the entry into the city of a group of *Zealots* led by John of Gischala[39] in November 67 CE. The existing rebel leaders lacked his fanaticism and the younger rebels were certainly swayed by John's oratory and the perception that the revolution was being overturned by the Romans. Throughout Judaea, divisions appeared between the militants and those opposed to war, and Jerusalem's food supplies dwindled as the population, already swollen by pilgrims unable to leave, endured large influxes of both rebels and refugees from the surrounding areas. The incoming militants joined forces with those already there and began murderous campaigns against those leading citizens whom they perceived as enemies. These so-called *Zealots* even went as far as occupying the Temple and using a lottery to elect a new high priest.[40]

Ananus b. Ananus led a counter movement against the *Zealots* and after a bloody and savage battle, the outnumbered militants took refuge in the inner sanctum of the Temple, which Ananus was loath to storm for religious reasons. John of Gischala, acting as a double agent, convinced the *Zealots* to request urgent assistance from the Idumaeans on the pretence that Ananus was about to surrender Jerusalem to the Romans. Twenty thousand Idumaeans responded and encamped outside the city gates after failing to gain admittance. Under the cover of darkness and a violent night-time storm, however, a group of militants evaded the guards and opened the gates to allow entry to the Idumaeans. Those guarding the Temple summoned help, but the combined strength of the *Zealots* and the Idumaeans inflicted an indiscriminate massacre upon the moderate opposition. After the Temple had been *deluged with blood*, the Idumaeans looted and murdered until the death count exceeded 8,500. Subsequently, the priests who had led the moderates were sought out and Ananus was amongst those executed.[41]

The *Zealots* and Idumaeans instigated a purge of all perceived opponents and potential adversaries, particularly the younger prominent members of Jerusalem's society. Arrest by day followed by torture and death by night became commonplace and allegedly 12,000 *of the youthful nobility thus perished*.[42] The Idumaeans eventually realized that their collaboration was based on a false premise and most left the city after releasing about 2,000 citizens from prison. Nevertheless, the *Zealots* continued to intimidate and slay those who gave them the slightest excuse. Anybody caught attempting to desert the city was allowed to leave upon the payment of a bribe, whereas those with neither money nor valuables were slaughtered by the guards. Corpses were left putrefying as the burial of so-called traitors was forbidden. While the *Zealots'* unremitting reign of terror raged, Vespasian restrained his generals from attacking Jerusalem, reasoning that as the Jews exhausted themselves with internal strife, the Romans grew stronger by merely observing the situation. The tyrannical treatment meted out to Jerusalem's inhabitants continued unabated, both before and after John of Gischala claimed sole leadership of the militant party, provoking the emergence of rival factions.[43]

Following a precedent set by the *sicarii* militants who had occupied Masada, groups of brigands began to plunder towns and villages throughout Judaea. Despite pleas from escapees from the city to liberate Jerusalem, Vespasian decided that before he could focus solely upon that task, he firstly had to eliminate all potential distractions and obstacles in the Judaean countryside. Between March and June 68 CE, his armies subjugated the towns and cities in the regions of Peraea, Samaria and Idumaea as well as central Judaea.[44] Everything was now in place for the commencement of the Roman assault upon Jerusalem and an end to the Jewish uprising. However, upon receiving news of the death of Emperor Nero, Vespasian desisted in his preparations while his son Titus left for Rome to obtain for fresh instructions. Before he arrived, the new emperor[45] was assassinated and, as the scale of Rome's internal conflicts became clear, Titus rejoined his father and the mooted attack upon Jerusalem remained on hold.[46]

Led by Simon bar Giora, an army of Jewish marauders that had previously skirmished with John of Gischala's militants surrounded Jerusalem intent upon taking control of the Judaean capital. Signs of internal disagreements were already apparent amongst the *zealots* inside the city, and the authority of John was challenged as those Idumaeans who had stayed loyal and remained when most had left, now turned against him. John's faction took refuge in the Temple, while in the Spring of 69 CE, the Idumaeans and senior priests allowed Simon to enter the city to become Jerusalem's new supremo.[47]

The ensuing brutal and prolonged conflict between the forces of John and Simon was exacerbated when a third faction detached themselves from John's *zealots*. This group, led by Eleazar b. Simon,[48] occupied the inner court of the Temple, while John's followers held the outer court and Simon controlled most of the city outside the Temple precinct. As well as those of the adversaries, the casualties of the civil war included huge numbers of innocent residents and worshippers. In order to deny food to rival groups, the warring factions destroyed most of Jerusalem's stockpiles of grain and other provisions, seemingly unmindful that famine in the city would ensure their own demise and doom the rebellion to catastrophic failure.[49]

Chapter 21

Destruction

The internal strife in Jerusalem was prolonged due in part to the internal conflicts raging amongst the Roman leadership. In the spring of 69 CE, the unpopular Vitellius was ruling in Rome, but in July the Roman armies in the east proclaimed Vespasian as their Emperor,[1] instigating a further five months of struggle for the imperial throne. Vitellius was executed in December 69 CE, ending the Roman civil war and enabling confirmation of Vespasian as the undisputed Emperor. With stability restored in Rome, in the spring of 70 CE, Vespasian sent his son Titus to regain control of Jerusalem.[2]

The Judaean capital was bursting at its seams with a population swollen by tens of thousands, including Passover festival pilgrims unable to leave, refugees from the countryside seeking safety and all manner of brigands and insurgents. It was confronted by an army of more than 60,000 men, comprising four Roman legions,[3] auxiliary troops supplied by client-kings and a number of mercenaries.[4] One of the most important figures accompanying Titus was his chief adviser Tiberius Alexander, who had previously served as the Judaean procurator from 46 to 48 CE. Of greater significance, however, was a former Jewish rebel who had since become a Roman collaborator.

The latter, born in Jerusalem, was originally named Yosef ben Matityahu and was from a distinguished Jewish priestly family. When the uprising began in 66 CE, he had been appointed as the commander-in-charge of the Jewish insurgents in Galilee. He became a Roman prisoner after Vespasian forced his surrender in 67 CE, but was released two years later, whereupon he defected and switched to the side of the Romans,[5] principally acting as an interpreter. Pensioned and granted Roman citizenship after the Jewish/Roman war, he changed his name to Titus Flavius Josephus in honour of his Roman patrons. The most comprehensive primary source for the events of the 70 CE siege of

Jerusalem is, of course, Josephus' *The Jewish War*, written in Rome between 75 and 79 CE. Josephus' version of the proceedings should be appreciated, therefore, as being written from a Roman perspective by someone who had betrayed the Jewish uprising, setting out to expose the iniquity and immorality of the rebels and depicting Titus and the Romans in a heroic framework.

Titus first experienced the fanaticism of the Jewish insurgents when he attempted to reconnoitre the city accompanied by only 600 cavalry and was lucky to survive an unexpected attack by the Jews. Further fierce fighting occurred when the temporarily allied Jewish rebel factions attacked the 10th Legion as it was preparing a camp on the Mt of Olives. The Jews were eventually driven back when Titus brought reinforcements from his main camp located on Mt Scopus.[6]

At the time of the Passover Feast, Eleazar b. Simon unwisely opened the Temple courtyard gates to admit pilgrims, whereupon John of Gischala's *zealots* took advantage and attacked Eleazar's rival faction. Many innocent citizens and pilgrims perished in the ensuing massacre, which eradicated Eleazar and his followers as a separate clique, leaving just the two rebel groups led by John of Gischala and Simon b. Giora.[7]

While the 10th Legion remained to the east on the Mt of Olives, the bulk of the Roman army moved from Mt Scopus to new camps closer to Jerusalem. One was in the north adjacent to Psephinus Tower and another in the west near Hippicus Tower (see figure 20), one of three strong fortifications built by Herod the Great in around 28 BCE. The repositioning of the camps was accompanied by the demolition of any intervening fences, trees and other obstacles, to ensure unimpeded lines for the transportation of provisions, particularly water, which was in short supply. Titus also had to act to improve the military safeguards on the routes used to convey goods and equipment in order to prevent disruption by surprise Jewish sorties.[8]

As the Romans constructed earthworks for the siege, both sides suffered casualties as their respective artilleries fired missiles[9] across the walls. The thunderous din that began in May 70 CE, as three Roman battering rams hammered against Jerusalem's walls in three different places, was the catalyst for the rebel factions to finally come together for the common cause. The attackers were subjected to a constant barrage from above and the defenders mounted several raids outside the walls. Three seventy-five-foot high wooden towers were constructed to house the Roman light artillery, which caused carnage amongst the Jews on the ramparts. As one particular battering ram made progress against the outer *Third Wall*, the under-fire exhausted Jews on night-duty abandoned their attempt to defend it and retreated to the *Second Wall*. Consequently, late in May 70 CE, fifteen days after the siege had begun, the Romans breached the *Third Wall* and destroyed parts of northern Jerusalem as they established a new camp inside the city.[10]

The Jews conducted frequent ardent raids against the Romans, who in turn ceaselessly attacked the wall between them and the defenders. Five days after breaking through the *Third Wall*, a battering ram enabled the Romans to create a gap in the *Second Wall*, but their penetration into the narrow streets beyond this breach was short lived as, amid ferocious hand-to-hand fighting, the rebels repulsed the incursion. Despite a tenacious Jewish defence, within a few days Titus' army retook and destroyed the northern section of the *Second Wall*. After a short pause, the Romans endured a constant lethal barrage from the ramparts above, as they began to construct earthworks to facilitate assaults on the *First Wall* and Fortress Antonia.[11]

If caught by the rebels, residents attempting to abscond from the city were killed, but nevertheless, many did manage to evade the guards and were allowed to pass by the Romans. Those who remained suffered unjust persecution by the followers of John of Gischala and Simon bar Giora and equally horrendous, the effects of the earlier reckless destruction of the food reserves. The awful famine was endured by the ordinary people, while the rebels used force, terror and torture to secure food for themselves. Large numbers of the starving population were caught by the Romans foraging for food outside the city and, in an unsuccessful bid to erode the morale of the defenders, hundreds of these unfortunate captives were crucified by the Romans in full view of the besieged Jews. Others were mutilated and sent back having had their hands cut off.[12]

By the middle of June 70 CE, the Romans had completed four separate huge earthworks to support their siege engines intended to overcome the Jewish defences at the *First Wall* and Fortress Antonia. John of Gischala's rebel faction, however, undermined and caused the collapse of the earthworks at Antonia, while the insurgents under the command of Simon bar Giora attacked the others. Battering rams were set ablaze and once the flames spread to the supporting-ramps, the Roman plans were in ruins. Their response was to build a blockading wall completely surrounding

Jerusalem, anticipating that hunger and despair would weaken the Jewish resolve and provide safer conditions for the construction of replacement supports for their war-engines. The Romans were able to commence new earthworks against Fortress Antonia without suffering attacks from the increasingly despondent rebels, who no longer able to bear the stench of the unburied victims of the famine, began to toss the decaying bodies into the ravines outside the city walls.[13]

Despite Jewish attacks on the Roman earthworks during July 70 CE, the battering rams were used against Antonia and by the end of the month the Romans had overrun the fortress and the struggle moved on for control of the Temple. In August, the rubble provided by the demolition of Antonia was used to construct a broad thoroughfare for the Roman army to ascend to the Temple. The use of war engines, assaults by ladder and hand-to-hand fighting had all failed to break the stalemate, but then in an attempt to hamper the Roman advance, the Jewish rebels set fire to the north-west portico between Fortress Antonia and the Temple. The Roman response was to wilfully do the same to the adjoining portico. This tactical use of fire by both sides, to frustrate their respective enemy objectives, heralded the ultimate demise of Jerusalem's glorious Temple.[14]

Since the fall of Antonia, one month had passed during which significant numbers of both rebels and Romans had been killed, as well thousands of the inhabitants of Jerusalem succumbing to the famine. By late August 70 CE, Titus recognized that the Roman battering rams could not overcome the strong Temple walls and as a consequence, he ordered that the outer gates to the Temple compound be set alight. Allegedly, to preserve the Temple, Titus gave orders for the proliferating conflagration to be extinguished. Amid the confusion and carnage of the armed struggle, however, the flames reached and eventually completely engulfed the Temple.[15]

The rebels retreated to the relative safety of the city, as the Romans, almost hysterical in their victory, slaughtered people indiscriminately. The temple compound presented a hellish scenario – it seemed as if *the temple-hill was boiling over from its base, being everywhere one mass of flame, but yet that the stream of blood was more copious than the flames and the slain more numerous than the slayers.*[16]

No mercy was shown to priests forced to capitulate due to lack food, but Titus offered to let the insurrectionists live if they surrendered and lay down their weapons. A counter-proposal from the rebels, that they and their families simply be allowed to pass through the surrounding wall built by the Romans, was treated with contempt. Titus took offence at this request and issued a death warrant against all of the insurgents, in conjunction with an order to his troops to destroy the city of Jerusalem.[17]

The first weeks of September 70 CE saw the Romans begin setting fire to public buildings and houses and the Lower City in particular was devastated. The more elevated ground of the Upper City proved more problematic and once again the Romans had to resort to building earthworks to facilitate the final stages of the siege. The construction of the ramps began on the eastern side of the Upper City and also to the west of Herod's palace, which had been taken over by the rebels. Desertion from the last remaining rebel held area became widespread, although Simon bar Giora was able to thwart an Idumaean plot to defect to the Romans.[18]

The supports for the battering rams were in place by the final week of September and a breach in the defenders' wall soon followed. Although the three strong towers named Hippicus, Phasael and Mariamne, built by Herod the Great on the northern side of his palace in around 28 BCE, were considered impregnable, they were abandoned by the rebels who knew full well that lack of food and water would ultimately achieve what force could not. Effectively, all resistance was now ended and the very last refuge of the insurgents was concealment in the city's secret subterranean passages. One senior rebel officer did manage to find a way out of the tunnels and subsequently rejoined the rebellion outside Jerusalem, but for the majority, death or capitulation were the only feasible options.[19]

The Roman soldiers entered the Upper City and slaughtered anybody that they came across while they plundered and set alight the houses, many of which by this time were home solely to the rotting corpses of those who had succumbed to the relentless famine. The following day most of the city was ablaze as during the night, the unchecked burning buildings had escalated into a vast conflagration.[20]

Lacking food, the threat of starvation induced the rebel leaders Simon bar Giora and John of Gischala to emerge from their respective underground sanctuaries and surrender to the Romans. Both were taken to Rome and later flaunted as prisoners in the traditional Roman victory march, following which Simon was executed. John was spared, but spent the rest of his life in captivity.[21]

The indiscriminate slaughter had ceased, but the fate of the surviving Jews was not pleasant. Only those presenting armed resistance were commanded to be put to death, but the Roman soldiers also took it upon themselves to slay the elderly and infirm. Vast numbers were herded into the Court of Women area of the ruined Temple, where thousands starved to death or were executed. Many of those who survived this internment were forced to accompany Simon bar Giora and John of Gischala to be triumphantly exhibited in Rome's victory celebrations. Others were compelled to become gladiators and thousands more were simply sold as slave labour.[22]

Titus made sure that the most revered Temple treasures were seized in order to be displayed in Rome. These included the golden Shrew-bread table, a copy of the Jewish Law, the fine purple drapes that screen the most holy part of the temple and the seven-branched candelabra known as the Menorah.[23] The huge amount of gold that the Romans plundered from Jerusalem, particularly its great Temple, caused the future price of this traditional store of value to fall drastically throughout the Middle East. Similarly, the Roman action of condemning so many of Jerusalem's captive Jews to bondage created an overwhelming disparity between the supply and demand for slaves, the prices of which also suffered acute deflation.[24]

The decision of Titus was that the whole city and the Temple were to be razed to the ground. The stones of the *Third Wall* were removed for secondary use, as the area north of the city reverted to being virtually uninhabited.[25] The towers of Hippicus, Phasael and Mariamne were allowed to endure, ostensibly to demonstrate that the Romans army was powerful enough to conquer cities even with such strong defensive structures, but possibly to avoid the laborious task of dismantling the huge edifices. Also, a portion of the wall bounding the city on the west was left standing, as partial protection for the Roman garrison, *Legio X Fretensis*, which was stationed in the ruined city to ensure the future maintenance of good order.

The rest of the city walls were levelled to such an extent that it was difficult to envisage that Jerusalem had ever been inhabited. *Such was the end to which the frenzy of revolutionaries brought Jerusalem, that splendid city of world-wide renown.*[26]

Chapter 22

The Bar Kokhba Revolt

Jerusalem had been devastated and so many of its inhabitants had perished, or been removed as slaves and prisoners of war, that the principal occupants were now the Roman legion, *Legio X Fretensis*, together with some auxiliary cavalry and infantry units and their families and service providers.[1] Following his victory, Titus took the treasures he had confiscated from Jerusalem and his Jewish captives to the coastal city of Caesarea, ready for embarkation to Rome once the weather allowed. He then travelled to the northern town of Caesarea Philippi, at the base of Mt Hermon, to enjoy celebrations, including compelling prisoners to take part in lethal gladiatorial contests.[2]

The city of Jerusalem and the territory of Judaea were now the responsibility of a new series of Roman Governors. The previous sequence of procurators were members of the equestrian order,[3] but from 70 CE the Judaean Governors were drawn from the higher-ranking senatorial class. Accordingly, the subordination to the Governor of Syria was a thing of the past and for the next forty-seven years, the Governors of Judaea would hold office as Praetorian legates. They continued the precedent, set by the earlier procurators, of having their official residence outside Jerusalem in the palace that Herod had built in Caesarea,[4] which was now known as the *Praetorium*.[5] The first such Governor was Sextus Vettulenus Cerialis, beginning a tradition of simultaneously holding the office of Governor of Judaea and commander of the Roman legion stationed in Jerusalem.[6]

One of the privileges that the Romans had previously afforded the Jews was the right to collect the *didrachm tax* for the upkeep of the Temple in Jerusalem. Vespasian, the 9th Roman Emperor, needed to oversee extensive repairs to his civil war-damaged capital and ordered the Jews to continue to make this payment, but now as the *Fiscus Judaicus*, to provide on-going support for the Jupiter Capitolinus Temple in Rome.

Formerly the tax had to be paid by all Jewish males over the age of twenty years, but it was now extended to Jews of both genders from the age of three years and was effectively a religious tariff. The ignominy of the subversion of the purpose of this levy was relatively minor compared with the degradation felt by many, following the redistribution of Jewish land amongst the victorious Romans. Former Jewish landowners often now had little choice other than to become tenant farmers or hired labourers.[7]

Despite the subjugation of Jerusalem, pockets of Judaean resistance lingered and, in 71 CE, Lucilius Bassus had arrived as the new Governor and Legate.[8] His early successes against the Jews included retaking the fortresses of Herodium and Machaerus and routing the rebels in the Jardes forest.[9] Before he could complete the eradication of Jewish opposition, Lucilius Bassus died and was replaced by Flavius Silva.[10] The last vestige of the rebellion ended in around April 74 CE, when Silva reclaimed the fortress of Masada, which had been overrun by the *sicarii* almost eight years earlier. When the Romans finally entered Masada, they found only two old women and five children still alive – of the rest, the *sicarii* had murdered their own families and then committed suicide.[11]

With no Jewish temple, no council of elders (Sanhedrin) and no high priest, Jerusalem was no longer the spiritual centre of Judaism. One of Jerusalem's most influential religious figures, Rabbi Yohanan ben Zakkai, allegedly escaped the city hidden in a coffin during the siege of 70 CE. With Roman acquiescence he founded a school for the study of the Torah in Jamnia, a coastal town to the west of Jerusalem. Effectively Rabbi Yohanan ben Zakkai and his acolytes took on the role previously exercised by the now defunct Sanhedrin, while the leader of the assembly, known as the *nasi* or patriarch, became the Jewish spiritual leader and interlocutor with the Romans. As well as Jewish acquiescence, the Romans also accepted this new order as it allowed for the convenient administration of local Jewish customs and laws. Throughout Judaea further Jewish theological schools emerged and especially due to the efforts of the scholar Rabbi Akiba ben Joseph, the Jewish Oral laws became codified and thenceforth known as the Mishnah.[12]

Vespasian, as Roman Emperor from 69 until 79 CE, undoubtedly caused resentment with his imposition of the *Fiscus Judaicus* and his reallocation of Judaean territory, and possibly an attempt to eradicate all Jews of Davidic descent.[13] However, more vindictive persecution of the Jews and their widespread diaspora appeared during the time of the third emperor of the Flavian dynasty, Domitian (81–96 CE).[14] Following his assassination, the new emperor was the elderly and ineffectual Nerva (96–98 CE), who died from a stroke and subsequent fever, to be replaced by Trajan (98–117 CE). The ambition of this emperor was to greatly expand the Roman world and when the majority of his armed forces were fighting in Parthia, the Jewish diaspora unleashed furious rebellions between 115 and 117 CE, particularly in Mesopotamia and the Roman territories of Cyrene, Egypt and Cyprus.

Incessant banditry and enduring Zealot influences in Palestine caused the Romans to remain anxious. Below the surface of relative calm in Judaea, tensions simmered in anticipation of a spark that would reignite Jewish opposition to Roman rule. One source, admittedly of dubious authorship and reliability, relates that *Palestine showed the spirit of rebellion*.[15] Certainly, the local population must have viewed the c.117 CE appointment of Lucius Quietus as Governor of Judaea[16] with trepidation and suspicion as this was the Roman general who had very brutally subdued the Jewish uprising in Mesopotamia.[17] Disputedly, either at this time, or perhaps a few years later, a second Roman legion was sent to Judaea and the Governorship was separated from command of *Legio X Fretensis*. As a consequence, beginning with Quietus, the Judaean Governors stepped-up further in rank to that of consul.[18]

Emperor Trajan died in August 117 CE and was succeeded by Hadrian, during whose reign Judaea's Jewish population would mutiny once again. This was the so-called Bar Kokhba revolt, various catalysts for which are often attributed directly or indirectly to Hadrian. One assertion was that the hostilities were instigated by the emperor issuing a decree prohibiting the practise of circumcision.[19] A rather implausible trigger for the insurgency is the Jewish legend that, having granted permission for the Jews to rebuild their holy temple, Hadrian was then persuaded by the Samaritans to retract his authorization.[20] It has also been maintained that Hadrian had made an early decision to establish *Aelia Capitolina* as a Roman colony on part of the desolated city of Jerusalem, and to erect a temple dedicated to the worship of Jupiter on the abandoned ruins of the Jewish temple, and that this initiated the hostilities.[21]

The historicity and logic of attributing culpability for a renewal of Judaean Jewish hostilities to the actions of Hadrian are questionable.[22] Ever since the sixth century BCE exile to Babylon, there had been a belief inherent in the Jewish psyche that eventually salvation and freedom would return to Judaea. The apocalyptic literature[23] of the first and second centuries CE fuelled this eschatological expectation and many perceived Simon Bar Kokhba as the messiah who would bring about their deliverance. It is possible that Bar Kokhba himself also subscribed to this viewpoint. One account that refrains from assigning the cause of the revolt to an ordinance of Hadrian, attributes the origins of the war to its leader, who *claimed to be a luminary who had come down to them from heaven.*[24] It is, of course, more than plausible that a number of grievances, real and imaginary, combined to cause the Jews to once more take up arms against the Romans.

The messianic credentials of Simon Bar Kokhba were enhanced by the support given to him by a number of religious leaders, including the figurehead of Palestinian Judaism, Rabbi Akiba ben Joseph. Poverty, deprivation and/or simply the desire to be free from foreign occupation also motivated significant numbers of the Jewish populace to join the revolutionary movement. On the other hand, Bar Kokhba's missive resulted in the uncompromising mistreatment of Christians,[25] probably including gentiles as well as Judaeo-Christians.

Despite a lack of detail concerning the conduct of the war, the rebellion is commonly dated from 132 CE, after Hadrian had supposedly completed a grand tour of his eastern provinces.[26] Nevertheless, fighting between various Roman legions and Jewish insurgents had already been raging for some years, possibly as early as 125 CE.[27] The Romans paid the price for initially failing to realize the seriousness of the uprising,[28] and by 132 CE, when Publius Marcellus the Governor of Syria came to the assistance of the Judaean Governor, Tineius Rufus,[29] it is likely that Simon Bar Kokhba had already secured control of most of southern Judaea.

Coins minted by the rebels indicate that they occupied Jerusalem for about two years.[30] However, there is no evidence that Bar Kokhba attempted to rebuild the fortifications and a damaged city without walls would have been vulnerable to reoccupation by the Romans whenever it suited them. Having learnt the lessons of the first Jewish/Roman war, the insurgents preferred to fight in the countryside, utilizing moveable defences in *advantageous positions* to avoid static sieges and open-field battles against the professional Roman legionnaires. Additionally, the caves of the Judaean desert, east of Jerusalem descending to the Dead Sea, afforded a series of tunnels and lairs for the rebels and their military and administrative command structures.[31]

By 135 CE, the guerrilla war waged against the Romans had become such a problem that further reinforcements were needed and Emperor Hadrian was persuaded to recall his highly regarded general, Julius Severus, from Britain to take over as the Governor of Judaea and oversee the Roman response. The strength of the rebels was now such, that it was the turn of the Romans to eschew open-field battles, but Severus had enough troops to capture bands of insurgents and to generally restrict the movements of the rebels. For a year or two before Severus had arrived, the rebels had utilized a stronghold named Betar (Beththera)[32] close to Jerusalem, but no fortress was going to be able to withstand the experienced Roman siege tactics for too long. In the summer of 135 CE, the Romans gained control of the fortress from the exhausted and starving rebels and Simon Bar Kokhba *paid the penalty he deserved.*[33]

The Bar Kokhba revolt was over, but for a number of the rebels and their families, the caves in the cliffs by the Dead Sea became a final refuge.[34] The last days of some are poignantly illustrated by the discovery, nearly 2,000 years later, of their skeletons wrapped in makeshift burial-shrouds and Roman arrows in the so-called Cave of Horror.[35] During the conflict, huge numbers of rebel bases and villages throughout Judaea had been laid waste and the fatalities on both sides were fearfully large.[36] In the aftermath of the conflict Rabbi Akiba was executed as a dissenting Jewish martyr, by having his flesh ripped with iron combs.[37]

It is not known for certain when exactly the Romans conceived the idea of building a pagan city-colony on the derelict site of Jerusalem, and if concerns over the proposal did or did not contribute to the Bar Kokhba revolt. In either case, the Romans were now obliged to find permanent solutions to the Judaean problem and the particular challenge presented by Jerusalem. The outcome was that Jews would be prohibited from entering the city, which was to be rebuilt and renamed. As further punishment, the Judaean province lost its Jewish identity by also being retitled and the very practice of Judaism was subjected to harsh constraints.

Chapter 23

Aelia Capitolina

The Rabbinic quotation: *Betar was taken and the city* [Jerusalem] *was ploughed up*,[1] is usually interpreted as meaning that *Colonia Aelia Capitolina* was founded after the Jewish rebel stronghold of Betar had been overcome by the Romans in the summer of 135 CE. Other ancient written sources[2] differ on the question of whether the Roman military colony preceded or post-dated the Bar Kokhba Revolt. The numismatic evidence,[3] however, clearly demonstrates that Hadrian's concept of *Aelia Capitolina* was at least celebrated in 130 CE, even if the structures of the new city are unlikely to have been fully completed until after the Jewish defeat, especially as there are indications the rebels may have occupied Jerusalem for a period during the war.

Hadrian's retribution for the Bar Kokhba Revolt was multi-stranded and included changing the name of the province to eliminate any association with its Jewish uniqueness. The exact date that *Provincia Syria Palaestina* came into being is unclear, but it is likely to have been very soon after the rebellion had been put down. The new name of the province may have been prompted by Judaea's non-Jewish inhabitants, who aspired to the older vague appellation of Coele-Syria.[4]

Following a recommendation from Hadrian, the Roman Senate passed a decree banning all Jews from entering Jerusalem and its immediate surrounding area.[5] The edict itself is no longer extant, but its consequences were cited by many early Christian writers to proclaim God's just punishment of the Jews.[6] The *Fiscus Judaicus*, levied upon the Jews to provide on-going support for the Jupiter Capitolinus Temple in Rome, was still in place, but sixty-five years after its imposition, in real terms this burden had diminished. A new punitive Jewish property tax was introduced,[7] and Rabbinic tradition relates the introduction of anti-Jewish measures including outlawing the ordination of rabbis, vetoing observance of the Sabbath, proscribing study of the Torah and forbidding circumcision.[8]

The Roman distaste of circumcision had its roots in the notion that genital mutilation, particularly castration, was barbaric. At an undetermined date, Hadrian increased the penalties for castration and this may have been interpreted as a ban on circumcision. In practice, the Roman authorities had nearly always accommodated Jewish customs, even after the 66–74 CE war. Accordingly, although it is possible that a ban on circumcision did contribute to the Bar Kokhba Revolt, it is more likely that this prohibition was enforced after 135 CE, as part of the solution and/or punishment for the uprising.[9] Even discounting the other Rabbinic claims of anti-Jewish measures, merely outlawing circumcision would in effect become an attack on the very practice of Judaism. After Hadrian's death in 138 CE, his successor Antoninus Pius appears to have taken a more conciliatory approach to the Jews by re-authorizing circumcision.[10]

As the limited archaeological remains dating to the Roman colony of Aelia Capitolina were not necessarily discovered *in situ*, a clear city plan is problematic. Nevertheless, it is possible to formulate a reasonable approximation (see figure 21), especially as it is considered likely that the Madaba map, a sixth-century mosaic, preserved many of Aelia's basic features.[11] Josephus' so-called *Third Wall* had been dismantled in 70 CE and the northern perimeter of Aelia Capitolina was analogous to the future northern line of Jerusalem's existing 'Old City', constructed in the sixteenth century CE. The archaeological evidence indicates that the area north of this line was uninhabited for at least the next three hundred years.[12]

Entry to the city from the north was via a great arched gate, the site of the present-day Damascus Gate.[13] It opened onto a semi-circular Piazza, the main feature of which was a great column celebrating the Roman victory and probably featuring a depiction of Hadrian. The Arabic name for the gate, *Bab al 'Amud*, is derived from the column, which together with the gate is clearly depicted on the Madaba map. The triumphal arch was bounded by a wall extending for a short distance from the gate both to the west and east. However, the hypothesis that the city had no defensive walls is sustained by the lack of any remnants discovered in excavations of the northern line and the other sides of the city pertaining to that period.[14] The strong military presence and absence of regional enemies appears to have precluded the necessity for protective fortifications.

Roman military city-colonies usually were of a standard format with a main north-to-south thoroughfare called the Cardo, intersected by a principal east-to-west street called the Decumanus. Aelia, however, had two Cardo emanating from the semi-circular Piazza in the north. The first went directly south as far as what we now know as the Jewish Quarter of the Old City.[15] An additional secondary Cardo led from the Piazza in a south-easterly direction following the natural route along the Tyropoeon Valley and then more directly south, parallel to the Temple Mount, but again ceasing at a similar latitude to the first Cardo. Thus, the southern perimeter of Aelia Capitolina followed closely the northern line of the now defunct Hasmonean *First (Ancient) Wall*. There were also two Decumanus, one of which intersected the north-south Cardo close to the southern perimeter and ran from the western wall of the Temple Mount to Aelia's western perimeter gate. The second Decumanus followed a line north of the Temple Mount from Aelia's eastern perimeter gate until it met the second Cardo.[16]

The 10th Roman Legion, the *Legio X Fretensis*, had been stationed in Jerusalem since the demolition of the city's walls in 70 CE. However, a section of wall on Jerusalem's western boundary was left intact to protect the Roman garrison.[17] As the source providing this information also mentions the great towers of Phasael, Hippicus and Mariamne being spared destruction as ongoing-evidence of the Romans' ability to overcome powerful defences, an inference was drawn that the section of surviving wall and therefore the location of *Legio X Fretensis'* camp was outside Aelia's southern perimeter on the Western Hill close to the towers.[18] An alternative theory is that the camp, as an integral part of Aelia Capitolina, would necessarily have been situated within the new city boundaries.[19]

The hub of Roman cities was the public meeting place known as the Forum. In Aelia Capitolina, the square that comprised the Forum was on the north-western side of the main Cardo-Decumanus junction. Adjacent to the Cardo and north of the Forum stood a Roman basilica providing cover against the weather for diverse functions such as local administration, legal decisions and a market place. The Roman Venus-Aphrodite temple, surrounded by a *temenos*,[20] was located to the west of the basilica and it is possible that the groundwork preparations for the construction of these buildings unintentionally concealed the sites of both the crucifixion and burial of Jesus.[21] The second Decumanus, north of the Temple Mount led through a triumphal arch, the Ecce Homo Arch, to a second 'Eastern' Forum.[22] This generally accepted city-plan is, however, challenged by alternative hypotheses. One is that only the largest Roman cities had more than one Forum and Jerusalem was far too small to have had anything other than the eastern Forum, and the site of the Forum in the west was in fact the camp of *Legio X Fretensis*, inside the new city perimeter.[23] Another is that the Ecce Homo Arch was a monumental entrance rather than a triumphal arch and that it was built during the second century, but later than the time of Hadrian's foundation of Aelia Capitolina.[24]

There is no evidence supporting the second/third-century CE source[25] which maintained that Hadrian built a pagan temple on the site of the ruined Jewish temple. To have done so would have created an unending Jewish problem for the Romans and greater credence is given to the evidence of a later observer[26] that the adornments on the Temple Mount were merely two statues and *a perforated* [pierced] *stone*. The statues would have been one of Emperor Hadrian and another dedicated to the venerated deity, Jupiter.

The establishment of Aelia Capitolina was not a unique venture as the Romans had previously initiated many such ventures throughout the territories under their control. Residing within the city were at least half of *Legio X Fretensis*' 5,000 legionnaires,[27] who facilitated the development of communities, as locals established nearby dwellings in order to provide supplies and services to the camp. It was not unusual for retired Legionnaires to carry on living in Aelia with their families.[28] The Roman *deductio* system applied to Aelia Capitolina, which meant that part of the territory was divided into lots and distributed to colonists, including Roman army veterans, who became assimilated into the local population. As Jews were excluded from the city, Syria Palaestina's Hellenistic peoples became the majority of Aelia Capitolina's local inhabitants. These comprised a virtually indistinguishable mixture of Hellenized Syrians and the descendants of Greek settlers.[29]

A population thought to number between 10,000 and 15,000 formed a fairly typical, if small, Roman city, and notwithstanding the presence of the Latin speaking Roman soldiers, the inhabitants mainly spoke Greek and worshipped pagan gods. In addition to the principal temple dedicated to the leading deity Venus-Aphrodite, evidence has been discovered of temples devoted to the Roman god of healing and medicine, *Aesculapius*, the patron god of Africa, *Genius Africae* and the Graeco-Egyptian god *Serapis*. The dwellings were characteristically Roman with the more affluent residents living in villas decorated with mosaics, depicting deities such as *Ge* and *Tyche* and the various seasons of the year.[30]

Notwithstanding that some *Legio X Fretensis* troops may have been stationed on the Western Hill, the area to the south of Aelia Capitolina was sparsely populated. The most significant group of inhabitants outside the city perimeter was Jerusalem's branch of Judaeo-Christians living on Mount Zion. To the developing Christian religion, Jerusalem was considered hallowed and since the beginning of the second century, pilgrims had been visiting the city, including the Cenacle on Mount Zion, which was traditionally held as being the site of the Disciples' Last Supper with Jesus.

Although a full reconciliation between the Judaeo and Gentile (Greek) Christians was still in the distant future, the gradual progression towards the gentile nature of the Church was reflected in the 135 CE appointment of Marcus, the first bishop of Jerusalem not to have been a convert from Judaism.[31] At this point in time, the highest episcopal rank in the Christian Church was known as a Metropolitan and it was under the authority of the Metropolitan of Caesarea that Marcus was appointed.

The capital city and residence of the Roman Governors of Judaea had been Caesarea and this arrangement continued for the province of Syria Palaestina. The senior officers of the two Roman legions in Syria Palaestina, including *Legio X Fretensis* in Aelia Capitolina, were of praetorian rank and subordinate to the consular ranked Governor in Caesarea, who no longer doubled as the commander of *Legio X Fretensis*.[32] Within the province of Syria Palaestina, Aelia Capitolina lacked the eminent position previously enjoyed by Jerusalem and additionally was viewed as a small polytheistic city of no great significance within the wider Roman Empire. The diminution in its political importance during the second century became manifest as detachments from *Legio X Fretensis*, which had symbolized Rome's military strength in Jerusalem since 70 CE, began to be redeployed elsewhere.

The surviving members of the Jewish assembly founded by Rabbi Yohanan b. Zakkai in Jamnia after the fall of Jerusalem in 70 CE, re-established a *Sanhedrin* in Galilee in around 140 CE. Gamaliel II, the leader or *nasi* of the previous assembly had since died and the position was conferred upon his son, Simeon II *ha-nasi*, whom the Romans accepted perforce as having authority over purely local Jewish matters. The enforcement of Rome's imperial power over the Jews necessitated a recognized authority to decide upon matters concerning the interpretation of Jewish law and thus introduced an element of stability to the potentially dangerous post-war era in Syria Palaestina. Where negotiations were necessary between the Romans and the Jews, these would take place through the office of the *nasi*, which was now acknowledged as hereditary.[33] In around 165 CE, the presidency of the Sanhedrin passed to Judah *ha-nasi* (Judah I), the son of Simeon II *ha-nasi*.

Late in the second century CE, Narcissus began his first spell as Bishop of Jerusalem, but following false accusations of impropriety, he voluntarily spent many years of isolation in the Judaean desert. Upon his return to Jerusalem in around 211, the aged Narcissus was once again appointed as Jerusalem's bishop. Eventually, however, owing to his advanced years he needed an assistant and Alexander, a former Bishop of Cappadocia in central Anatolia was compelled to take the position of bishop coadjutor. In 216 CE, at the alleged age of 116 years, Narcissus died and Alexander became Jerusalem's, or more precisely, Aelia Capitolina's bishop in his own right.[34]

Before his death in 217 CE, the Sanhedrin *nasi* Judah I established good relations with the Roman emperors known as *the Severi*, who ruled from 193 until 235 CE. It is possible that during the third century, Jewish Sages, taking advantage of the more relaxed Jewish/Roman relationship began to visit Jerusalem and this may in turn have led to the establishment of a Jewish community in the city. Rabbinical literature makes references to a settled community or *kehillah*, and various unproven theories contend that the edict prohibiting Jews from entering Jerusalem may have been lifted or eased or even whether the ban actually extended to visits.[35]

In addition to his own doctrinal contributions, using documents written by contemporary theologians, Bishop Alexander assembled a library in Jerusalem, which Church historian Eusebius of Caesarea acknowledged as assisting his labours in penning the his fourth-century tome, *Ecclesiastical History*.[36] Earlier in his life, Alexander had endured Roman persecution and in 250 CE, he fell foul of Roman Emperor Decius' edict, to the effect that everyone in the Empire should perform a sacrifice to the Roman pagan gods. Alexander was made to appear before the governor's court in Caesarea, but declining to renounce his faith, the aged bishop was sent to prison where he subsequently died.[37]

The last of *the Severi*, Severus Alexander was assassinated in 235 CE, following which the Roman Empire descended into the chaos known as the Crisis of the Third Century, when there were over twenty claimants for the title of Emperor during the next forty-nine years. Amongst territories that attempted to secede from the empire was an important Syrian frontier city called Palmyra, which under the leadership of Queen Zenobia, took control of Anatolia, Syria, Palestine, Arabia and Egypt. Any effects of the brief Palmyrene domination of *Syria Palaestina* on Aelia Capitolina have faded into unrecorded history, as most likely the city was simply not particularly important to the rival forces, and by the end of 272 CE, Roman Emperor Aurelian had reconquered Rome's eastern territories.

In all probability a defensive wall around Aelia Capitolina had been unnecessary due to the safeguarding presence of *Legio X Fretensis* for the past two centuries. However, the gradual redeployment of the legion culminated in its complete withdrawal at the end of the third century, leaving the city largely undefended. Archaeological evidence suggests that this potential problem was addressed late in the third or early in the fourth century, by the construction of a new city wall (the so-called Roman-Byzantine Wall) largely on top of or alongside the remnants of the Second Temple period First Wall.[38] At this point in its annals, however, Jerusalem was a fairly obscure town within a relatively minor Roman province, although subsequently it would regain its former status, to eventually become the most important religious centre in the Byzantine Christian Empire.

Chapter 24

The Beginnings of a Christian City

Civil conflicts blighted the early years of the fourth-century Roman Empire, until Constantine I (the Great) gradually began to exert his influence. The persecution of Christians was officially ended in 313 by the Edict of Milan,[1] and by 324 CE, the Empire had been reunited under the exclusive authority of Constantine, at a point in time when the Christian population of Palestine was still relatively insignificant.[2] That it was Constantine who had eventually emerged victorious from amongst the opposing Roman factions was pivotal in the transformation of Jerusalem (*Aelia Capitolina*) into a Christian city. Nevertheless, theological conflict became a more pronounced feature of Christianity during the era that began with its freedom from oppression.

Constantine's Christian tendencies, however, did not preclude a pragmatic approach to the ever-present challenge presented by his Jewish subjects. Importantly, the decree banning all Jews from entering Jerusalem was amended by Constantine to allow access to the site of the ruined temple once a year on the 9th Av.[3] A pilgrim who witnessed this ceremony of lamentation in 333 CE, recorded: *there is a perforated* [pierced] *stone to which the Jews come every year and anoint it, bewail themselves with groans, rend their garments, and so depart.*[4]

Despite some ambiguity concerning exactly when Constantine converted to Christianity, the fact that he attempted to unify Christian theology by summoning a meeting of the Christian bishops in May 325 CE, is indicative of both his faith and intentions shortly after attaining sole leadership of the Roman Empire. What came to be known as the very first Christian Ecumenical Council met in Nicaea[5] to discuss, *inter alia*, the rift caused by the views of Arius[6] that the God the Son was subordinate to God the Father. The doctrines of Arius were rejected in

159

favour of an interpretation that came to be known as the Nicene Creed and which promulgated that Christ was *consubstantial with the Father.*

Notwithstanding that Caesarea remained metropolitan See for Palestine, of great significance to Jerusalem's Christians was the Council of Nicaea's decision to accord special status to the bishop of Jerusalem:

> *Since custom and ancient tradition have prevailed that the Bishop of Ælia* [i.e. Jerusalem] *should be honoured, let him, saving its due dignity to the Metropolis, have the next place of honour.*[7]

Amongst Jerusalem's Christians there was a generally held belief that Jesus' burial site was somewhere beneath the Roman temple, completed almost two hundred years earlier to the north of Aelia Capitolina's main *Forum.* The authenticity of the location is disputed, partly due to the uncertainty surrounding the line of the so-called Hasmonean *Second Wall,* which had been demolished in 70 CE. The New Testament relates that *Jesus suffered outside the gate,* also that *the place where Jesus was crucified was near the city* and that *the tomb was close at hand.*[8] It therefore adds to the probable legitimacy of the site if it were located to the west of the *Second Wall.*

In order to uncover the place of Jesus' resurrection, Constantine ordered the dismantling of the Roman Venus-Aphrodite temple and the removal of its foundations.[9] It has been speculated that the desire to find Jesus' tomb originated with an entreaty made to the emperor by Aelia Capitolina's bishop Macarius, at the meeting of the Christian bishops in Nicaea.[10] Probably the most reliable source of information that we have is Eusebius, who was the Bishop of Caesarea at that time (c.314–340 CE), and although he makes no mention of Macarius' request, this should be viewed in the context that the two bishops were on opposite sides of the Arian debate and were rivals for the leadership of Palestine's Christians. Eusebius simply relates that an empty cave was unearthed and declared be to the place of Jesus' burial and resurrection.[11]

A Christian legend attributes Constantine's mother, Helena, with ordering the destruction of the Roman temple and the subsequent discovery of Jesus' tomb and the cross upon which he was crucified. Cyril, the bishop of Jerusalem for much of the second half of the fourth century, may have propagated this narrative in order to elevate the position of the episcopal See of Jerusalem in the Christian hierarchy. Alternative speculation is that the myth originated with Cyril's nephew Gelasius, bishop of Caesarea in the later fourth century, whose unpublished manuscripts have unfortunately not survived. The story was, nevertheless, repeated by a number of subsequent Christian writers,[12] albeit without gaining credence. Eusebius' work heaped a great deal of high praise upon Helena,[13] and undoubtedly if he thought she played any part in the detection of either the sepulchre or the cross, he would have mentioned it.

The Church of the Holy Sepulchre was instigated as Constantine issued instructions that close to the cave, a basilica was to be erected *on a scale of rich and royal greatness.*[14] Work began on two distinct projects, one of which was the extraction of huge volumes of stone from around the cave to be reused in the construction of its monumental Rotunda and the other to build Constantine's Basilica, which may well have been given precedence.[15]

As evidenced by the actions of Narcissus, the late-second/early-third-century bishop of Jerusalem, opting for a solitary contemplative lifestyle in the Judean wilderness was not a new phenomenon. The early fourth century progression of this concept was the establishment of monasteries, led by pioneers such as Chariton, who established three monasteries in the region around Jerusalem and Hilarion, whose example near Gaza led to monasteries springing up *throughout the whole of Palestine.*[16]

For some time, past Roman emperors had been prone to establishing regional headquarters, where they could better defend the far-flung empire and also avoid interference from the Senate in Rome. At the same time that his grand building projects in Jerusalem were commencing in c.326, Constantine chose to inaugurate a new capital at Byzantium, where the Bosphorus Strait separates Europe and Asia and connects to the Sea of Marmara. In 330 CE, the city was dedicated as his official capital city, henceforth called Constantinople, the first city of the new Roman Byzantine Empire.

The First Council of Nicaea had rebuffed the views of Arius, but advocates of this theology remained a potent force and when Maximus became bishop of Jerusalem in 333 CE, he was considered to have Arian sympathies. The Arian creed also held sway in Caesarea, whose Bishop Eusebius was a favourite of the Emperor. In 335 CE, Constantine used the opportunity presented by the attendance of the Christian bishops for the dedication of the Church of the Holy Sepulchre to convene the

Council of Jerusalem,[17] and used his influence to allow the Arians back into the Church.[18]

Although at this time the Rotunda was still five years from completion, the basilica had been finalized and the Church of the Anastasis or Holy Sepulchre was consecrated. The Church comprised three buildings enclosed in one precinct on Mount Golgotha where Jesus was crucified, buried and resurrected. Furthest east, three gates led to twelve columns encircling the domed apse and the naves of the magnificent basilica, the interior of which was overlaid with gold. The basilica was separated from the columned Rotunda in the west by a large open courtyard of polished stone.[19] The anniversary of the Feast of Dedication of the Church became an integral part of Jerusalem's Christian calendar, commemorated annually with a celebration lasting eight days, when *people from every region under the sun resort to Jerusalem during this festival and visit the sacred places.*[20]

The languor of Aelia Capitolina was overtaken by a new vibrancy as Christian Jerusalem began to expand during the fourth century. New buildings appeared, not only within the confines of the city, but also outside its perimeter walls. To mark the site of Christ's ascension to heaven, Constantine, or possibly his mother Helena, initiated the construction of the Church of Eleona on the Mount of Olives.[21] In the south-west of the city, the Church of the Apostles was replaced by the grandiose Basilica on Mount Zion,[22] spoken of as the *Mother of all churches.*[23]

Despite the continuing expansion of Jerusalem and its growing importance in the eyes of Christian pilgrims, economic progress was not without interruption. Scientific analysis, including that of pollen grains from lake beds, indicate a small climate shift from about 300 to 500 CE towards a slightly drier and warmer environment.[24] Consequentially, *Jerusalem and the neighbouring country was at one time visited with a famine, and the poor appealed in great multitudes to Cyril, as their bishop, for food.*[25] About five years after his appointment in 350 CE, Cyril sold valuable church artefacts in order to help feed those in need, but by doing so presented his enemies with an opportunity to have him removed from office. Cyril's struggles to remain in office were a microcosm of the theological battle being fought by those supporting the opposing Nicene and Arian views. In 357 CE, he was initially exiled from Jerusalem by a church council, sympathetic to Arian beliefs, for selling church property. During the next twenty-one years Cyril was frequently banished and then reinstated as bishop of Jerusalem, but he finally held uninterrupted office from 378 until his death in 386 CE.

In 361 CE, Constantine's nephew Julian became the Roman emperor when he was thirty years old. As a child he had been brought up as a Christian, but as an adult he was vehemently anti-Christian and favoured the polytheistic worship of the ancient Greek and Roman gods. There is a lack of unanimity amongst the ancient sources concerning Julian's decision to rebuild Jerusalem's Jewish temple. Generally, the Christians thought he was favouring the Jews solely in order *to grieve the Christians*,[26] whereas a more neutral Roman view was that Julian was *eager to extend the memory of his reign by great works*.[27] Julian's financing of the project was augmented by Jewish contributions and labour and the site was cleared in readiness for foundations to be laid for the renascent temple. Christian anti-Jewish mythology involving fire and images of the cross obfuscate the abandonment of the temple project, but the principal reason for the cessation of work was an earthquake in Palestine in May 363 CE.[28]

The attempt to reconstruct Jerusalem's temple contributes to the clarification of two historical uncertainties. Firstly, it indicates that when Aelia Capitolina was created, no Roman temple was erected on the site of the destroyed Jewish holy sanctuary, as Julian simply would not have allowed the replacement of a shrine dedicated to a Roman god. Secondly, although technically all Jews were banned from the city, there was in fact a Jewish presence in Jerusalem by the middle of the fourth century.

In June 363 CE, Julian was fatally wounded in battle against the Persians, and the re-establishment of Christianity throughout the Roman Empire by Julian's successors ensured that the temple rebuilding project was never resumed. Conversely, Christian building ventures continued unabated. Likely to have been before 378 CE, Poemenia, a wealthy Roman noblewoman, built the Church of the Holy Ascension on the Mount of Olives.[29] Understandably, due to their proximity and their common purpose of commemorating the site of Christ's ascension to heaven, historical references to the Church of the Holy Ascension and the earlier Church of Eleona were occasionally muddled. In around 379 CE, Melania,[30] an immensely wealthy Spanish woman, widowed at a young age from her Roman husband, came to Jerusalem and funded a monastery and a convent to provide hospitality to pilgrims and local clergy.[31]

However, the Christianity that the Roman/Byzantine world had once again embraced remained doctrinally divided. Although in the west, co-emperor Gratian was a devotee of the Nicene dogma, the eastern part of the empire was ruled by Valens, who opposed the Nicene decisions and supported a version of Arian views. In 379 CE, Valens was succeeded by Theodosius I,[32] who began a campaign to reassert the Nicene doctrine, which included propagation of the so-called Nicene Creed and promulgated a substantial number of edicts to suppress the Arianers as heretical. Nicene Christianity became the Empire's sole authorized religion and state church on 27 February 380 CE, with the proclamation of the Edict of Thessalonica.[33]

Economically, Jerusalem prospered as a Christian city. Its invigoration owed much to the *successive crowd of pilgrims from the shores of the Atlantic Ocean and the most distant countries of the East.*[34] The organized parties and individual pilgrims were augmented in no small measure by the commoditization of holy relics such as fragments of the *true cross*, which had been assigned to the care of the bishop of Jerusalem. However, prospective fourth century pilgrims were warned that in the holy city: *there is no form of uncleanness that is not perpetrated amongst them; rascality, adultery, theft, idolatry, poisoning, quarrelling, murder, are rife,*[35] and that they: *will have to tolerate in its full dimensions an evil from which you desired to flee when you found it partially developed elsewhere.*[36]

The mid-fourth-century famine, partly attributable to the slightly drier and warmer climate shift that had so affected Jerusalem's poor and prompted Bishop Cyril to sell church artefacts, was a symptom of the escalating agrarian problems affecting *Provincia Syria Palaestina* during the century. A warning against agricultural workers approaching the aqueduct leading to Jerusalem used terms thought to refer to sharecroppers (*georgoi*), suggesting that most of the land in the region belonged to the wealthy property owners. Partly to forestall the abandonment of farmland, the Byzantine law of *Colonatus* was extended to Palestine in around 386 CE. This prohibited landowners and sharecroppers from relinquishing their agricultural lands and obliged sharecroppers to remain subservient to the land owner. Farmers who were unable to meet their tax obligations were actively encouraged to go and work for wealthier land owners.[37]

Following the death of Cyril in 386 CE, John II was inaugurated as Bishop of Jerusalem. At approximately the same time, the Latin priest, theologian and historian, Jerome[38] began his sojourn in a Bethlehem monastery to work on his revision of the old Latin translation of the Bible, which eventually became the definitive and officially promulgated Latin version of the Bible in the Roman Catholic Church.[39]

John and Jerome certainly knew one another and Jerome spent time in Jerusalem to improve his understanding of the Jewish scripture and make use of the Hebrew texts in his epic translation project. Before eventually becoming friends, however, they were initially on opposite sides of an early Christian theological dispute, principally concerning the pre-existence of souls, espoused by the third-century early Christian ascetic theologian, Origen of Alexandria. Jerome disputed Origen's interpretations, whereas despite his denials, John was often suspected and accused of Origenist tendencies. Bishop John II is particularly remembered for negotiating a reconciliation of the Judaeo-Christian minority with the rest of the Christian Church of Jerusalem. To commemorate the bringing together of these factions, John blessed the altar of the Jewish Christian Church on Mt Zion in 394 CE.

Notwithstanding the city's religious shift towards Christianity, administratively Jerusalem, or *Aelia Capitolina*, had formed part of Roman *Provincia Syria Palaestina* since 135 CE. Over time, the peripheral boundaries of the province had undergone changes,[40] but in the late-fourth/ early-fifth centuries, as the Byzantine/Roman empire moved towards a permanent east/west partition,[41] *Provincia Syria Palaestina* was broken up into three smaller Byzantine administrative regions. Jerusalem was situated within the central *Palaestina Prima*, with *Palaestina Secunda* to the north and *Palaestina Tertia* occupying the southern region of the now defunct Roman administrative area. Each of the three new provinces had its own civil governor, with a military commander (*dux Palaestina*) resident in Caesarea having overall authority for all three provinces. The Church was organized along the same lines with a bishop ministering to each city, but a more senior bishop in each of the three civil capitals (Caesarea, Scythopolis and Petra) overseeing ecclesiastical matters in their respective provinces.[42]

Chapter 25

Christology

During the fifth century, it became commonplace for monks who came to Jerusalem to remain, leading to a further proliferation of monasteries in or close to the city. Visitors, whether monks or otherwise, on pilgrimages to the holy sites, required places to stay for food and shelter and have any medical needs attended to. Hostels for these purposes were most common as annexes to monasteries near cities, close to places of worship and on the routes taken by the pilgrims.

Melania the Younger, the granddaughter of Melania the Elder, arrived in Jerusalem in 417 and founded a monastery for women and another for men, both located between Poemenia's Church of the Ascension and the Eleona Church on the Mount of Olives.[1] An influential figure before his death in 428 CE, was the rural bishop (*chorepiscopus*) known as Passarion, who founded an almshouse outside the east gate of Jerusalem and a large monastery *inside the walls of holy Zion*.[2] He was an inspiration to many other monks, including Peter the Iberian, a Georgian prince turned pilgrim, monk and theologian, who built Jerusalem's Monastery of the Iberians as a hostel for pilgrims.[3] As the monks increased in number, a symbiotic relationship developed as their support became important to the church leaders in Jerusalem and, correspondingly, it was helpful to the monks to have an outside arbiter to mediate in their disputes.[4]

The fourth-century endowment of magnificent churches and ancillary buildings in and around Jerusalem was replicated during the fifth century. Of importance to the Armenian Christians,[5] was the Church of St James built in around 420, in the western precincts of Jerusalem. Also, in the west of the city, but further north, the erection took place of a church dedicated to John the Baptist. Despite the increase in the number of church buildings, Jerusalem's Christian hierarchy felt they lacked the status that was merited by the strength of the association of the Son of God with the city. Notwithstanding the special status granted to Jerusalem's bishop by the Council of Nicaea, Caesarea remained the metropolitan see for *Palaestina Prima* and Antioch endured as the supreme capital of the Diocese of the East.

In 417, John II was succeeded by the relatively meek Praulius, but in 422, the ambitious and politically astute Juvenal was ordained as Bishop of Jerusalem. Juvenal's overriding aim was to secure the elevation of his episcopal see, expand its reach and eventually secure Jerusalem's independence from both Caesarea and Antioch. Although not decisive, the prestigious stature accompanying the residency of Empress Eudocia in Jerusalem for most of Juvenal's episcopy could not but have aided his aspirations, at least until theological differences disrupted their relationship.

Eudocia had converted to Christianity when she married emperor Theodosius II in 421 and undertook a pilgrimage to Jerusalem in around 438. During this pilgrimage, Eudocia instigated the construction of a grand basilica to St Stephen, the first Christian saint,[6] outside the northern gate of Jerusalem.[7] The construction of this church was the catalyst for Jerusalem's renewed expansion, with the area beyond the boundaries of its northern walls becoming a congested, extramural residential suburb, with additional facilities for pilgrims and religious functions. Archaeological evidence indicates that during the Byzantine period, the area to the north of the gate contained, *inter alia*, four monasteries and two hostelries for pilgrims as well as a cemetery.[8]

At the invitation of Eudocia, Archbishop Cyril of Alexandria presided over a ceremony of interment of the relic remains of St Stephen at the new basilica.[9] The following day Cyril conducted a service during which the relic bones of Persian and Armenian martyrs were deposited on the Mount of Olives;[10] *a gesture symbolizing the internationalization of Jerusalem and its centrality in a new map of Christian religiosity.*[11] A few years later, Empress Eudocia returned to spend the rest of her life in Jerusalem following a deterioration in her relationship with Emperor Theodosius.[12]

An unverifiable verisimilitudinous account of her time in the city concerns the struggle between Jewish and Christian factions for the very spiritual essence of Jerusalem. According to this story, when approached by a delegation of Jews from Galilee, Eudocia appears to have granted an extension to the Jewish privilege of entry to the city on days other than 9th Av.[13] The Galilean Jewish priests allegedly wrote a letter proclaiming the official restoration of Judaism in Jerusalem and calling upon the diaspora to come to the city for the Feast of Tabernacles. Consequently, 103,000 Jews assembled on the Temple Mount to lament the destruction of the temple.

However, according to this account, the extremist anti-Jewish Syriac monk Barsauma[14] and his disciples also entered the city, with some of the monks going to observe the Jewish ritual. Either from divine providence or hurled by the monks, stones rained down, ostensibly causing the death of many of the Jewish participants. The accused monks resisted arrest, but on the orders of Eudocia, the Roman army quelled the disorder and the monks were taken into custody. Following an inquiry, the Jewish priests conceded that divine wrath was responsible for the carnage and asked Eudocia to release the monks. Evading responsibility, Eudocia sent for the governor to come from Caesarea to authorize the release of the monks and subsequently Barsauma marched out to a massed throng of supporters, declaring a triumph for Christianity.[15]

Eudocia's abundant resources enabled her to finance the construction of *a huge number of churches to Christ*, both within and also beyond the walls of Jerusalem. As well as initiating the building and consecration of the churches, she ensured their economic viability by *assigning a sufficient income to each one*.[16] When the great cross in the Church of the Ascension on the Mount of Olives was destroyed in a fire, Eudocia arranged for an expensive huge brass replacement.[17] In addition to her expenditure on churches, the infrastructure projects financed by the empress were quite diverse and included the development and future upkeep of a palace for the bishops of Jerusalem during the episcopacy of Juvenal.[18] The palace, or *episcopeion*, was situated just to the west, or north-west of the Church of the Holy Sepulchre, allowing the bishop private access to the Church.[19]

Eudocia's significant involvements with the architectural landscape of Jerusalem include either repairing or redirecting the city fortifications around Mt Zion and Siloam's Pool in order to protect the proliferating Christian suburbs.[20] To provide a place of rest and sustenance for pilgrim visitors to Jerusalem, Eudocia founded the Patriarchal Hospice on the Jaffa road about two miles west of the city,[21] and built *more monasteries and homes for the poor and elderly than I am able to count*.[22] In the mid-fifth century, the Church of St Sophia was inaugurated, but without any known link to Eudocia. There is little certainty over the actual location of this church.[23]

Juvenal's rise to prominence amongst the eastern church hierarchy reached a peak at the Second Council of Ephesus[24] held in the summer of 449. Executing the will of Emperor Theodosius and his chief minister Chrysaphius, the attending bishops effectively endorsed the doctrine that was widely accepted in Palestine, the so-called Monophysite belief in the single divine nature of Christ. Juvenal's support of this judgement pleased the Palestinian Christians and especially the increasingly powerful monks. In terms of his position in the Church hierarchy, his authority appeared to have overtaken that of the archbishops of the other prominent episcopal sees, as he clearly occupied the second-most senior position at Ephesus.

In July 450, Theodosius II died and, within a month, strong military influences brought about the marriage of Marcian to Theodosius' sister Pulcheria, and his inauguration as the new Byzantine emperor. Marcian, Pulcheria, Pope Leo and the majority of senior bishops, especially those outside Palestine and Egypt, opposed the judgements issued at Ephesus. Essentially to reverse the decisions of the so-called *Robber Council* of Ephesus, the Council of Chalcedon[25] was convened in October 451, with over 500 bishops in attendance. Pope Leo had declined to recognize the gathering of bishops at Ephesus as a synod and in a definition of faith, the bishops at Chalcedon repudiated the doctrine of Monophysitism and agreed that *Jesus Christ, the only-begotten Son [of God] must be confessed to be in two natures, unconfusedly, immutably, indivisibly, inseparably [united].*[26]

The position of Juvenal was complex as he was viewed as one of the six foremost Ephesus transgressors, who were excluded in the early stages of the Chalcedon synod. Dioscorus of Alexandria,[27] who had presided at Ephesus, was made a scapegoat as his former colleagues, including Juvenal, abandoned him in order to save themselves. Juvenal's *volte-face* not only gained him readmittance to the Council, but even secured him a place on the committee selected to draw up the authoritative formula of the synod's confession of faith.[28]

Earlier, the three provinces of Phoenicia I and II and Arabia had been transferred to Juvenal's diocese, but at Chalcedon, however, Juvenal realized that this realignment was unsustainable. At a session discussing ecclesiastical jurisdictions, the bishops confirmed that the three provinces would belong permanently to the diocese of Antioch, but Jerusalem's bishop would henceforth have authority over *Palaestina*

Secunda and *Palaestina Tertia* as well as *Palaestina Prima*. The See of Jerusalem now appeared autonomous from the Metropolitan of Caesarea and although it was not made clear whether or not ecclesiastically it remained under the jurisdiction of Antioch, in practice Jerusalem had secured its independence.[29]

Unfortunately for the returning Juvenal, his achievements at Chalcedon were viewed as betrayals by the majority of Palestine's Christians, who supported the Monophysite doctrine espoused at Ephesus. The monks were especially furious and only prevented from confronting him at Caesarea by the refusal of the governor to allow them entry into the city. Juvenal's refusal to repudiate the decisions made at Chalcedon provoked such a violent reaction that he fled to Constantinople to request assistance from the Byzantine emperor Marcian.[30]

Peter the Iberian was one of the leading figures in the cabal of monks, who set about creating their own anti-Chalcedonian ecclesiastical hierarchy.[31] Another of their leaders, Theodosius, who had attended the proceedings at Chalcedon, was chosen as the Bishop of Jerusalem in place of Juvenal, who was effectively deposed,[32] shortly followed by all other Palestinian bishops who did not support the Monophysite creed. Theodosius had the backing of the monks and the support of the populace, and indeed that of the dowager Empress Eudocia.[33]

Letters from the Byzantine Emperor and Empress Pulcheria, as well as Pope Leo, failed to persuade the monks to accept the Chalcedon declaration of faith and in the summer of 453 CE, the Byzantine army was used to bring about the forced restoration of Juvenal. Many of the monks were slain, although the regally-connected Peter the Iberian was spared. Theodosius fled, but was eventually apprehended and died soon after being released from a four-year period of very unpleasant incarceration in Constantinople. The reinstated Juvenal officiated as Patriarch[34] of Jerusalem, but he was deeply resented by the Christians in his diocese.

Eudocia resisted calls to return to the orthodox cause until 456 CE, when her apparent change of heart was inspired more by political rather than religious considerations.[35] Indicative of Eudocia's continued Monophysite leanings, on land that she owned and at her request, the monk Romanus established an anti-Chalcedonian monastery thirty-three miles south-west of Jerusalem at Eleutheropolis.[36] Nevertheless, such was the esteem in which Eudocia was held, that her return to the Chalcedon communion encouraged many others to follow her example.[37] In 458, Anastasius became Jerusalem's Patriarch upon the death of Juvenal. Two years later, Eudocia, in the knowledge that she was coming to the end of her life, arranged for him to consecrate St Stephen's basilica, the construction of which she had previously orchestrated. Within a few months Eudocia, in accordance with her wishes, was buried in the grounds of the basilica, just outside the northern gate of the city.[38]

Before joining the priests at the Church of the Holy Sepulchre in 474, A monk named Martyrius established a significant monastic complex, including a hospice, north-east of Jerusalem on the Jericho–Jerusalem road.[39] Subsequently, upon the death of Anastasius in 478 CE, the founder of the Martyrius Monastery took on the mantle of Patriarch of Jerusalem. It was during his episcopacy that a vain attempt was made by the Byzantine emperor Zeno to resolve the dispute between the adherents and opponents of the Council of Chalcedon. In 482, Zeno promulgated an irenic formula devised by Acacius, the Patriarch of Constantinople. The *Henotikon*,[40] however, failed to satisfy the hard-line Monophysites in Alexandria and was repudiated in Rome by the pro-Chalcedon Pope Felix III, leading to the excommunication of Acacius in 484 and the beginning of the so-called Acacian schism between Rome and Constantinople.

Born in Cappadocia in around 439 CE, an ascetic monk known as Sabas became symbolic of Judaean Desert monasticism. His chosen isolation in the cliffs at the southern end of the Kidron valley, half-way between Jerusalem and the Dead Sea was intruded upon by pilgrims and would-be followers and eventually led to the founding of the *Great Laura* monastery in 483 CE.[41] With assistance from his fellow monks, Sabas established further recluse monasteries (*laurae*) and communal monasteries (*coenobia*) in the Judean desert, and other older monasteries also came under his authority. Of enduring consequence was the set of written rules that he established to direct daily life in the monasteries.

In 486 CE, the death of Martyrius and the consecration of Sallustius as Patriarch of Jerusalem provided the opportunity for some dissatisfied monks to seek a change in the leadership of the *Great Laura*. Hoping for a more sympathetic hearing than they would have received from Martyrius,[42] they approached Sallustius, denouncing Sabas' lack of education and requesting the appointment of an ordained priest as their archimandrite. Sallustius, however, refused to accede to the demands of the dissident monks and in 491 CE, he ordained Sabas.[43] In the same year, Anastasius[44] was chosen by Emperor Zeno's widow as her new husband, and was enthroned as the succeeding Byzantine emperor.

Shortly before he died and was succeeded by Elias in 494 CE, Sallustius appointed Sabas the archimandrite in charge of those monks living solitary (*anchoritic*) existences.[45] The mutually supportive association of Patriarch Elias with Sabas saw the former build a new monastery close to the episcopal palace, and the latter establish two new hospices in Jerusalem.[46] In around 500 CE, the Church of the House of Caiaphas was established on Mt Zion, close to the fourth-century Basilica on Mt Zion.[47]

During the last decade of the fifth century, Elias and Sabas oversaw a gradual acceptance of the Chalcedonian doctrine amongst the Palestinian monks.[48] Nevertheless, those monks who questioned Sabas' leadership qualifications increased in number and in 503 CE, they brought about a protracted rebellion, following which Sabas retired into self-imposed exile. The rebel monks sought a replacement, but their contention that Sabas had died was exposed when the archimandrite returned to Jerusalem for the annual celebration of the dedication of Church of the Holy Sepulchre.[49] Elias ensured that Sabas was reinstated, but scores of anti-Sabaitic monks left and established a *New Laura* at Tekoa,[50] about twelve miles south of Jerusalem and the site of an old monastery originally founded by the monk Romanus.

Due to his support of the Chalcedonian dogma, the position of Elias as Patriarch of Jerusalem was always tenuous, as the Emperor Anastasius supported his predecessor's *Henotikon* formula and sympathized with the monophysites. In particular, after receiving a letter from Elias appearing to reject the Council of Chalcedon, Anastasius had felt betrayed when it later became clear that this was anything but the Patriarch's true theological perspective.

In 511 CE, in order to defend the interests of the Christian Church in Jerusalem, Elias implored Sabas to accompany a delegation of senior monks to Constantinople. Part of Sabas' mission was to try to alleviate the Byzantine tax burden on Jerusalem. Thirteen years earlier, Anastasius had annulled the *collatio lustralis* and on this occasion Sabas persuaded him to reduce the *superflua discriptio* levy.[51] Although the emperor made it clear to Sabas that he wished to replace the Patriarch of Jerusalem, the archimandrite managed to secure a reprieve for Elias by extolling the moderation of his views.[52] Two years later, Sabas once again intervened to save Elias, when he orchestrated a mass demonstration of monks to thwart an imperial force led by Severus, the Patriarch of Antioch and leader of the so-called *Acephaloi*.[53]

Elias' refusal in 516 CE, to accede to the emperor's demand that he accepts Severus into his communion, led Anastasius to finally supplant him with a supposedly more compliant leader of the church in Jerusalem. Olympus, the imperial military commander in Palestine (*dux Palaestina*) exiled Elias and replaced him with John III,[54] who had promised to hold communion with Severus and to anathematize the Council of Chalcedon. The desert monks, including Sabas, began to gather together and plead for the promises to be broken. Either John was intimidated by the large numbers of monks or emboldened by their support, but in either case he had a change of mind and theological stance. Olympus appears to have been replaced, as an angry Emperor Anastasius despatched a new *dux Palaestina*, known as Anastasius, son of Pamphilus, with orders to arrest the new Patriarch. In his prison cell, John was paid a visit by Zacharias, the governor of Caesarea, and advised to agree to carry out his original pledges if he were released, which the *dux* then arranged.[55]

The vacillating John summoned the monks to Jerusalem and, as they numbered around 10,000, they assembled just north of the city at the basilica of St Stephen, where the complex of the church, its porticoes, hospice, monastery and gardens provided sufficient space for them all. The *dux Palaestina* together with the governor of Caesarea, and even the Emperor's nephew Hypatius, coincidentally on a pilgrimage to the city, went to the basilica expecting John to fulfil his undertakings to the emperor. In the event, the archimandrites Sabas and Theodosius joined John on the pulpit as the monks chanted a chorus of: *anathematize the heretics and confirm the council* [of Chalcedon]. John, Sabas and Theodosius then anathematized the leading Monophysite and non-Chalcedonian theologians. In the face of such vociferous intimidation, the *dux* fled to the safety of Caesarea, while Hypatius disowned Severus and made generous donations to Jerusalem's major churches and to the Palestinian monks.[56]

Archimandrites Theodosius and Sabas sent a lengthy humble petition to Byzantine emperor Anastasius explaining their position, but in the event it was a rebellion closer to home and threat to Constantinople itself that forestalled immediate imperial retribution against the Patriarch of Jerusalem and the desert monks.[57] Longer term, it was the death of Anastasius and the election of pro-Chalcedonian Justin as the new Byzantine emperor in 518 CE, that secured the positions of John, Sabas and Theodosius.

Chapter 26

Justinian

Justin's reign as Byzantine emperor began in September 518 and ended in August 527 CE. Importantly, his attachment to the orthodox anti-Anastasian party, together with the support of his nephew and foremost adviser, Justinian, facilitated a resolution to the Acacian schism between the pro-Chalcedonian church of Rome and the previously Monophysite-inclined church of Constantinople. Jerusalem appears to have been relatively peaceful during Justin's reign, although the city endured a lengthy drought from possibly 515 until 520 CE.[1] The exiled Patriarch Elias died in around 518 and his successor John passed away in 524. However, the more elderly archimandrites, Sabas and Theodosius, outlived Justin. His successor, Justinian, was determined to recover the territory that had been lost by the Roman world during the fifth century,[2] and to unite the Roman/Byzantine empire under the banner of Christian orthodoxy.

The Persian Sasanian Empire, however, presented a potential threat to the fulfilment of Justinian's policies. The Romans and the Persians were traditional enemies and although they had experienced a period of peace during the second half of the fifth century, the two super-powers had gone to war at the beginning of the sixth century and again in 527 CE, just prior to Justin's death.

In 530 CE, despite now being over ninety years of age, Sabas once again journeyed to Constantinople as an envoy, this time on behalf of Jerusalem's Patriarch Peter and other senior clerics. Partly as a consequence of another Samaritan rebellion,[3] and partly caused by the imperial army during its brutal repression of the uprising, Palestine's infrastructure had incurred a great deal of damage. Ostensibly, Sabas' remit was to request a reduction in the level of imperial taxation for *Palaestina Prima* and *Palaestina Secunda*, as compensation for the destruction that had occurred.[4]

Encouraged by a welcoming and reverential reception, Sabas' successful entreaties to Emperor Justinian were far reaching and included direct financial assistance, the rebuilding of churches and the expulsion of three 'heresies'. Of particular significance to Jerusalem was Justinian's promise to implement Sabas' plea *to found a hospital in the holy city for the care of sick strangers, and to build and appoint the church of the Mother of God whose foundations were laid some time ago by our archbishop Elias.*[5] The protracted construction of the 'New Church of St Mary, Mother of God' (*Nea Theotokos*) project began, although Sabas, who fell ill and died in December 532, did not survive to see its completion.

One of the 'heresies' that Sabas referred to Justinian was that of the Origenists. Two and a half centuries after the doctrines of Origen of Alexandria had first been expounded, a number of early-sixth-century Palestinian monks adopted an interpretation[6] of this complex theology, as part of the endeavour to resolve the dispute between the advocates of and those opposing the Council of Chalcedon. The restraint previously exercised against the spread of these views amongst the monks ended with the death of the uncompromising Sabas,[7] and the influence of the Origenist monks began to take hold in the monastic communities around Jerusalem.

To bring an end to the Roman/Byzantine-Persian war that had been fought primarily in Mesopotamia, Justinian and the new shah, Khusro I, signed a peace treaty in 532 CE. This so-called 'eternal' truce proved to be a misnomer and lasted only eight years and geographically more diverse hostilities were renewed in 540 CE.[8]

In 541 CE, the Mediterranean region began to experience a plague that would kill millions of people and irrevocably weaken the Byzantine Empire. The most likely source was flea-infested rats, inadvertently transported by traders from East Africa. Subsequently, sufficient numbers of the rat-fleas transferred to human bedding or clothes to initiate an outbreak of the highly-contagious bubonic plague (*Yersinia pestis*). The pandemic known as the Plague of Justinian was first identified in Pelusium in the north-eastern delta of the river Nile, from where it spread remorselessly northwards to Alexandria and eastwards to Palestine and *there was a pestilence, by which the whole human race came near to being annihilated.*[9]

During the summer months of 542, Constantinople suffered incredible mortality rates with reports of deaths reaching up to 5,000 people each day, and which at its most virulent *even came to ten thousand and still more than that*,[10] and *it happened that 5,000 and 7,000, or even 12,000 and as many as 16,000 of them departed in a single day.*[11] An account of the effects of the plague in Antioch noted the plague's incessant fifteen-year resurgent cycles *in this its 52nd year* (593/4),[12] and another laments the plague's longevity: *the eastern regions were overwhelmed by the same (horrors) which have not yet come to an end.*[13]

The narratives of the suffering were chilling:

i. *In some it began with the head, making eyes bloodshot and face swollen, went down to the throat ... In others a flux of the stomach occurred. While in some buboes swelled up, and thereafter violent fevers.*[14]

ii. *The trouble began with a wound that formed in the palm of the hand, and progressed until the afflicted one could not take a step. The legs swelled, then the buboes burst and pus came out. The city began to stink and so the bodies were thrown into the sea, but the bodies kept resurfacing.*[15]

iii. *In those cases where neither coma nor delirium came on, the bubonic swelling became mortified and the sufferer, no longer able to bear the pain, died.*[16]

iv. *Others who perished falling in the streets to become a terrible and shocking spectacle for those who saw them, as their bellies were swollen and their mouths wide open, throwing up pus like torrents, their eyes inflamed and their hands stretched out upward, and the corpses rotting and lying on comers and streets and in the porches of courtyards and in churches and martyria and everywhere, with nobody to bury (them).*[17]

The greatest loss of life would have been in the urban centres[18] and, as in the major cities of Constantinople and Antioch, the suffering in Jerusalem would have been just as gruesome and terrifying. A letter from a devout monk and recognized counsellor, whose hermit cell near Gaza lay within the jurisdiction of the church of Jerusalem, offered reassurance that three venerated holy men would pray to prevent *the whole world from complete and sudden annihilation.*[19] That the plague reached *Palestine and the region of Jerusalem* is substantiated in a contemporaneous chronicle.[20]

Despite the havoc wrought by the 'plague of Justinian', around twelve years after Justinian's work had commenced on the *Nea Theotokos* in Jerusalem, a service of dedication was held in 543 CE. Justinian's builders had continued Aelia Capitolina's main thoroughfare (the *cardo maximus*) southwards beyond its original second-century boundary,[21] and the church together with its associated buildings were completed on either side of the extended boulevard. The extension of the *cardo* connected the Church of the Holy Sepulchre in the north of the city with the *Nea Theotokos* and thereby facilitated frequent celebratory processions between Jerusalem's two foremost churches, along a broad and imposing colonnaded avenue.

Undoubtedly the new road was also convenient for the transportation of the flame-coloured columns that adorned the basilica, the tall cedar trees used for the roof and also the huge blocks of stone for the south-eastern foundations of the church, which was constructed on a hillside.[22] The site of the *Nea Theotokos* complex was in Jerusalem's present-day Jewish Quarter (see figure 22), with one section protruding slightly to the east of what later became the 'Old City Walls.' The contemporary accounts were full of praise for the completed structure, describing *interior doors of such grandeur as to show those passing what a spectacle they are about to meet with,*[23] and that *it is superfluous to describe the size, dazzling splendour and rich decoration of the venerable edifice.*[24]

In addition to a church dedicated to the Mother of God, Sabas had asked Justinian to build a hospital for ailing visitors. Contemporaneous narratives describe Justinian's financing of *two hospices* [...] *one of which is destined for the reception of strangers, while the other is an infirmary for the sick poor,*[25] and alternatively *a hospital of one hundred beds* [...] *to expand subsequently to two hundred beds.*[26] A slightly later account written by a pilgrim, probably between 560 and 570 CE, refers to hospices for strangers, but presumably exaggerates the number of *more than three thousand beds for sick persons.* This pilgrim also writes that at the basilica there was *a large congregation of monks,*[27] suggesting a nearby monastery.

Subterranean vaults, underpinning the artificial platform accommodating part of the *Nea Theotokos* complex on the southern slope of the hill, were excavated in the 1970s. An inscription was rather unexpectedly discovered and this confirmed that the construction had been carried out on behalf of the emperor Justinian under the supervision of Constantinus. This section of the vaulting provided the foundations for an annex to the church and supported a monastery constructed in 549/550 CE.[28]

In the absence of Sabas, the Origenist monks increased in number to such an extent that in 537 CE, the Superior of the *Great Laura*, Abba Gelasius,[29] ejected forty of them from the monastery. Nevertheless, the theological quarrel continued to rage in and around Jerusalem, as the ousted monks joined the *New Laura* at Tekoa, which had been established some thirty years earlier. Justinian's 543 CE Edict against the doctrines of the Origenists failed to resolve the increasingly violent dispute, at least in the context of Jerusalem, and in 547 CE, a combination of intrigue and armed guards allowed the Origenist monks to install their own Superior at the *Great Laura*. This led to the persecution and temporary expulsion of non-Origenist monks. In the following year, however, the investiture of the orthodox Abba Conon as the monastery's Superior, allowed the dispersed monks to return to the *Great Laura*.[30]

Notwithstanding a serious internal doctrinal divergence, the Origenists remained powerful enough in 552 CE to have their own choice, a monk named Macarius,[31] ordained as Jerusalem's new Patriarch in succession to Peter, and *war resulted in the holy city*.[32] In December, Justinian agreed to Abba Conon's request that Macarius should be replaced by an orthodox Patriarch named Eustochius, and events moved on to the Second Council of Constantinople,[33] which opened on 5 May 553 CE.

For Jerusalem's clergy, the most relevant and important aspect of the convocation concerned the position of the Origenists in Christian doctrine.[34] The Council's anathematization of Origen[35] was accepted by almost all the bishops of Palestine, but the hostile reaction of monks of the *New Laura* was to secede from the orthodox church. Eustochius' attempts to rehabilitate them were rebuffed and in February 554 CE, the imperial military commander (*dux*) was asked to expel the Origenists and the *New Laura* was repopulated with orthodox brethren from various other desert monasteries.[36]

Based on estimates of the size of the city and its density of population, one twentieth century calculation of the number of residents in Jerusalem at that time was 55,000–60,000.[37] However, there is no historical data that may be relied upon concerning the size of Jerusalem's mid-sixth-century population, the density of which must have been distorted by the 'plague of Justinian'. The numbers of reported casualties and prisoners of war, resulting from the early-seventh-century Persian capture of Jerusalem, indicate a larger population, but these figures themselves may be inaccurate and/or include non-residents seeking shelter in the city during a period of armed conflict.[38]

In 562 CE, the Roman/Byzantine and the Persian Sasanian empires reached agreement on a new peace settlement intended to prevail for 50 years. Three years later in November 565 CE, Byzantine emperor Justinian died aged approximately eighty-three.

Justinian is particularly remembered for the codification of laws that became known as the *Corpus Juris Civilis*, which had a profound influence on future ecclesiastical and civil laws. His fervent discrimination against virtually all religions other than Christianity, as defined by the Ecumenical Councils of Nicaea (325), Constantinople (381), Ephesus (431) and Chalcedon (451), included the re-emergence of anti-Jewish decrees.[39] This legislation may not have been the cause of the bitterness between the Jewish and Christian residents of Jerusalem, but certainly would have added to it. The elevation of Jerusalem's Christian ecclesiastical status was confirmed during Justinian's reign by virtue of several official proclamations[40] jointly addressing, and thus giving legal form to the five Patriarchs of Rome, Constantinople, Alexandria, Antioch and Jerusalem, commonly known as the Pentarchy.

Chapter 27

The Persians

As 565 drew to a close, Justin II succeeded as the new Byzantine emperor and in 572, hostilities with the Persian empire erupted once more. The next twenty years, covering the remainder of Justin II's reign, that of his successor, Tiberius Constantine, and the early years of Maurice,[1] was a period punctuated by intermittent wars and treaty negotiations. In 591, however, Maurice restored friendly relations between the Roman/ Byzantine and Persian Sasanian empires, when he assisted Khusro II to recover his throne following the Shah's overthrow some months earlier.[2]

In the winter of 602, faced with a mutiny by his Balkan army and lacking public support, Maurice deserted his capital city of Constantinople. Phocas, commander of the troops, was declared emperor in place of Maurice, who was captured near Chalcedon and executed a few days later.[3] The Byzantine empire was plunged into turmoil as *in all regions of the land they took up the sword and slaughtered each other.*[4]

The demise of Maurice relieved Khusro II of any perceived obligations of friendship and presented with a Byzantine empire weakened by civil war, he seized the opportunity to attack its border defences. The final struggle between the two great rivals of the ancient world had begun. Previously, hostilities had tended to be confined to particular regions, but this conflict took on the nature of unrestrained total war. For a quarter of a century battles raged across the entire Middle East, including Mesopotamia, Anatolia, Syria, Palestine and Egypt. Fighting was experienced from Gandzak on the Iranian plateau to Chalcedon on the Bosphorus, as well as in Yemen, the Transcaucasus and the steppes of Central Asia.[5]

From the very beginning of Phocas' reign, this usurper of the Byzantine throne was unpopular with many of his subjects, both in Constantinople and in the outlying regions of the empire. Phocas' position was constantly under threat, with those who plotted against him risking torture and death. In 609, serious anti-Phocas movements occurred in Antioch, Jerusalem and Alexandria, where the rebellion was supported by the Byzantine governor of Africa, Heraclius. The Jewish revolt in Antioch may have been triggered by Phocas deciding that all Jews should become Christians, but the disorder was crushed by Phocas' brutal henchman, Bonosus.[6] The unrest in Jerusalem was also subdued by Bonosus, whose reaffirmation of Byzantine control included replacing the patriarch Issac (Isacius) with Zachariah (Zacharius), a senior church official from Constantinople.[7]

Early in October 610, the violent reign of Phocas ended with his overthrow and replacement by Heraclius, the son of the similarly named rebellious Byzantine governor of Africa. Although he had wrested the empire from Phocas, Heraclius was not yet in a position to mount an effective opposition to the Persian invaders.[8] The Shah's army overran Syria and Palestine late in 613, and established a base in the coastal city of Caesarea, which surrendered without resistance.[9]

The Christian population of Palestine was mainly Orthodox, but Monophysite and other nonconformist Christian communities were also present, enduring the displeasure of and occasional repression by their Orthodox-inclined emperors. The Christian reaction to the Persian invasion was muted and it is possible that the Christians in Caesarea deserted the city before the Persians arrived.[10] There was certainly no popular uprising in support of the Byzantine Empire and significantly, the population included large numbers of Jews and Samaritans who were so disenchanted with the persecution perpetrated by their Christian emperors, that they collaborated with the invading forces. Jewish troops had served in the Persian army for at least the past few decades.[11]

Early-seventh-century Jerusalem was recognized as an international centre of Christianity. The thousands of pilgrims that stayed for prolonged periods, or even permanently, had ensured its transition into a cosmopolitan city, the principal language of which was Greek, but where Hebrew, Latin, Syrian, Aramaic, Armenian and Coptic were also spoken.[12] The lack of resistance so far experienced during the conquest of Palestine led the Persians to believe that Jerusalem too *should willingly submit and be left in peace and prosperity*.[13] Jerusalem's patriarch Zachariah initially agreed, and during the winter of 613/614 CE, Persian provincial governors were duly appointed to oversee affairs in the city.

Zachariah, however, had not reckoned with the disruptive power of the organizations known as the Blues and the Greens. During the fifth to seventh centuries, Byzantine public life involved these so-called Circus Factions,[14] whose origins lay in supporting opposing charioteers racing in the hippodromes of Roman and Byzantine cities. These consortia had developed from enthusiastic spectators of sport into groups with considerable political influence and physical presence, who would express their feelings in passionate demonstrations that sometimes turned into violent riots with deadly consequences.[15]

In Palestine the hippodromes of Caesarea and Gaza were renowned venues for chariot racing, but not withstanding its dominant ecclesiastical orientation, such events also took place in Jerusalem, probably in a hippodrome built by Herod the Great.[16] The rival factions transposed into street-gang hooligans, who would make inscriptions on buildings, such as *The Tyche*[17] *of the Blues wins; long live.*[18] The arrival of the Blues and Greens in the early-seventh century, and their subsequent malevolent behaviour towards each other and Jerusalem's inhabitants was *full of all villainy ... banded together for bloodshed as well and for homicide.*[19]

The two major primary sources describing the events in Jerusalem during the late-spring of 614 are Antiochus Strategius and Sebeos. Strategius, a monk from the *Great Laura* monastery founded by Sabas in the late-fifth century, was an eye-witness to the events, and understandably his record has strong Christian religious overtones. The anonymous work attributed to the Armenian historiographer Sebeos, written in the mid-seventh century, is more detached. Although there are minor differences in their respective chronologies, the siege and destruction of Jerusalem occurred in April/May 614.[20]

According to Strategius, the accord reached between the Persians and Zachariah was overturned when the Blues and Greens objected *and assailing him like wild beasts*, forcibly dissuaded Zachariah from *making peace with the enemy.*[21] Fearing for his own life and the safety of the city, Zachariah dispatched a senior monk, Abba Modestus, to the Byzantine garrison at Jericho to request military aid.

Sebeos relates that the Persian officials were in Jerusalem for some months and that although generally the city inhabitants had accepted the situation, *the youths of the city killed the officers of the Persian king, and themselves rebelled against his authority.*[22] The uprising developed into ferocious hostility against Jerusalem's minority Jewish population, undoubtedly as the latter were suspected of conspiring, or at least co-operating, with the Persians. In the resulting civil conflict, the overwhelming numbers of Christians prevailed, and those Jews that did not perish *jumped from the walls and went to the Persian army*.[23]

The furious Persians besieged Jerusalem and although Abba Modestus returned from Jericho with a contingent of Byzantine troops, this was to no avail because as soon as the would-be liberators realized how heavily they were outnumbered, they immediately panicked and abandoned their mission.[24] It took the Persians less than three weeks to overwhelm Jerusalem's defences, as the city walls were demolished by barrages of missiles fired from ballistae,[25] and/or the foundations of the walls crumbled as they were undermined by the Persians.[26] It is, of course, quite feasible that both devices were used simultaneously. Those whose task it was to defend the walls deserted their positions and sought whatever hiding places were available, and having breached the city walls, the anger of the Persians was unleashed:

> *For the enemy entered in mighty wrath ... and slew all whom*
> *they found ... and respected none at all, neither male nor*
> *female, neither young nor old, neither child nor baby, neither*
> *priest nor monk, neither virgin nor widow ... they destroyed*
> *persons of every age, massacred them like animals.*[27]

Eventually, the Persian commander ordered a halt to the carnage and promised peace to the remaining Christians, who had hidden to avoid the indiscriminate slaughter. The assurance of safety was too late for many, however, as thousands of those who had concealed themselves had perished from thirst and starvation, in whatever available covert shelters they had managed to find. The more fortunate survivors, adjudged to have skills that would be useful to the Persians, were singled out, and with echoes of the Jewish deportation to Babylon one thousand years before, the artisans, together with their Patriarch Zachariah, were forcibly transported eastwards to Persia. Those considered to have little value were herded into an empty Roman reservoir in western Jerusalem, outside the Jaffa Gate, known as the Mamilla Pool. Their plight was particularly awful:

> *... people suffocated ... owing to the confinement of the place*
> *... Death on every side declared itself, since the intense heat,*
> *like fire, consumed the multitude of people, as they trampled*

on one another in the press, and many perished without the sword.[28]

The prisoners confined inside the harsh conditions of the Mamilla Pool suffered the further misfortune of Jewish revenge for their earlier treatment at the hands of the Christians. Jewish retribution took the form of ransoming detainees[29] from the Persians and offering them the choice of converting to Judaism or being slaughtered like animals.[30]

The Persians were determined to mark their victory in Jerusalem by removing the most precious symbol of Christianity – the Cross upon which Jesus was said to have been crucified. Under threat of torture and death, the clerics were forced to reveal where the remnants of the Holy Cross were hidden, and these relics were removed to Persia along with any gold or silver found in the city.[31]

Several historical accounts point to huge numbers of Christians perishing during the assault upon Jerusalem and its aftermath.[32] Even assuming some contemporaneous inaccuracies, the total death toll was certainly very high. One source informs us that the Persians slew 17,000 people and took 35,000 prisoners.[33] The laments of the Christian eye-witness allude to the deaths of incalculable numbers of those hiding from the Persians, and similarly those who perished in the Mamilla Pool, and others being ransomed and slaughtered by the Jews.[34] The latter source also relates that once the Persians had left, a devout Christian called Thomas organized the search for those who had died and recorded the numbers of corpses and where they were found. The details are painstakingly listed with the conclusion that *the total number of all was 66,509.*[35]

Seven sites of the intentional accumulation of large quantities of corpses associated with the Byzantine period have been discovered, and although they cannot all be positively dated to 614 CE, there is reasonable evidence to do so.[36] These lend credence to the story that huge numbers were killed during the Persian conquest of Jerusalem and one or two of these mass burial sites can be correlated with Strategius' account of Thomas' discoveries of the deceased. Nevertheless, the total of 66,509 dead Christians is probably an exaggerated miscalculation, on the basis that the entire population of early-seventh century Jerusalem was probably not much higher than this figure.[37] Of course, during a period of foreign invasion, the number of people inside the city was most likely to have been swollen by those from the surrounding areas seeking refuge within the perceived safety of the city walls.

The Persians withdrew leaving Jerusalem under the control of the Jews, whose leader was a somewhat obscure figurehead named Nehemiah.[38] There was a resumption of the Jewish practice of making sacrifices, presumably on the ruins of the Temple on Mount Moriah, and further damage was inflicted on the Christian places of worship.

The main thrust of the Persian war against the Byzantine empire now took the form of a pincer movement. The northern army having advanced through Anatolia was threatening Constantinople, while the army in Palestine was moving on to conquer Egypt. It suited the Persians to make allies of the Jewish militia, who were assigned the responsibility of capturing the Phoenician seaports to prevent the superior Byzantine navy from interfering with Persian supply lines. Initially, the Jews were successful and, with the assistance of the local Jewish inhabitants, seized the port of Acre. Further north, however, the port of Tyre resisted more strongly and the Jewish assailants were forced to mount a prolonged siege.

The bond between the Persians and the Palestinian Jews was not particularly strong and possibly during the first half of 616, the Persians assumed direct control over the whole of Palestine. Mooted possible causes include a failed Jewish promise to unearth vast treasures beneath the Church of the Holy Sepulchre, and growing Christian influence at the Persian imperial palace. A more plausible combination of reasons is that Jewish usefulness as a military ally was waning at a time when the Persians sought the co-operation of the more populous Christian community. The Jewish minority in Jerusalem accounted for possibly only 10–15 per cent of the population. They would never be reconciled with Byzantium and were therefore not a threat to Persian interests, but the Palestinian Christians were in a position to choose sides and therefore needed to be managed with greater tact and sensitivity.[39]

Although a ban prohibiting any new Jewish immigration into the city had been imposed by the Persians,[40] the current Jewish inhabitants led by Nehemiah had held power in Jerusalem for three years. Perhaps commensurate with the failure of the two-year siege of Tyre by the Jewish militia in 617 CE,[41] the sixty-seven-year-old Shah of the Persian Sasanian empire, Khusro II, became convinced that the Persians should bring the Jewish control to an end and ordered their expulsion from the city. Robust resistance by the disappointed Jews proved futile as

Persian troops enforced the directive and Nehemiah was duly executed in Emmaus, a small town not far from Jerusalem.[42]

Abba Modestus, who was serving as locum-tenens Patriarch in the absence of the Persian detainee Zachariah, was now at liberty to begin the reconstruction of Jerusalem's great churches. The restoration work with which Modestus is credited raises the question of how much destruction had occurred in Jerusalem during 614 CE. The Christian eye-witness describes churches being burned and demolished by the hysterical Persian assailants, with further destruction being perpetrated by the Jews after the forced Christian exodus, and the marching deportees gazing back upon Jerusalem and seeing *a flame, as out of a furnace, reached up to the clouds*.[43] The Armenian history describes three days of slaughter, following which the Persians stayed for another twenty-one days and then withdrew to an outside encampment *and burnt the city with fire*.[44] A seventh-century Greek Christian chronicle records that *The Lord's tomb was burnt and the far-famed temples of God, and, in short, all the precious things were* destroyed.[45]

Modestus' letter to the head of the Armenian Church mentions renewals to the Church of the Holy Sepulchre, the Basilica of Mount Zion and Church of the Ascension, although his plea for financial assistance for the rebuilding suggests an element of premature exaggeration.[46] A tenth-century source informs us that the Persians had destroyed the church of Gethsemane and the church of Helena, *both of which remain in ruins to this day*.[47] This same source, however, confirms that upon his return to Jerusalem, Modestus *built the churches of the Resurrection, of the Holy Sepulchre, of Calvary, and of St Constantine*.[48] Undoubtedly, some churches would have suffered irreparable damage and perhaps especially so on the Mount of Olives. Nevertheless, it appears that the harm done to many of the major churches inside the city walls was superficial enough to allow Modestus to have them repaired during the next thirteen years or so. Additional evidence also points to timely renovations having been carried out, as some of the major churches were in use during the Early Islamic period.[49]

The long-drawn-out conflict between the two super-powers continued with the Roman/Byzantine empire also experiencing increasing threats from its European enemies. Encouraged by the Persians encamped in Chalcedon, across the Bosphorus Straits from Constantinople, the Avars of Eastern Europe besieged the Byzantine capital city during the summer of 626 CE.[50] The ultimate failure of the siege, however, was followed by Byzantine emperor Heraclius' successful incursion into Mesopotamia in 627, and a Persian coup d'état that saw the imprisonment and death of the increasingly unstable Shah Khusro II in 628 CE. Heraclius and Kavad II (Siroes[51]), the son and short-lived successor of Khusro agreed a peace treaty, the main conditions of which were the restoration of all Byzantine territories that the Sasanian empire had annexed, the release of all Byzantine prisoners being held by the Persians and the return of the relics of Christ's Cross.[52]

On 21 March, 630 CE,[53] Heraclius made a triumphant entry into Jerusalem, accompanied by his wife Martina, complete royal entourage and his army. The patriarch Zachariah had not survived his deportation to Persia sixteen years earlier, and, no doubt partly in recognition of his work rebuilding the city's churches, the emperor officially appointed Modestus as the new patriarch of Jerusalem.[54]

The major event of the highly charged emotional celebrations was the return to Jerusalem of the relic of the True Cross, which despite its travels and possible misuse by the Persians, was *sealed as before in a chest, just as it had carried away.*[55] The joyous spectacle, which rendered some of the witnesses speechless, symbolized the triumph of Christianity over great adversity and the re-establishment of Byzantine authority in this most auspicious province. Emperor Heraclius generously distributed blessings and money and the Cross was returned to its rightful place in Jerusalem's Church of the Holy Sepulchre.[56]

Epilogue

Any feelings of relief at the end of the war, and of the restoration of God's grace upon the Christians of Jerusalem, were not to last. Not in Jerusalem, nor in Palestine, nor anywhere in the Near East. As the Middle Ages dawned, the Arab Muslims emerged from Arabia to occupy Syria and Palestine in around 636 CE.

The twenty-five-year war between the Roman/Byzantine and Persian Sasanian empires had exhausted the resources of both and neither was in any sort of condition to withstand the Muslim advance. Following the 630 CE celebrations in Jerusalem, savage revenge was meted out upon the city's Jews, and indeed upon the Jewish inhabitants of all Palestine, as payback for their collaboration with the Persians. Thousands of Jews were massacred and thousands fled. Thus, the creed that regarded Palestine and Jerusalem as its homeland, and that for centuries had fought intruders such as Babylonians, Seleucids and Romans, was also unable to resist the Muslim encroachment, even if it had been inclined to do so in the circumstances of that period in time.

In 637 CE, Jerusalem surrendered to the Muslim forces and new chapters were about to begin in the extraordinary history of this unique city.

Notes

Chapter 1 Foundation

1. Isaiah 9:1.
2. 1 Kings 1:33.
3. 1 Kings 1:9. En Rogel was alternatively known as Bir 'Ayyub or Job's Well.
4. Gibson, 2014, pp. 362–363.
5. Wilkinson, 1974, p. 33.
6. Alternatively referred to as *'Ain Umm el Daraj* or *the Virgin's Fountain.* 'Gihon' is derived from the Hebrew verb to gush forth.
7. Kenyon, 1975, p. 78
8. Ibid., pp. 94–96.
9. Present-day Lebanon.
10. Bryan, 2000, p. 243.
11. Thutmose's first campaign and the battle at Megiddo are recorded on the Armant Stela and the Annals carved on the walls of the Temple of Karnak [Pritchard, 1969, pp. 234–238. The Egyptians referred to Palestine and its people as *Retenu*].
12. About 377 cuneiform tablets were discovered at Tell el-Amarna in middle Egypt. Nearly all of the letters belonged to the royal archives of Pharaohs Amenhotep IV (Akhenaten) and Amenhotep III. Most were written by Canaanite (occasionally Egyptian) scribes and around half originated in Palestine [Pritchard, 1969, p. 483].
13. Extracts from Amarna Letters Nos 286–290 [Pritchard, 1969, pp. 487–489].
14. Old land-based enemies of the Hittites as well as the 'Sea Peoples' contributed to the destruction of the Hittite empire (Liverani, 2014, pp. 384–388).
15. Later known as Ptolemais (Hellenistic and Roman periods) and Acre (Middle Ages).
16. Lipiński, 2000, p. 25.
17. Liverani, 2014, p. 391; Pioske, 2013, p. 7.
18. Judges 21:25.

Chapter 2 David

1. Miller and Hayes, 1986, p. 159.
2. Gelinas, 1995, p. 228.
3. Genesis 10:15–16; Joshua 15:63; 1 Chronicles 11:4.
4. 1 Samuel 4:1–10.
5. Miller and Hayes, 1986, p. 168.
6. 1 Samuel 16:21.
7. 1 Samuel 19–27.
8. 1 Samuel 31:1–6.
9. 2 Samuel 2:8–10.
10. 1 Samuel 29:1–7.
11. 2 Samuel 2:1–4.
12. 2 Samuel 5:1–3.
13. 2 Sam 5:8. However, the equivalent passage in the Septuagint (II kings V:8) makes no mention of a water shaft.
14. Gill, 1991, p. 1470.
15. Jos. *War* V, 137.
16. Kenyon, 1975, p. 196.
17. Kenyon, 1967, p. 30.
18. Mazar, 1982, p. 3.
19. Broshi, 1978, p. 11.
20. Wilkinson, 1974, p. 33.
21. Present-day Khirbet Seilun.
22. 2 Samuel 6:17.
23. Judges 6:36–37.
24. 2 Samuel 24:18–25.
25. Ahlström, 1993, pp. 470–471.
26. Mendelsohn, 1942, p. 15.
27. 2 Samuel 20:24 and 12:31.
28. A kingdom around the area of Aleppo in present-day southern Syria/Lebanon. Zobah was previously at war with Saul (1 Samuel 14:47) and subsequently attacked by Solomon (2 Chron. 8:3).
29. 2 Samuel 8:1–13.
30. 1 Chronicles 26.
31. Gibeon was a Canaanite city north of Jerusalem.
32. 2 Samuel 21:1–9.
33. The biblical concept of bloodguilt includes liability to punishment for murder and attaches to the killer and his family.
34. 2 Samuel 15–19.
35. 2 Samuel 20.

36. Ahlström, 1993, p. 543.
37. 1 Kings 1:5–10.
38. 1 Kings 1:32–35; 1 Chronicles 23:1.

Chapter 3 Solomon

1. 1 Kings 1:38–39.
2. 1 Kings 2:24–46.
3. 1 Chronicles 22:2–4.
4. 1 Kings 6:1. McFall, 1991, p. 10 concludes the foundation date of the Temple was virtually certain to be 968 BCE. If so and also Solomon's fourth year, then Solomon's date of ascension must earlier than 970 BCE.
5. 1 Kings 6:2.
6. 1 Kings 5:6; 5:18; 7:13.
7. 1 Kings 6:15–35.
8. Ahlström, 1993, p. 533.
9. 1 Kings 7:13–38.
10. 1 Kings 6:38; 7:1; 9:10.
11. 1 Kings 7:6–7.
12. 1 Kings 10:18–20.
13. Kenyon, 1975, p. 128.
14. 1 Kings 3:1; 7:8; 9:16; 9:24; 11:1–2; 2 Chronicles 8:11.
15. 1 Kings 7:2–5.
16. 1 Kings 10:16.
17. Broshi, 1978, pp. 10–11.
18. 1 Kings 11:27.
19. 2 Samuel 5:9.
20. Variously referred to by slightly different spellings as Adoram (2 Sam. 20:24; 1 Kings 12:18); Adoniram (1 Kings 4:6; 1 Kings 5:14) and Hadoram (2 Chron. 10:18).
21. 1 Kings 5:13–16.
22. Mendelson, 1942, p. 16.
23. Ibid.
24. 1 Kings 10:14–15.
25. 1 Kings 9:26–28.
26. 1 Kings 10:10.
27. 1 Kings 11:1–13.
28. Miller and Hayes, 1986, p. 202.

Chapter 4 Separate Kingdoms

1. 1 Kings 9:20–22.
2. 1 Kings 11:28.

Notes

3. 1 Kings 11:30–32.
4. Ahlström, 1993, p. 543.
5. 1 Kings 12:18.
6. 1 Kings 14:21
7. Present-day Jordanian city of Dhiban.
8. The territory of Tribe of Benjamin was originally more extensive (Joshua 18:11–28).
9. Founded in 945 BCE by Sheshonq, who was of Libyan descent.
10. Miller and Hayes, 1986, p. 237.
11. 2 Chronicles 11:5–12.
12. 1 Kings 14:25; 2 Chronicles 12:2–4.
13. 1 Kings 14:25–26.
14. Taylor, 2000, p. 335, states that the *Karnak inscriptions record a major military expedition c.925 BC*. As Sheshonq's arrival in Jerusalem was meant to be in Rehoboam's fifth year, some observers have concluded that the date of Solomon's death and the accession of Rehoboam was in fact 930 BCE. The Judean kings tended to use zero year counting for the partial year of ascension, so that if Rehoboam became king in 931 BCE his first full year would be 930 and his full fifth year would be 926. Sheshonq died soon after his return to Egypt in 925 and therefore to set out for Palestine, arrive at Jerusalem, attack several other cities and then return to Egypt and die, makes it quite reasonable to surmise that the campaign began in 926 and ended in 925 BCE.
15. 1 Kings 15:6–7.
16. 2 Chronicles 13:1–21.
17. 1 Kings 15:9–15.
18. 2 Chronicles 14:8–12. The numbers of the opposing armies are clear exaggerations.
19. Ahlström, 1993, p. 566.
20. 2 Chronicles 16:1 places this event *in the thirty-sixth year of the reign of Asa*, i.e. 875 BCE, by which time Baasha had been dead for 10 years. This is an error or misinterpretation of the 36th year since the beginning of the separation of Israel from Judah and, therefore, 895 BCE is the correct date. (Thiele, 1983, p. 84).
21. 1 Kings 15:16–22.
22. 2 Chronicles 16:12.
23. Compare 1 Kings 22:43 and 2 Chronicles 17:6.
24. 2 Chronicles 19:2 and 20:35.
25. 2 Chronicles 19:5–8
26. 2 Chronicles 17:7–9; 19:4; 1 Kings 22:46.
27. 2 Chronicles 17:1–2.

28. 2 Chronicles 17:5 and 17:11.
29. 2 Chronicles 17:13–19.
30. For conclusive proof of this date: Thiele, 1983, p. 95, and note 13.
31. Pritchard, 1969, pp. 278–279.
32. 1 Kings 22:47–49 and 2 Chronicles 20:35–37.
33. 2 Chronicles 20:1–23.
34. Also known as Ben-hadad II.
35. 1 Kings 22:4. Jehoshaphat also repeats the phrase to the later king of Israel, Jehoram (2 Kings 3:7).
36. 2 Kings 1:17.
37. 2 Chronicles 21:4.
38. Septuagint IV Kings I:18.
39. Tanakh 2 Kings 1:17.
40. Miller & Hayes, 1986, pp. 280–281.
41. Thiele, 1983, p. 101.
42. 2 Kings 8:20–22 and 2 Chronicles 21:8–10.
43. 2 Kings 6:24–31 referring to Hadadezer by his alternative title of Ben-hadad [i.e. Ben-hadad II].

Chapter 5 Syrians and Assyrians

1. 2 Kings 9:14–15.
2. Ahlström, 1993, pp. 593–4.
3. 2 Kings 10:1–25.
4. Now in the British Museum.
5. Alternatively referred to as Jehoash.
6. 2 Kings 11:1; 2 Chronicles 22:10.
7. 2 Kings 10:12–14.
8. Ahlström, 1993, p. 600.
9. 2 Kings 11:4–12; 2 Chronicles 23:1–11
10. Miller and Hayes, 1986, p. 304; Ahlström, 1993, p. 600, note 1.
11. 2 Kings 11:16; 2 Chronicles 23:15.
12. 2 Kings 12:4–15.
13. 2 Kings 12:17–18.
14. 2 Chronicles 24:15–25.
15. Miller and Hayes, 1986, p. 305.
16. 2 Kings 14:1–5.
17. Evidence provided by a broken Assyrian inscribed stone slab record found at Calah (Nimrud). Pritchard, 1969, p. 281.
18. 2 Chronicles 25:5–13, but the numbers of men in Amaziah's army, the number of Israelite mercenaries and the numbers of Edomites killed are typical Chronicles' exaggerations.

19. Described disparagingly by Jehoash after the kings had fallen out as *A thistle on Lebanon sent to a cedar on Lebanon* (2 Chron. 25:18).
20. 2 Kings 14:13; 2 Chron. 25:23. This section of the wall was undoubtedly repaired before the Babylonian destruction of 586 BCE and again by Nehemiah in the second half of the fifth century BCE when the respective gates are referred to as the Fish Gate and the Old Gate (Nehemiah 3:3–6).
21. 2 Kings 14:14.
22. Azariah is alternatively referred to as Uzziah (particularly so in 2 Chronicles).
23. 2 Kings 14: 17–21; 2 Chron. 25:25–26:1.
24. 2 Kings 15:2; 2 Chron. 26:3.
25. 2 Chronicles 26:9.
26. 2 Chronicles 26:15.
27. Jeroboam II's co-regency with his father Jehoash from 793 BCE and his sole monarchy between 781 and 753 BCE account for the assertion that *he reigned forty-one years* (2 Kings 14:23).
28. 2 Kings 14:22; 2 Chron. 26:2.
29. 2 Chronicles 26:6–8.
30. Archaeological evidence was unearthed during the 1969/1972 excavations in the Jewish Quarter of the Old City of Jerusalem. See Avigad, 1970a, 1970b and 1972.
31. 2 Kings 15:5; 2 Chron. 26:21.
32. 2 Chronicles 27:3.
33. 2 Chronicles 27:4–5; Jos. *Ant.* IX, 237–8.
34. Pritchard, 1969, pp. 282–284.
35. 2 Kings 16:2–4; 2 Chronicles 28:2–4.
36. The so-called *Syro-Ephraimite War.* 2 Kings 16:5; Isaiah 7:1.
37. Compare 2 Kings 15:37 when Jotham was alive with 2 Chronicles 28:5 after Jotham's death.
38. 2 Chronicles 28:17–18.
39. 2 Kings 16:7–8; 2 Chronicles 28:16.

Chapter 6 Hezekiah

1. For a full explanation see Siegfried Horn, 1964, pp. 50–51 and McFall, 1989, pp. 393–404.
2. 2 Kings 18:4–6.
3. 2 Chronicles 29:3–36 and 31:2–19.
4. 2 Chronicles 30:1 to 31:1.
5. Jos. *Ant.* IX, 283–287 [citing Menander of Ephesus' translation of the Tyrian Archives].
6. 2 Kings 17:6; 17:24.
7. Pritchard, 1969, p. 287.

8. Ibid., p. 286.
9. Ibid., p. 285.
10. 2 Chronicles 32:28–29.
11. Miller and Hayes, 1986, pp. 354–356.
12. 2 Chronicles 32:5–6.
13. 2 Chronicles 32:3–4.
14. Sirach 48:17 and see also 2 Kings 20:20 and 2 Chronicles 32:30.
15. Pritchard, 1969, p. 321. *The Siloam Inscription* was removed and is now housed in Istanbul's Museum of the Ancient Orient.
16. Faust, 2015, p. 262.
17. 2 Kings 22:14; Zephaniah 1:10.
18. Zephaniah 1:11.
19. Isaiah 22:10.
20. 2 Chronicles 32:5.
21. Avigad, 1970b, pp. 130–135 and Avigad, 1972, pp. 193–194.
22. Faust, 2015, pp. 266–267.
23. Isaiah 31:1–3.
24. 2 Kings 20:12–13 places this meeting after rather than before Hezekiah's rebellion, but this would have been impossible after 701 BCE because by then Merodach-baladan was no longer king of Babylon (Ahlström, 1993, p. 695, note 7).
25. Pritchard, 1969, pp. 287–288 (The Annals of Sennacherib).
26. Ibid., p. 288.
27. 2 Kings 18:15–16.
28. Pritchard, 1969, p. 288.
29. 2 Kings 19:35–36 and Isaiah 37:36–37.
30. Herodotus, *The Histories*, 2:141.
31. Jos. *Ant.* X, 21.
32. 2 Kings 18:14.
33. Pritchard, 1969, p. 288.
34. 2 Kings 20:1.
35. 2 Kings 20:18.

Chapter 7 Babylon

1. 2 Kings 21:1; 2 Chronicles 33:1.
2. Isaiah 1:7.
3. The Hebrew term for the Valley of the Son of Hinnom was *ge-hinnom*, a Greek transliteration of which is *gehenna* – the Greek word for hell.
4. Tanakh Isaiah 30:33.
5. 2 Chronicles 33:6.
6. 2 Kings 21:10–14.

Notes

7. 2 Chronicles 33:11.
8. Compare 2 Chronicles 33:14 with 2 Chronicles 32:5–6.
9. Compare 2 Chronicles 33:15–17 with 2 Chronicles 33:22.
10. Pritchard, 1969, p. 291.
11. Ibid., pp. 534–541.
12. 2 Kings 21:3–5 and 2 Chronicles 33:3–5.
13. Isaiah 3:5 and 2 Kings 21:16.
14. 2 Kings 21:19–26 and 2 Chronicles 33:21–25.
15. 2 Kings 23:15.
16. 2 Kings 22:3 – 23:20 and 2 Chronicles 34:8–33.
17. Goddess/consort of Yahweh/Queen of Heaven.
18. Grayson, 2000, p. 91.
19. Near the village of Altınbaşak in present-day south-eastern Turkey.
20. 2 Kings 23:29–30 and 2 Chronicles 35:20–24.
21. 2 Kings 23:30.
22. Grayson, 2000, p. 96.
23. 2 Kings 23:33–35.
24. Jeremiah 22:13–17.
25. Jeremiah 26:1–24.
26. Grayson, 2000, p. 99.
27. Normally referred to as Nebuchadnezzar II, to distinguish him from a twelfth century BCE Babylonian monarch of the same name.
28. Grayson, 2000, p. 100.
29. Ibid., p. 101.
30. Herodotus, *The Histories*, 2:159.
31. Jeremiah 47:1.
32. Grayson, 2000, p. 101.
33. 2 Kings 24:1.
34. Pritchard, 1969, p. 564.
35. 2 Kings 24:2.
36. Jos. *Ant.* X, 97; 2 Chronicles 36:6.
37. 2 Chron. 36:9 is referring to his co-regency when it says he became king when he was eight years old, whereas 2 Kings 24:8 is referring to his sole monarchy when it states he was eighteen years old when he became king.
38. The 2nd day of the month of Adar in the seventh year of Nebuchadnezzar (Grayson, 2000, p. 102).
39. 2 Kings 24:14–16.
40. Broshi, 1975, p. 5, note 2: *Assuming that the length of life in antiquity was the same as that of contemporary eastern agricultural communities, we have assumed that the proportion of male adults in ancient societies was 1:36 or 28%*; Duncan-Jones, 1963, p. 87, *It is found that in the modern society whose*

mortality pattern corresponds most closely with that of Roman Africa, this age group [men of 18 years and above] constitutes about 1/3.6 [= 28%].

41. Jeremiah 35:11.
42. Jos. *Ant.* X, 102.
43. Grayson, 2000, p. 102.
44. 2 Kings 25:1.
45. Pritchard, 1969, p. 322.
46. Jeremiah 52:6–11.
47. 2 Kings 25:27–30.
48. Jeremiah 52:14.
49. Kenyon, 1975, p. 170.
50. Jeremiah 52:12–13.
51. Jeremiah 52:17–19.

Chapter 8 The Second Temple

1. Jeremiah 52:16.
2. Barstad, 2003, p. 4.
3. Ezekiel 11:15.
4. Barstad, 2003, p. 11.
5. Jeremiah 39:10.
6. 2 Kings 22:8–10.
7. Jeremiah 40:7–12.
8. Jeremiah 41:1–3.
9. Grayson, 2000, pp. 109–110. Cyrus is referred to as Cyrus II, as his grandfather, also named Cyrus, had ruled part of Persia (Anshan) between c.640 and 580 BCE.
10. Ezra 1:1–3.
11. Ezra 1:4–11.
12. Ezra 7:7
13. Levine, 2002, page 4.
14. Compare Ezra 3:6–10 with Ezra 5:16.
15. Ezra 5:14.
16. Herodotus, *The Histories*, 3:89. Referred to as Cambyses II, as his grandfather, also named Cambyses, had ruled part of Persia (Anshan) between c.580 and 559 BCE.
17. Ibid., 3:88.
18. Ezra 2:1–61 and Nehemiah 7:5–63.
19. Ezra 3:2, 3:8, 5:2, Haggai 1:1 and Nehemiah 12:1 all refer to Zerubbabel as the son of Shealtiel, although the lists in 1 Chronicles 3:16–19 name Pedaiah as Zerubbabel's father. Both Shealtiel and Pedaiah were sons of Jehoiachin (Jeconiah) and therefore in either case, Zerubbabel was the grandson of Jehoiachin.

20. Haggai 1:1.
21. Ezra 3:7 and see also Ezra 5:2; Haggai 1:14; Zechariah 4:9.
22. Ezra 5:3 – 6:12.
23. Haggai 1:1–11.
24. Ezra 4:1–4.
25. Bedford, 1995, p. 71, note 1.
26. 2 Kings 17:7.
27. Psalms 74:10 and 79:5; Isaiah 64:5; Lamentations 5:20–21.
28. 2 Chronicles 36:21; Zechariah 1:12; Jeremiah 25:12 and 29:10.
29. Ezra 6:15.
30. Ezra 6:16.

Chapter 9 Nehemiah

1. Nehemiah 3:9–12.
2. The Holy Bible (RSV – 2nd Catholic Edition, San Francisco, 2006), Ezra, footnote on page 346.
3. Nehemiah 1:3.
4. Jos. *Ant.* XI, 161.
5. Jos. *Ant.* XI, 168.
6. Nehemiah 2:1.
7. Nehemiah 4:1–21.
8. Nehemiah 3:1–32.
9. Nehemiah 2:13–15.
10. Cahill and Tarler, 2000, pp. 40–41.
11. Nehemiah 3:15.
12. Nehemiah 2:8, 7:2.
13. Compare Nehemiah 6:15 with Jos. *Ant.* XI, 179.
14. Nehemiah 11:1–2.
15. Mazar, 1975, p. 200.
16. Nehemiah 5:1–13.
17. Nehemiah 5:14–19.
18. Nehemiah 13:6–30.
19. Bagoas was a fairly common Persian name and he was possibly Nehemiah's immediate successor as the Persian-appointed governor of Judah.
20. A Jewish military fortress was originally established at Elephantine (now part of the modern city of Aswan), an island in the river Nile, during the reign of the king Manasseh to assist the Egyptians in a military campaign against the Nubians. The Jewish community maintained their own temple where animal sacrifice formed part of the customary religious rites. When the Persians arrived, they allowed the fortress and the temple to remain, as it was undoubtedly helpful

in maintaining their authority. Egyptians, encouraged by a local Persian official, had destroyed the Jewish temple during an anti-Semitic rampage in 410 BCE.

21. Pritchard, 1969, pp. 491–492; Jos. *Ant.* XI, 297–301.
22. Ezra 7:11–14.
23. Ezra 7:15–26.
24. Nehemiah 8:1–4.
25. Ezra 10:3.
26. Tcherikover, 1959, p. 39.

Chapter 10 The Greeks

1. Close to the present-day Turkish town of Iskenderun.
2. Diodorus, *Lib. hist.* XVII, 40, 2 – 46, 5.
3. Jos. *Ant.* XI, 321–339.
4. Nehemiah 4:1–9.
5. Babylonian Talmud, *Yoma*, 69a.
6. Diodorus, *Lib. hist.* XVII, 49, 1.
7. Tcherikover, 1959, p. 4.
8. Ibid., pp. 40–41.
9. Zechariah 9:13.
10. 2 Maccabees 4:13.
11. The sequence of Alexander's appointments of satraps in Coele-Syria in 332/331 CE is complicated and unclear. See Bosworth, 1974, pp. 46–64.
12. Near Mosul in present-day Iraq.
13. *Heidelberg Epitome, FdGH* 155, 1, 2. This document describes Arrhidaeus as *dull-witted, and also epileptic.*
14. Coele-Syria principally refers to Phoenicia and Palestine and comprises the lands south of the River Eleutherus, now known as the Nahr al-Kabir al-Janoubi (Southern Great River), along the northern border of present-day Lebanon with Syria.
15. *Heidelberg Epitome, FdGH* 155, 2, 2–3.
16. Diodorus, *Lib. hist.* XVIII, 43, 1.
17. Tcherikover, 1959, p. 9.
18. Diodorus, *Lib. hist.* XIX, 93, 4–7.
19. Diodorus, *Lib. hist.* XX, 93, 1–2.
20. A village in central Anatolia.
21. Tcherikover, 1959, p. 53.

Chapter 11 The Ptolemies

1. A city perimeter of 50 *stades* (approximately 9,500 metres) is a gross miscalculation.
2. The population figure of 120,000 is also an obvious exaggeration.

Notes

3. About 150 metres.
4. An unlikely 46 metres. Ezra 6.3 states that the decree of the Persian king Cyrus specified a breadth of 60 cubits (28 metres).
5. Jos. *Apion* I, 197–99 credits this passage to Hecataeus of Abdera, the c.300 BCE author of the lost work, *History of Egypt* (quoted in Diodorus, *Lib. hist.*), but probably the source is a lost work of a first-century BCE writer: *On the Jews* by (Pseudo-)Hecataeus, a Jewish writer, perhaps a priest from Jerusalem.
6. Diodorus, *Lib. hist.* XVIII, 43, 1–2.
7. Tcherikover, 1959, p. 57.
8. Jos. *Ant.* XII, 6, quoting second-century BCE Greek historian Agatharchides (only fragments of his major works survive).
9. Diodorus, *Lib. hist.* XXI, 1, 5.
10. A south coastal region of Asia Minor.
11. Grainger, 2010, p. 212.
12. *The Letter of Aristeas*, 10–50.
13. *The Septuagint* or *LXX.*
14. Levine, 2002, p. 58.
15. *The Letter of Aristeas*, 105. 40 stades is c.7,600 metres and an exaggeration, as in note 1 above.
16. Polybius, *Hist.* XVI, 22a.
17. Grainger, 2010, p. 257 *The battle of Panion is nowhere precisely dated, but it seems to have happened in the second half of 200.*
18. Polybius, *Hist.* XVI, 39; Jos. *Ant.* XII, 133.
19. Jos. *Ant.* XII, 154; Polybius, *Hist.* XXVIII, 20, 9.
20. Grainger, 2010, pp. 270–271.
21. Tcherikover, 1959, p. 128.

Chapter 12 The Seleucids

1. Tcherikover, 1959, p. 117.
2. Probably Ptolemy, the son of Thraseas, Governor of Coele-Syria and Phoenicia.
3. *Gerousia* or γερουσία (Greek). This was the Council of Elders, the forerunner of the *Sanhedrin*.
4. The number of *artabae* is not given. One *artabae* = c.40 litres.
5. One *medimni* = c.50 litres.
6. October.
7. Jos. *Ant.* XII, 138–144. The similarities between Antiochus' early-second-century BCE letter, reproduced by Josephus, to *The Letter of Aristeas* (verses 35–40, purporting to be the mid-third-century BCE letter from Ptolemy II, *Philadelphus*, to Jerusalem's high priest Eleazar), give rise to scepticism regarding the authenticity of Antiochus III's letter.
8. Near Mt Sipylus in present-day Turkey.

9. Polybius, *Hist.* XX1, 43.
10. Grainger, 2010, pp. 284–286.
11. Schürer (1890), 2012 reprint, 2nd div. vol. II, pp. 25 and 33.
12. Schürer (1890), 2012 reprint, 1st div., vol. I, p. 286.
13. Tcherikover, 1959, pp. 125–126.
14. Grainger, 2010, p. 288.
15. 2 Maccabees 4:9.
16. Tcherikover, 1959, p. 162. See also 2 Maccabees 4:40.
17. 2 Maccabees 4:32–50.
18. 2 Maccabees 13:5–8. From about 164 BCE, however, Menelaus was unable to fulfil the duties of High Priest because Judas Maccabee had taken control of Jerusalem and the pro-Greek factions had been driven out.
19. The mother of Ptolemy VI was Antiochus IV's sister, Cleopatra, who had married Ptolemy V.
20. Polybius, *Hist.* XXIX, 27, 11–13.
21. Hence history recalls the incident as 'The Day of Eleusis'.
22. Polybius, *Hist.* XXIX, 27, 1–6.
23. Grainger, 2010, p. 308.
24. 1 Maccabees 1:20–24.
25. 1 Maccabees 1:29–32.
26. 2 Maccabees 5:1–26.
27. 1 Maccabees 1:54–60; 2 Maccabees 6:1–11; Jos. *War* I, 34–5.
28. *Sinful people, lawless men* [1 Macc. 1:34]; *Macedonian garrison* [Jos. Ant. XII, 252]; *Syrian garrison* [Schürer (1890), 2012 reprint, div. 1, vol. 1, p. 206].
29. 1 Maccabees 1:33; 2:31; 7:32; 14:36.
30. Schürer (1890), 2012 reprint, div. 1, vol. 1, pp. 206–7, n. 35.
31. Kenyon, 1975, pp. 196–7.
32. Simons, 1952, pp. 144–157, believes that the Akra covered the entire south-east hill; Shotwell, 1964, pp. 10–19, concludes that the Akra and the S.E. hill are not necessarily co-extensive.
33. Jos. *Ant.* XII, 251–2.
34. Jos. *Ant.* XIII, 215.
35. Kenyon, 1975, p. 198.
36. 1 Maccabees 9:53.
37. 1 Maccabees 12:36; 13:49.

Chapter 13 The Maccabean Revolt

1. See Chapter 10, *The Greeks*, note 14.
2. The author of 1 Maccabees is unknown; 2 Maccabees is said to be an epitome of a larger work by Jason of Cyrene, of whom very little is known. Both date to the second century BCE.

3. The date upon which the Seleucid Era began in 312 BCE is 1st Dios in the Macedonian calendar, whereas the Era of Antioch began in 300 BCE on 22nd Artemisios, falling in October and May respectively in the Gregorian calendar.

4. 1 Maccabees 2:15–28.

5. 2 Maccabees 5:27 and 8:1.

6. Tcherikover, 1959, pp. 204–5.

7. A flat region that straddles present-day Afghanistan and Tajikistan.

8. 1 Maccabees 4:36–56. The eight-day celebration was the precursor of the Jewish *Hanukkah*, the Greek *Encaenia* and the Christian *Feast of the dedication of the Church of the Holy Sepulchre*.

9. After the sixth-century BCE Babylonian destruction of Judah, many Edomites had migrated northwards into southern Judah/Judea, forming the origins of Idumaea.

10. 1 Maccabees 6:18–31.

11. 1 Maccabees 6:43–46.

12. Present-day Aleppo.

13. 2 Maccabees 13:3–8 places Menelaus' demise at the beginning of the invasion of Judea, whereas Josephus suggests it was later at the time of the subsequent peace negotiations (Jos. *Ant.* XII, 384–385).

14. 1 Maccabees 6:55–63. Here the reference to Mt Zion is the name often used in antiquity for the area of Mount Moriah and the Ophel rather than the southern section of Jerusalem's Western Hill, which later came to be known as Mount Zion.

15. Polybius, *Hist.* XXXI, 11–15.

16. 1 Maccabees 7:1–4.

17. Jos. *Ant.* XII, 386. 1 Macc. 7:5–9, 2 Macc. 14:3 and 14:13 are inconsistent on this point.

18. 1 Maccabees 7:14.

19. 1 Maccabees 7:15–18.

20. 1 Maccabees 7: 20.

21. 1 Maccabees 7:31–35.

22. Near Beth-horon, about twelve miles north-west of Jerusalem.

23. 1 Maccabees 7:39–43. The 13th day of Adar falls in early March of the Gregorian calendar.

24. 1 Maccabees 9:35–42.

25. 1 Maccabees 9:57; Jos. Ant. XIII, 22.

26. Tcherikover, 1959, p. 232.

27. Present-day Mukhmas, a village in ruins on the northern ridge of Wadi Suweinit.

28. 1 Maccabees 9:73.

Chapter 14 Independence

1. Schürer (1890), 2012 reprint, 1st div. vol. I, p. 239.

2. Diodorus, *Lib. hist.* XXXI, 32a, 40a; Jos. *Ant.* XIII, 35–36.

3. Polybius, *Hist.* XXXIII, 18.
4. The present-day Israeli city of Acre.
5. 1 Maccabees 10:3–11; Jos. *Ant.* XIII, 37–42.
6. 1 Maccabees 10:18–20; Jos. *Ant.* XIII, 45.
7. Jos. *Ant.* XVIII, 18–22; Jos. *War* II, 119–161.
8. 1 Maccabees 10:25–45.
9. 1 Maccabees 10:51–66; Jos. *Ant.* XIII, 83–85.
10. 1 Maccabees 10:67; Jos. *Ant.* XIII, 86.
11. Respectively the present-day Israeli cities of Jaffa and Ashdod.
12. 1 Maccabees 11:17; Jos. *Ant.* XIII, 117.
13. Diodorus, *Lib. hist.* XXXII, 9d and 10.1.
14. Schürer (1890), 2012 reprint, p. 246.
15. 1 Maccabees 11:20–37; Jos. *Ant.* XIII, 121–129.
16. Jos. *Ant.* XIII, 131–132.
17. 1 Maccabees 11:57.
18. 1 Maccabees 11:60–12:38.
19. Tryphon may have been pre-empting any possible intervention by Jonathan on behalf of Antiochus VI, if he were to seize the Seleucid throne for himself. 1 Maccabees 12:39–40 and Jos. *Ant.* XIII, 187.
20. 1 Maccabees 13:12–24; Jos. *Ant.* XIII, 203–209.
21. 1 Maccabees 13:31–32. Other sources [Jos. *Ant.* XIII, 218; Diodorus, *Lib. hist.* XXXIII, 28; Livy, *Hist.* 55.11; App. *Syrian Wars* XIV, 67–68] place the murder of Antiochus VI after Demetrius had been taken prisoner by the Parthians in 139 BCE. Schürer (1890), 2012 reprint, pp. 176–177 argues strongly in support of the chronology of 1 Maccabees in this instance.
22. 1 Maccabees 13:41.
23. 1 Maccabees 13:49–51 and 14:37.
24. Jos. *Ant.* XIII, 215.
25. 1 Maccabees 14:8–13.
26. 1 Maccabees 14:41.
27. 1 Maccabees 15:15–24.
28. By then Demetrius II may already have been captured by the Parthians, but Rome's intent was clear.
29. Characene and Elymais.
30. 1 Maccabees 15:1–9.
31. 1 Maccabees 15:28–35.
32. Tryphon was reportedly killed in 138 BCE. Jos. *Ant.* XIII, 224; Strabo, *Geog.* XIV, 5, 2; App. *Syrian Wars*, XIV, 68.
33. 1 Maccabees 16:4–10.

Chapter 15 The Hasmoneans

1. 1 Maccabees 16:11–16.
2. Jos. *Ant*. XIII, 228–229; Jos. *War* I, 54–55. Contradicting 1 Maccabees 16:16, Josephus relates that Mattathias and Judas were not killed at the same time as Simon, but were taken prisoner by Ptolemy along with their mother.
3. Jos. *Ant*. XIII, 230–231; Jos. *War* I, 57. Again, Josephus additionally includes John Hyrcanus' brothers.
4. Doubts exist over the chronology of the ancient Jewish Sabbatical Years and this could have been 135 or 134 BCE, with implications for the date Simon was murdered. See Schürer (1890), 2012 reprint, 1st div. vol. I, pp. 40–46.
5. Jos. *Ant*. XIII, 236–241.
6. Jos. *Ant*. XIII, 242–247.
7. Jos. *Ant*. VII, 393; XIII, 249.
8. Jos. *Ant*. XIII, 247; Diodorus, *Lib. hist.* XXXIV/V, 5.
9. Jos. *Ant*. XIII, 273.
10. Jos. *Ant*. XIII, 257.
11. Jos. *Ant*. XIII, 275–281; Jos. *War* I, 64–65.
12. Jos. *Ant*. XIII, 288–296.
13. Schürer (1890), 2012 reprint, pp. 287–288.
14. Jos. *Ant*. XIII, 299.
15. Jos. *Ant*. XIII, 302; Jos. *War* I, 71.
16. The Ituraeans were originally nomads who had settled in the mountains of Lebanon. Their territorial domain was uncertain, but probably included Galilee, whose population was predominantly non-Jewish and until now had lain outside Judean hegemony. See Schürer (1890), 2012 reprint, pp. 293–294.
17. Jos. *Ant*. XIII, 318–319.
18. Jos. *Ant*. XIII, 301 relates that Aristobulus 'was the first to put a diadem on his head,' whereas Strabo *Geog*. XVI, 2, 40 states that 'Alexander [Janneus] was first to declare himself king instead of priest.'
19. Jos. *Ant*. XIII, 320; Jos. *War* I, 85.
20. Ptolemy Lathyrus (Ptolemy IX, *Soter II*) was then ruling Cyprus, having been deposed as the Pharaoh of Egypt, a position that he held on three separate occasions. (116–110, 109–107 and 88–81 BCE).
21. Jos. *Ant*. XIII, 324–364; Jos. *War* I, 86–87.
22. Jos. *Ant*. XIII, 372–373; Jos. *War* I, 88.
23. Jos. *Ant*. XIII, 375–379; Jos. *War* I, 90–95.
24. Schürer (1890), 2012 reprint, p. 302.
25. Jos. *Ant*. XIII, 379–383; Jos. *War* I, 96–98.
26. Jos. *Ant*. XIII, 389–394; Jos. *War* I, 99–105.

27. Schürer (1890), 2012 reprint, pp. 306–307.
28. 1 Maccabees 10:10–11; 1 Maccabees 13:10; Jos. *Ant.* XIII, 40–42.
29. 1 Maccabees, 16:23.
30. Jos. *War* V, 142.
31. Jos. *War* V, 142–145.
32. Mishnah, *Kodashim*, Middoth 5(4).
33. Jos. *Ant.* XV, 403. The *baris* was the forerunner of Herod the Great's 'Fortress Antonia'.
34. Broshi, 1978, p. 13; Levine, 2002, p. 92.
35. The problems involved in arriving at accurate estimations of populations in antiquity and the wildly different figures arrived at are discussed, inter alia, in McGing (2002, pp. 88–106) and Reinhardt (1995, pp. 237–265).
36. Jos. *Ant.* XIV, 476.
37. Jos. War V, 146.
38. Amongst others see: G. A. Smith, 1907, Vol. 1, pp. 247–249 and map 6 (facing p. 241); Ross, 1942, pp. 72–75; Avi-Yonah, 1968, pp. 122–125.
39. Polyhistor, 'Metrical Survey of Syria' in Euseb. *PE* IX, xxxvi.
40. Mackowski, 1980, p. 87.
41. Patrich, 1982, p. 34.
42. Jos. *Ant.* XIII, 407; Jos. *War* I, 107.
43. Jos. *Ant.* XIII, 408–409; Jos. *War* I, 110–111.
44. Jos. *Ant.* XIII, 410–417; Jos. *War* I, 113–114.
45. Jos. *Ant.* XIII, 409; Jos. *War* I, 112.
46. Ptolemy the son of Mennaeus ruled a nearby territory, including the mountain country of the Ituraeans.
47. Jos. *Ant.* XIII, 422–429; Jos. *War* I, 117–118.

Chapter 16 The Romans

1. Grainger, 2010, p. 273.
2. Present-day Manisa in the Aegean region of Turkey.
3. 'The Day of Eleusis.'
4. Sartre, 2005, pp. 35–36.
5. Great-grandson of Antiochus VII.
6. The first amongst equals.
7. Jos. *Ant.* XIV, 4–6.
8. Kokkinos, 2010, p. 96.
9. Jos. *War* I, 181.
10. The Nabataeans were originally an Arab nomadic people, who had begun to settle in southern Palestine as the Edomites migrated northwards during the sixth century BCE following the Babylonian destruction of Judah. A capital

city was established at Petra and Nabataean power gradually expanded as far as the region east of the river Jordan. The collapse of the Ptolemaic and Seleucid empires facilitated the foundation of a major independent state, which included parts of Syria. In 80 BCE, Antipater had married Cyprus, a Nabataean noblewoman related to the Nabataean royal family.

11. Jos. *Ant.* XIV, 8–19; Jos. *War* I, 123–126.
12. Jos. *Ant.* XIV, 28.
13. Dio, *Hist.* XXXVII, 11, 4.
14. Pompey subjugated Armenia and annexed Pontus and Syria, declaring both to be Roman provinces.
15. Jos. *Ant.* XIV, 29–33; Jos. *War* I, 127–130.
16. Diodorus, *Lib. hist.* XL, 2.
17. Jos. *Ant.* XIV, 46.
18. Jos. *Ant.* XIV, 47–58; Jos. *War* I, 132–143.
19. Jos. *Ant.* XIV, 63–66; Jos. *War* I, 145–149; Strabo *Geog.* XVI, 2, 40; Dio *Hist.* XXXVII, 16, 1–5.
20. In c.47 BCE, Julius Caesar granted permission to Hyrcanus and Antipater to repair the damaged walls.
21. Jos. *Ant.* XIV, 69; Jos. *War* I, 150–151.
22. Livy, *Hist.* 102.4.
23. Cic. *Flac.* 67; Jos. *Ant.* XIV, 72; Jos. *War* I, 153. Josephus and Cicero's statements concerning Pompey's restraint are at slight variance with Dio *Hist.* XXXVII, 16, 4, but Dio's comment *'all the wealth was plundered'* may be referring to the enforced tributary payments – see Jos. *Ant.* XIV, 78.
24. Kokkinos, 2010, p. 97.
25. Jos. *Ant.* XIV, 79; Jos. *War* I, 157–158.
26. App. *Mithridatic Wars* 117.
27. Jos. *Ant.* XIV, 82; Jos. *War* I, 160.
28. Following Pompey's conquest, the initial sequence of Governors of Syria was Scaurus 65–62 BCE, Marcius Philippus 61–60 BCE, Lentulus Marcellinus 59–58 BCE and Aulus Gabinius 57–55 BCE.
29. Jos. *Ant.* XIV, 82–90; Jos. *War* I, 157–158.
30. Jos. *Ant.* XIV, 90–91; Jos. *War* I, 169–170.
31. Jos. *Ant.* XIV, 92–97; Jos. *War* I, 171–174; Plutarch, *Antony*, 3.
32. Jos. *War* I, 483.
33. Jos. *Ant.* XIV, 98–103; Jos. *War* I, 175–178.
34. Jos. *Ant.* XIV, 104–109, 119–120; Jos. *War* I, 179–180.
35. Ascalon or Ashkelon, on the southern coast of Palestine had strong links with Herod and his forebears.
36. Jos. *Ant.* XIV, 123–126; Jos. *War* I, 183–186.

37. Although now aged around fourteen years, three years earlier Ptolemy XIII had married his co-ruler and sister, Cleopatra VII, but was now attempting to become the sole authority in Egypt.

38. Jos. *Ant.* XIV, 127–136; Jos. *War* I, 187–193.

39. As Ethnarch, Hyrcanus is appointed protector of the Jews living outside as well as inside Judea, whereas Antipater holds Judean territorial leadership as procurator. See Sharon, 2010, pp. 474–483.

40. Jos. *Ant.* XIV, 137–144, 151, 190–195; Jos. *War* I, 194–200.

41. Jos. *Ant.* XIV, 158–184; Jos. *War* I, 203–215.

42. Cassius and his brother-in-law, Marcus Brutus, had conspired to murder Julius Caesar and were now at war against Mark Antony and Octavian.

43. Jos. *Ant.* XIV, 271–292; Jos. *War* I, 220–235.

44. Including Ptolemy (son of Mennaeus) the ruler of Ituraea (Chalcis) and Marion, the prince of Tyre.

45. Jos. *Ant.* XIV, 294–299; Jos. *War* I, 236–240.

46. Jos. *Ant.* XIV, 300 accurately states 'an agreement of marriage'; Jos. *War* I, 241 is premature in stating 'now he married'. Kokkinos, 2010, pp. 114–115 maintains that the betrothal would have taken place in Ascalon and that Alexandra II and Mariamne I followed Herod to Jerusalem.

47. App. *Roman Civil Wars*, V, 7.

48. Jos. *Ant.* XIV, 302–303, 324–329; Jos. *War* I, 242–247.

49. Lysanias who was a Parthian ally, had recently succeeded his father Ptolemy as the Ituraean ruler.

50. Jos. *Ant.* XIV, 330–348; Jos. *War* I, 248–260.

51. As Masada was too small to accommodate everybody, Herod left his contingent's women with supplies and bodyguards in the fortress, while he continued his journey.

52. Jos. *Ant.* XIV, 352–362, 370–380; Jos. *War* I, 263–267, 274–281.

53. The Hasmonean, Antigonus I, did not ever rule in Judea. He was the great-uncle of Antigonus II and was assassinated in 104 BCE by his rival sibling, Aristobulus I.

54. Jos. *Ant.* XIV, 363–369; Jos. *War* I, 268–273.

Chapter 17 The Herod the Great

1. Jos. *Ant.* XIV, 384–387.

2. Jos. *Ant.* XIV, 390–393; Jos. War I, 286–289. Dio *Hist.* XLVIII, 41, 4–5 also mentions Ventidius' extortion, and additionally states that he 'frightened the king, Antigonus, out of the country.'

3. An ancient city on the west bank of the Euphrates, whose ruins were flooded in 1992 as part of the Atatürk Dam project.

4. Roman governor of Syria 38–37 BCE.

5. Jos. *Ant.* XIV, 434–461; Jos. *War* I, 317–339.

6. Kokkinos, 2010, pp. 208–209.

7. Jos. *War* I, 431–433.

8. Sartre, 2005, p. 52.

9. Jos. *War* I, 352.

10. Jos. *Ant.* XIV, 470–486; Jos. *War* I, 347–356.

11. Schürer (1890), 2012 reprint, 1st div. vol. I, pp. 397–399, note 11.

12. Jos. *Ant.* XIV, 490; XV, 8–10; Jos. *War* I, 357; Dio *Hist.* XLIX, 22, 6; Plutarch, *Antony*, 36.

13. Jos. *Ant.* XV, 5–6; Jos. *War* I, 358–359.

14. Jos. *Ant.* XV, 264. In debt to Herod or Antigonus or simply unpaid state taxes is not elucidated.

15. Menahem Stern, 1982, page 42.

16. Kokkinos, 2010, pp. 216–217; Jos. *War* I, 563; Jos. *Ant.* XVII, 19.

17. Jos. *Ant.* XV, 22. In Mishnah, *Parah*, 3.5, this high priest is referred to as *Hanamel the Egyptian*.

18. Jos. *Ant.* XV, 21.

19. Plutarch, *Antony*, 36 and Dio *Hist.* XLIX, 32, 4–5 do not differentiate between the 37/6 and 34 BCE sets of territorial gifts to Cleopatra. Euseb. *Chron.* 60 (quoting Porphyry as his source) mentions only the most significant of the former bequests – *Chalcis and the surrounding regions* – whereas Jos. *Ant.* XV, 95–96 and *War* I, 361–362 relate the chronology of the territorial gifts with greater accuracy – see Schürer (1890), 2012 reprint, 1st div. vol. I, pp. 402–403, note 5.

20. Jos. *Ant.* XV, 23–49.

21. Jos. *Ant.* XV, 50–56; Jos. War I, 437.

22. Jos. *Ant.* XV, 62–87; Jos. *War* I, 441–444 is premature in stating that Mariamne is also executed.

23. Jos. *Ant.* XV, 292, 409, XVIII, 91; Jos. *War* I, 401; Tac. *Hist.* V, 11. For a very detailed description of Fortress Antonia see Jos. *War* V, 238–247.

24. Jos. *Ant.* XV, 107–160; Jos. *War* I, 364–385.

25. Jos. *Ant.* XV, 161–182; Jos. *War* I, 434.

26. Jos. *Ant.* XV, 195; Jos. *War* I, 392. Dio *Hist.* LI, 7, however, relates the incident with no mention of any participation by Herod.

27. Jos. *Ant.* XV, 187–200, 217; Jos. *War* I, 387–396. The additional territories were Gadara, Hippus, Samaria, Gaza, Anthedon, Joppa and Strato's Tower (Caesarea).

28. Jos. *Ant.* XV, 220.

29. Jos. *Ant.* XV, 218–246.

30. Jos. *Ant.* XV, 247–252. The disloyal friends included Costobar, the second husband of Herod's sister Salome, and the enemies included the Sons of Baba, whom Costobar had kept hidden.
31. Jos. War I, 402. Kokkinos, 2010, pp. 221–222 infers work on the palace began c.29/28 BCE, citing the statement in Jos. *Ant.* XV, 292 that the palace preceded the rebuilding of Samaria/Sebaste in 27 BCE.
32. Jos. Ant. XV, 320–322.
33. Kokkinos, 2010, pp. 221–222.
34. Jos. *Ant.* XVII, 19–22; Jos. *War* I, 562.
35. Jos. *Ant.* XV, 292–298; Jos. *War* I, 403. Schürer (1890), 2012 reprint, 1st div. vol. I, pp. 405–406, note 8, places the rebuilding of Samaria *probably in the year 727* (Roman dating *Ab urbe condita* – equivalent to 27 BCE).
36. Jos. *Ant.* XV, 268.
37. Schick, 1887, pp. 161–166; Reich and Billig, 2000, pp. 175–184. Jos. *Ant.* XVII, 255 mentions a hippodrome.
38. Patrich, 2002, pp. 231–239.
39. Jos. *Ant.* XV, 267–276.
40. Vermes, 1997, p. 481.
41. Jos. *Ant.* XV, 277–290.
42. The date may be approximated by virtue of Petronius' Egyptian prefecture during 24–21 BCE.
43. Jos. *Ant.* XV, 299–316.
44. Jos. *Ant.* XVI, 1–5.
45. Jos. *Ant.* XVII, 42–44.
46. Jos. *Ant.* XV, 365; XVI, 64.
47. Jos. *Ant.* XV, 331–341; XVI, 136; Pliny, *Natural History*, V, xiv. For a discussion of the dates see Kokkinos, 2010, Appendix 2, Section 3, p. 370.
48. Jos. War V, 161, 176–181; Jos *Ant.* XV, 318.
49. Jesus son of Phiabi took over from Hananel as high priest c.30 BCE.
50. Compare Jos. Ant. XV, 320–322 with Kokkinos, 2010, pp. 221–222.
51. Sartre, 2005, p. 92.
52. Jos. *Ant.* XV, 323–325; XVI, 18–19, 142–149; Jos. *War* I, 416–425.
53. Jos. *Ant.* XV, 380 '18th year of his reign'. Jos. *War* I, 401 '15th year' is probably just a clerical error.
54. Jos. *Ant.* XV, 380–390.
55. To an unlikely square of 500x500 cubits according to Mishnah, *Kodashim, Middoth*, 2, 1.
56. Jos. *Ant.* XV, 412.
57. Luke 4:9.
58. Jos. *Ant.* XV, 390.
59. Mishnah, *Kodashim, Middoth*, 1–5; Jos. *Ant.* XV, 380–425; Jos. *War* V, 184–226; Philo, *Spec. Laws* I, XIII (71–75).

60. Jos. *War* I, 401.
61. Philo, *Special Laws* I, XIII (72).
62. Babylonian Talmud, *Mo'ed Sukkah*, 51B.
63. Jos. *War* VI, 317.
64. Jos. *Ant.* XV, 420–423.
65. John 2:20; Jos. *Ant.* XX, 219.
66. Kokkinos, 2010, Appendix 2, Section 2, pp. 369–370. They had been sent to Rome for training and education some years earlier. Their younger brother died in Rome (Jos. *War* I, 435).
67. Jos. *Ant.* XVI, 66 ff; Jos. *War* I, 445 ff.
68. Jos. *Ant.* XVI, 356–394; Jos. *War* I, 535–551. Berytus (present-day Beirut) was a Roman colony.
69. Most modern historians use the name of Herod-Philip for the son of Herod and Mariamne II. Kokkinos, 2010, p. 223, prefers the nomenclature Herod III.
70. Jos. *Ant.* XVII, 61–145; Jos. *War* I, 582–640.
71. Jos. *Ant.* XVII, 149–167; Jos. *War* I, 648–655.
72. Jos. *Ant.* XVII, 182–190; Jos. *War* I, 661–665.

Chapter 18 Herod's Legacy

1. Antipas is frequently referred to as Herod-Antipas by Josephus and in the New Testament.
2. The nomenclature 'Herod IV' is somewhat arbitrary, on the basis that Herod the Great was Herod II and Herod-Philip (son of Mariamne II) was Herod III. See Kokkinos, 2010, p. 223 and p. 236.
3. The authority of the Roman emperor was supreme despite the assertion that, in c.24 BCE, Augustus granted Herod *the right to secure in the possession of his kingdom whichever of his offspring he wished* (Jos. *Ant.* XV, 343).
4. Jos. *Ant.* XVII, 200–218; Jos. *War* II, 1–13.
5. Jos. *Ant.* XVII, 219–316; Jos. *War* II, 14–92; Nicholas of Damascus, *Autobiography*, 8–10.
6. Jos. *War* II, 95–97. The territories on the north-eastern side of the river Jordan were Gaulanitis, Batanaea, Trachonitis and Auranitis. See Aharoni & Avi-Yonah, 1978, p. 140, map 222. Paneas was later (14 CE) renamed Caesarea Philippi.
7. Jos. *Ant.* XVII, 318–320; Jos. *War* II, 93–97; Nicholas of Damascus, *Autobiography*, 11.
8. Sharon, 2010, pp. 483–484. See Chapter 16, *The Romans*, note 41.
9. Jewish law prohibited marriage to a brother's widow (Lev. 18:16, 20:21), unless the previous union had been childless (Deut. 25:5).
10. Jos. *War* II, 117; Jos. *Ant.* XVII, 351–353.
11. Jos. *Ant.* XVII, 339–341.

12. Jos. *War* II, 111–113; Jos. *Ant.* XVII, 342–344; Dio *Hist.* LV, 27, 6; Strabo, *Geog.* XVI, 2, 46.
13. Judea, Idumaea and Samaria were thenceforth often referred to collectively as (Roman) Judaea.
14. Jos. *Ant.* XVIII, 23–25; Jos. *War* II, 118; Acts 5:37.
15. Jos. *Ant.* XVIII, 26, 33–35, 95, 123.
16. Jos. *Ant.* XX, 251.
17. Coponius 6–9 CE, Marcus Ambivulus 9–12 CE and Annius Rufus 12–15 CE.
18. Ishmael ben Phabi replaced Ananus ben Sethi in 15 CE, followed by Eleazar ben Ananus in 16 CE and Simon ben Camith in 17 CE, before Joseph Caiaphas (the son-in-law of Ananus) in 18 CE. Jos. *Ant.* XVIII, 33–35.
19. Jos. *Ant.* XVIII, 55–59; Jos. *War* II, 169–174.
20. Jos. *Ant.* XVIII, 60–62; Jos. *War* II, 175–177; Euseb. *EH* II, vi, 6–7.
21. Reportedly stoned to death for complaining that the widows of Hellenistic Jews were being treated less well than the widows of Hebraic Jews in the distribution of alms. See Acts 6:1 and 7:58.
22. Acts 8:1–3.
23. Although Acts 4:5–6 refers to 'Annas the high priest and Caiaphas...' the latter was in fact the High Priest at that time.
24. Jos. *Ant.* XVIII, 85–89.
25. Jos. *Ant.* XVIII, 90. The robe had been in the custody of the Romans since 6 CE (Jos. Ant. XV, 403–404).
26. Euseb. *EH.* II, vii.
27. Jos. *Ant.* XVIII, 124.
28. They married c.23 CE. Cyprus III was the daughter of cousins Salampsio (a daughter of Herod the Great) and Phasael II (a son of Herod the Great's brother Phasael I).
29. Jos. *Ant.* XVIII, 108.
30. Herodias I was the granddaughter of Herod the Great and the daughter of Aristobulus IV. She was briefly married to her uncle Herod-Philip and they had a child (Salome III), shortly after which she abandoned him. In 6 CE, Herodias married her uncle Philip the *tetrarch*, and in 34 CE she married her uncle Antipas the *tetrarch*. There is contradiction in the sources and later works concerning Herodias' marriages and also the marriage, if any, of her daughter, Salome III. Kokkinos, 2010, pp. 264–271 makes a coherent case for the sequence presented here.
31. Commissioner of markets.
32. Jos. *Ant.* XVIII, 148–149.
33. Jos. *Ant.* XVIII, 150–162.
34. Jos. *Ant.* XVIII, 187–191; Jos. *War* II, 179–180.

35. Jos. *Ant.* XVIII, 237; Jos. *War* II, 181; Philo, *Flaccus* VI (39).
36. Jos. *Ant.* XVIII, 240–252; Jos. *War* II, 181–183.
37. Philo, *Leg. Ad Gaium* XXX (198).
38. Philo, *Flaccus* I–XXI (1–190).
39. Jos. *Ant.* XVIII, 257; Philo, *Leg. Ad Gaium* XLVI (370).
40. Philo, *Leg. Ad Gaium* XLIV–XLVI (349–373).
41. Philo, *Leg. Ad Gaium* XXX (200–203); Jos. *Ant.* XVIII, 261.
42. Philo, *Leg. Ad Gaium* XXX (331–333); Jos. *Ant.* XVIII, 287–301; Jos *War* II, 201–203.
43. Jos. *Ant.* XIX, 274–277; Jos. *War* II, 215–217; Dio *Hist.* LX, viii, 2–3.
44. Jos. *Ant.* XIX, 335–337.
45. Jos. *Ant.* XIX, 300–311.
46. Jos. *Ant.* XIX, 293 and 331; Mishnah, *Zeraim*, Bikkurim 3:4.
47. Jos. *Ant.* XIX, 294.
48. Mishnah, *Nashim*, Sotah 7:8.
49. Jos. *Ant.* XIX, 299 and 330.
50. Acts 12:1–3.
51. Jos. *Ant.* XIX, 338–342.
52. Jos. *Ant.* XIX, 327; Jos. *War* II, 218–219; Jos. *War* V, 147–161. Also see Tac. *Hist.* V, 12.
53. *NEAEHL*, vol. 2, pp. 744–745.
54. Tzaferis et al, 2000, p. 287.
55. Jos. *Ant.* XIX, 326–327; Jos. *War* II, 152; Jos. *War* V, 218–219.
56. Tzaferis et al, 2000, p. 288.
57. Jos. *War* II, 563–564, 648; Jos. *War* V, 155
58. Jos. *Ant.* XIX, 343–350; Jos. *War* II, 219; Acts 12:19–23.

Chapter 19 Roman Procurators and Temple Curators

1. Jos. *Ant.* XIX, 356–359.
2. Jos. *Ant.* XIX, 360–363; Jos. *War* II, 220.
3. Jos. *Ant.* XX, 15–16, 103.
4. Jos. *Ant.* XX, 2–14.
5. Jos. *Ant.* III, 320, XX, 49–51, 100–102; Acts 11:28–29; Euseb. *EH* II, xi–xii.
6. Jos. *Ant.* XX, 104 and 222–223. Compare Schürer (1890), 2012 reprint, 1st div. vol. II, p. 193, note 5, with Kokkinos, 2010, pp. 318–319 and notes 184–185.
7. Acts 15:1–30.
8. Jos. *Ant.* XX, 105–112; Jos. *War* II, 224–227. The large, but inconsistent casualty numbers given by Josephus are likely to be exaggerations.
9. Jos. *Ant.* XX, 113–117; Jos. *War* II, 228–231.
10. Jos. *Ant.* XX, 121 and 124.

11. Mishnah, *Nashim*, Sotah 9, 1–9.
12. Jos. *Ant.* XX, 118–136; Jos. *War* II, 232–246; In Tac. *Annals* XII, 54, Cumanus is merely the governor of Galilee, with Markus Antonius Felix already *in situ* as procurator of Judaea.
13. The *sagan* was second in rank to the High Priest of the Temple and acted as his deputy whenever necessary.
14. Jos. *War* II, 243; Jos. *Ant.* XX, 162. Ananias was the incumbent High Priest, whereas Jonathan had held the position in 36–37 CE. Even after removal from office, the title and influence of the position endured. See Jeremias, 1967, p. 157 and Schürer (1890), 2012 reprint, 2nd div, vol. I, pp. 202–203.
15. Jos. *Ant.* XX, 141–143. Acts 24:24.
16. Tac. *Hist.* V, 9. Note, however, that Tacitus mistakenly refers to Felix' first wife as Drusilla.
17. Jos. *Ant.* XX, 138–159; Jos *War* II, 247–252.
18. Jos. *Ant.* XX, 160–161; Jos *War* II, 253.
19. Jos. *War* II, 254–257; Jos. *Ant.* XX, 162–166. The involvement of Felix in the murder of Jonathan is reported by Josephus in the latter reference, but not the former.
20. Jos. *Ant.* XX, 167–172; Jos *War* II, 258–265.
21. Jos. *Ant.* XX, 179–181. In 15 CE, Roman Prefect Gratus appointed a different person also named Ishmael ben Phabi as High Priest. For the rabbinical lament of the priestly dispute see Babylonian Talmud, *Pesahim* 57a.
22. Acts 8:3, 9:1–22, 24:24–27.
23. Jos. *Ant.* XX, 173–178; Jos *War* II, 266–270.
24. Jos. *Ant.* XX, 182; Jos *War* II, 271. Although 60 CE is the probable date for the recall of Felix, this is disputed. See Schürer (1890), 2012 reprint, 1st div. vol. II, pp. 182–184.
25. Jos. *Ant.* XX, 183; Acts 23:12, 28:30–31.
26. Jos. *Ant.* XX, 185–188; Jos *War* II, 271.
27. In 61 CE, Agrippa II enlarged Caesarea Philippi and renamed it Neronias (Jos. *Ant.* XX, 211) until the death of Nero in 68 CE, when it reverted to the name of Caesarea Philippi. The locale is presently known as Banias, in the disputed territory of the Golan Heights.
28. Jos. *Ant.* XX, 189–192.
29. Jos. *Ant.* XX, 193–196.
30. Euseb. *EH* II, xxiii. Jerusalem's early Christians were guided by a Council of Elders and considered itself part of the wider Jewish community.
31. Jos. *Ant.* XX, 197–203.
32. Jos. *Ant.* XX, 219–222. 'Over 18,000' redundancies is typical of Josephus' tendency to exaggerate numbers. The concluding work on the Temple was likely to have been maintenance and ornamental finishing.

33. Jos. *War* V, 36–37; Jos. *Ant.* XV, 391. The timber was, however, never used for the intended purpose due the advent of Jewish/Roman hostilities.
34. Jeremias, 1967, pp. 58–77.
35. Mark 13:1.
36. Babylonian Talmud: *Kiddushim* 49b; *Succah* 51b.

Chapter 20 Insurrection

1. Sartre, 2005, p. 107. Forced servitude in Judaea lasted six years.
2. Babylonian Talmud, *Shabbat 33b.*
3. Sartre, 2005, p. 104.
4. Jos. *Ant.* XX, 204.
5. Jos. *Ant.* XX, 208–210.
6. Jos. *War* II, 273.
7. Jos. *Ant.* XX, 220.
8. Jos. *Ant.* XX, 206–207.
9. Jos. *Ant.* XX, 214; Jos. *War* II, 418.
10. Jos. *War* II, 277–279; Jos. *Ant.* XX, 252–256.
11. Jos. *War* II, 280–283.
12. Jos. *War* II, 284–295. Seventeen talents was a relatively insignificant amount. In 54 BCE Crassus plundered 2,000 talents from the Temple (Jos. *Ant.* XIV, 105; *War* I, 179) and in 44 BCE Cassius demanded tribute of 700 talents from Judaea (Jos. *Ant.* XIV, 272; *War* I, 220).
13. One tenth of a Roman legion.
14. Jos. *War* II, 296–314.
15. Jos. *War* II, 315–332.
16. Jos. *War* II, 333–341.
17. Jos. *War* II, 342–407.
18. Led by the Temple captain (*sagan*) Eleazar, the son of former High Priest Ananias ben Nedebaeus (Jos. *War* II, 409). The incumbent High Priest was Matthias ben Theophilus (Jos. *Ant.* XX, 223).
19. Jos. *War* II, 408–410.
20. Jos. *War* II, 418–424.
21. Ananias ben Nedebaeus became Jerusalem's High Priest in 47 CE. He was replaced by Ishmael ben Phabi in 59 CE, at a time of class warfare between the high priests. As was customary, Ananias retained the title of High Priest even after his dismissal from the post and he remained an influential figure in Jerusalem. The aristocratic and wealthy Ananias was not popular with the poorer classes and as well as being associated with the theft of priestly tithes (Jos. *Ant.* XX, 205–207), the Babylonian Talmud refers to his alleged gluttony (*Pesahim 57a*, using the name *Yohanan ben Nidbai*).
22. Jos. *War* II, 425–429.

23. The son of Judas of Galilee, the founder of the *Zealots*, a sect which participated actively in the Jewish rebellion of 66 CE (Jos. *Ant.* XVIII, 23–25).
24. Jos. *War* II, 430–440.
25. Jos. *War* II, 441–448.
26. Jos. *War* II, 449–456.
27. Present-day Amman in Jordan.
28. Jos. *War* II, 457–498; Jos. *Life*, 25–27.
29. Euseb. *EH* III, v, 2–3; Epiphanius, *Panarion* I, 29, 7:8.
30. Jos. *War* II, 499–528. Mount Scopus is the present-day site of the Hebrew University of Jerusalem.
31. Josephus' so-called *Second* and *Third Walls* (Jos. *War* V, 146–161; Jos. *War* II, 218–219; Jos. *Ant.* XIX, 327).
32. Jos. *War* II, 529–555.
33. Jos. *War* II, 562–568. Ananus b. Ananus had previously been removed by Agrippa II as High Priest after only three months in 62 CE.
34. Vermes, 1997, p. 84.
35. Jos. *War* II, 647–649.
36. Jos. *War* III, 1–8; Tac. *Hist.* V, 10.
37. Jos. *War* III, 64–69.
38. The campaign in Galilee is recounted in Jos. *War*, III, 29 – IV, 120.
39. John's resistance to the Romans and flight from Gischala in Galilee is narrated in Jos. *War* IV, 84–111.
40. Jos. *War* IV, 121–157.
41. Jos. *War* IV, 193–318.
42. Jos. *War* IV, 326–333.
43. Jos. *War* IV, 334–397.
44. Jos. *War* IV, 398–450.
45. Roman Emperors immediately following the death of Nero: Galba (9 June 68 – 15 January 69); Otho (15 January – 16 April 69); Vitellius (16 April – 22 December 69 CE).
46. Jos. *War* IV, 497–502; Tac. *Hist.* II, 1–4.
47. Jos. *War* IV, 556–576.
48. This Eleazar was possibly the son of Simon bar Giora (See Jos. *War* IV, 225 and Jos. *War* V, 5).
49. Jos. *War* V, 2–35; Tac. *Hist.* V, 12; Babylonian Talmud, *Gittin* 56a relates how the Zealots *went and burned the stores of wheat and barley, so there was a famine.*

Chapter 21 Destruction

1. Jos. *War* IV, 592–604; Tac. *Hist.* II, 79–81; Suetonius, *Vespasian* 6.
2. Jos. *War* IV, 658.

3. The 5th, 10th and 15th legions, plus the 12th legion that Cestius Gallus had used in his earlier attack on Jerusalem.
4. Tac. *Hist.* V, 1; Jos. *War* V, 41–49.
5. Jos. *War* III, 336–398; Jos. *War* IV, 621–629.
6. Jos. *War* V, 52–97.
7. Jos. *War* V, 98–105; Tac. *Hist.* V, 12 implies that thereafter the two remaining factions co-operated in the fight against the Romans, but not so according to Jos. *War* V, 248–257.
8. Jos. *War* V, 106–108; 130–135; Dio *Hist.* LXV, 4, 5.
9. Varying from hand-thrown javelins and long-bow propelled arrows to bolts, spears and stones fired from catapults of varying complexity (ballistae and polyboloi).
10. Jos. *War* V, 259–303; Dio *Hist.* LXV, 5, 2.
11. Jos. *War* V, 305–359; 446.
12. Jos. *War* V, 420–459.
13. Jos. *War* V, 466–518.
14. Jos. *War* VI, 15–28, 68–80, 93, 149, 164–168.
15. Jos. *War* VI, 220–229, 233–243, 260–266.
16. Jos. *War* VI, 271–280.
17. Jos. *War* VI, 321–322, 350–353.
18. Jos. *War* VI, 354–355, 358, 363, 374–386.
19. Jos. *War* VI, 392–402, 370; VII, 26–28, 215.
20. Jos. *War* VI, 404–408.
21. Jos. *War* VI, 433–434; VII, 23–36, 118, 153–155; Dio *Hist.* LXV, 7, 1.
22. Jos. *War* VI, 414–419.
23. Jos. *War* VII, 148–151, 162. The fate of the Menorah has given rise to much speculation, including being removed to Africa by Geiseric the Vandal in 455 CE, subsequently taken to Constantinople by Belisarius in 534 CE, and returned to Jerusalem by Justinian (Procopius, *Hist.* IV, ix). Subsequently, it may have been destroyed, looted or even hidden in the desert at the time of the Persian attack in 614 CE. Alternatively, it may simply have been destroyed in Rome by the fire which engulfed Vespasian's Temple of Peace in 191 CE.
24. Jos. *War* VI, 317, 384.
25. Tzaferis et al., 2000, p. 288.
26. Jos. *War* VII, 1–4.

Chapter 22 The Bar Kokhba Revolt

1. Jos. *War* VII, 5.
2. Jos. *War* VII, 19–24.
3. The equestrian order constituted the second rank of the property-based classes of ancient Rome.

4. Jos. *War* VII, 407; Tac. *Hist.* II, 78.
5. Acts 23:35.
6. Initially Cerialis commanded the 5th Legion and after the siege, the 10th Legion (Jos. *War* VI, 237; VII, 163).
7. Jos. *War* VII, 216–218.
8. Lucilius Bassus appears to have been assisted by a procurator, L. Laberius Maximus (Jos. *War* VII, 216).
9. Jos. *War* VII, 163–164, 190–214. Herodium (seven miles south of Jerusalem) and Machaerus were close to the respective western and eastern coasts of the Dead Sea. The present-day location of the Jardes forest is unknown.
10. Jos. *War* VII, 252. The full name of the new Governor and Legate was L. Flavius Silva Nonius Bassus.
11. Jos. *War* VII, 389–401.
12. Graetz, 1893, volume II, pp. 321–359.
13. Euseb. *EH* III, xii, 1, derived from Hegesippus, but not mentioned in any other source material. For similar claims against Domitian and Trajan: Euseb. *EH* III, xix–xx and III, xxxii, 3–4.
14. Suetonius, *Domitian* 12, 2; Dio *Hist.* LXVII, 14, 1–2.
15. *SHA, Hadrian* 5, 2.
16. William Smith, 1844, p. 633.
17. Euseb. *EH* IV, ii; Dio *Hist.* LXVIII, xxxii, 1–5; Schürer (1890), 2012 reprint, 1st div. vol. II, p. 262.
18. Sartre, 2005, p. 128; Cotton and Eck, 2005, p. 26.
19. *SHA, Hadrian* 14, 2.
20. Midrash *Bereshit* (*Genesis*), *Rabbah* 64:8.
21. Dio *Hist.* LXIX, 12, 1.
22. Mantel, 1968, pp. 224–242 and pp. 274–296; Rubenstein, 2002, pp. 61 and 261; Schürer (1890), 2012 reprint, 1st div. vol. II, pp. 289–295.
23. E.g. *The Testament of Moses* (early first-century CE Essene-style work), the third book of *The Sibylline Oracles* (first-century CE work published in Alexandria) and from the first century BCE, Psalm 17 of *The Psalms of Solomon*.
24. Euseb. *EH* IV, vi, 2.
25. Hegesippus in Euseb. *EH* IV, viii, 4,
26. Dio *Hist.* LXIX, 12, 2.
27. Mantel, 1968, pp. 237–242.
28. Dio *Hist.* LXIX, 13, 1.
29. Euseb. *EH* IV, vi, 1.
30. Kanael, 1971, pp. 39–46; Meshorer 1967, pp. 95–96; There is also a reference to Hadrian having to destroy (retake?) Jerusalem in App. *Syrian Wars* VIII, 50.

31. Dio *Hist.* LXIX, 12, 3.
32. Probably present-day Battir, about six miles south-west of Jerusalem.
33. Dio *Hist.* LXIX, 13, 2–3; Euseb. *EH* IV, vi, 3; Jerusalem Talmud, *Ta'anit* 4:6 (68d–69a).
34. Indicated by the discovery of utensils, coins, and miscellaneous artefacts as well as documents and letters (some signed by Simon Bar Kokhba) found in the caves – see Avigad et al., 1961/2, pp. 6–62 and pp. 167–262.
35. Aharoni, 1962, pp. 186–199.
36. Dio *Hist.* LXIX, 14, 1–3.
37. Babylonian Talmud, *Berakhot* 61B.

Chapter 23 Aelia Capitolina

1. Mishnah *Ta'anit* IV, 6.
2. Compare Dio *Hist.* LXIX, 12, 1 with Euseb. *EH* IV, vi, 3–4.
3. Rocca, 2018; Meshorer, 1967, p. 93.
4. Eck, 1999, pp. 88–89. See also Chapter 10, *The Greeks*, note 14.
5. Euseb. *HE* IV, vi, 3 (quoting Aristo of Pella).
6. Harris, 1926, pp. 199–206.
7. App. *Syrian Wars* VIII, 50.
8. Babylonian Talmud: *Sanhedrin* 14A, *Me'ilah* 17A, *Baba Batra* 60B and *Berakhot* 61B.
9. Smallwood, 1959, p. 335–341.
10. Ibid., pp. 340–347 for possible dates and *raison d'être* for the lifting of the ban.
11. *NEAEHL*, vol. 2, pp. 758–759; Donner, 1992, pp. 87–94 and pull-out map.
12. Tzaferis et al., 2000, p. 288.
13. Magen, 2000, p. 286.
14. Geva and Bahat, 1998, p. 230; Avigad, 1983, p. 207.
15. Avigad, 1983 pp. 213–229 details the evidence demonstrating that the more southerly extension of the Cardo was constructed in the later Byzantine period.
16. *NEAEHL*, vol. 2, pp. 762–765 reviews the archaeological evidence of the first Cardo, the first Decumanus, the secondary or Eastern Cardo and the second west-to-east thoroughfare, without using the term 'Decumanus'.
17. Jos. *War* VII, 1–4.
18. *NEAEHL*, vol. 2, pp. 759–760 accepts this view, but concedes that the archaeological evidence is 'fragmentary' and 'difficult to identify'.
19. Bar, 1998, pp. 8–19.
20. Holy precinct around a temple.
21. *NEAEHL*, vol. 2, p. 763; Sartre, 2005, p. 129; Coüasnon, 1974, p. 12.
22. *NEAEHL*, vol. 2, pp. 764–765.
23. Bar, 1998, pp. 15–16.

24. Arnould, 1997, pp. 45–48.
25. Dio *Hist.* LXIX, 12, 1.
26. Bordeaux Pilgrim, *Jerusalem*.
27. Shanks, 2014, p. 27; Tsafrir and di Segni, 1999, p. 261.
28. Before the military reforms enacted in 193 CE by Emperor Severus, legionnaires were not officially permitted to marry, but this rule was often disregarded and in any case many legionnaires took common-law-wives.
29. Sartre, 2005, p. 152.
30. Sartre, 2005, pp. 155–156; Tsafrir and di Segni, 1999, pp. 262–263; Shanks, 2014, p. 29.
31. Euseb. *EH* IV, vi, 4.
32. Cotton and Eck, 2005, pp. 26–27.
33. *Nasi* meaning 'prince' had formerly indicated descent from King David, but now the title denoted president of the Sanhedrin.
34. Euseb. *EH* VI, viii, 7 – xi, 3.
35. Sartre, 2005, p. 321; Alon, 1980, pp. 695–696.
36. Euseb. *EH* VI, xx, 1.
37. Euseb. *EH* VI, xxxix, 1–3. The Roman Catholic and Eastern Orthodox Churches venerate Narcissus of Jerusalem as a Saint and venerate Alexander of Jerusalem as a Martyr and a Saint.
38. *NEAEHL*, vol. 2, pp. 770–772. Apropos the NE and NW corners of the Roman-Byzantine wall, see *NEAEHL*, vol. 5, pp. 1820–1822.

Chapter 24 The Beginnings of a Christian City

1. Issued by joint Emperors Constantine and Licinius.
2. Sivan, 2008, p. 3.
3. The 9th Av in the Jewish calendar varies in the Gregorian calendar and generally falls between mid-July and mid-August. It is the anniversary of the respective destructions of the Temple by both the Babylonians and the Romans and also the fall of Betar, effectively ending the Bar Kokhba Rebellion.
4. Bordeaux Pilgrim, *Jerusalem*.
5. Nicaea was a Hellenic city in north-western Anatolia, within the present-day Turkish city of İznik.
6. A Christian presbyter of Berber origin.
7. *Canon VII*, Council of Nicaea, 325 CE (reproduced in *NAPNF 2*, vol. XIV, p. 17).
8. Hebrews 13:12; John 19:20 and 19:42.
9. Euseb. *VC* III, xxv–xxvii.
10. Coüasnon, 1974, pp. 12–13; Walker, 2000, pp. 85–87. This inference rests upon the letter that Constantine wrote to Macarius (Euseb. *VC* III, xxx) and the

Council of Nicaea's *Canon VII*, granting special status to the Bishop of Aelia Capitolina.

11. Euseb. *VC* III, xxviii.
12. E.g. Ambrose, *Theodosius* 41–47 (pp. 325–328); Socrates, *EH* I, 17; Sozomen, *EH* II, 1; Theodoret, *EH* I, 17; Michael the Syrian, *Chron.* 45.
13. Euseb. *VC* III, xli–xlvii.
14. Euseb. *VC* III, xxix.
15. Coüasnon, 1974, pp. 14–15.
16. Di Segni, 1990, pp. 393–421; Jerome, *Hilarion* 24.
17. A previous convocation of Christian bishops in Jerusalem had occurred in c.49 CE (Acts 15:1–30), but neither meeting has been accorded the eminence of Ecumenical Council.
18. Athanasius, *De Synodis 21*; Soz. *EH.* II, 27; Socrates, *EH* I, 33.
19. Euseb. *VC* III, xxxiii–xxxix.
20. Sozomen, *EH* II, 26.
21. Euseb. *VC* III, xli–xliii; (Sulpitius) Severus, *SH* II, XXXIII.
22. Conjectured dates: Built by Constantine, therefore no later than 337 [Avigad, 1983, p. 208]; c.340 [Donner 1992, p. 92]; in 340 by Bishop Maximus III or later in the time of Bishop John II, 386–417 [*NEAEHL 2*, 1993, p. 778].
23. Theodosius, *De Situ Terrae Sanctae* 43.
24. Haldon, 2012, p. 23.
25. Sozomen, *EH* IV, 25.
26. Sozomen, *EH* V, 22.
27. Ammian, *History*, XXIII, 1.
28. Sozomen, *EH* V, 22; (Pseudo-)Cyril, Harvard Syriac 99, folios 188b–190a.
29. Rufus, *Peter the Iberian* §43.
30. Later referred to as Melania the Elder to distinguish her from her granddaughter, Melania the Younger.
31. Palladius, *Hist. Laus.* XLVI.
32. This and the next chapter mention five different persons named Theodosius:
    i. Roman Emperor Theodosius I, 379–395.
    ii. Byzantine Emperor Theodosius II, 408–450.
    iii. Theodosius, Archbishop of Jerusalem. 451–453.
    iv. Theodosius the Archimandrite, 494–529.
    v. Theodosius, pilgrim and author of *De Situ Terrae Sanctae*, c.530.
33. Declaration made by joint emperors Theodosius I, Gratian and Valentinian II.
34. Gibbon, Oxford, 1997, p. 119.
35. Gregory of Nyssa, *Letter on Pilgrimages*. The Bishop of Nyssa had doubts about the efficacy of pilgrimages to Jerusalem and in context his words may be viewed as somewhat slanted.

36. Jerome, *Letter LVIII*.
37. Safrai, 1998, pp. 40–41.
38. St Jerome was originally named Eusebius Sophronius Hieronymous.
39. The *Vulgate*.
40. At the end of the second century, Emperor Septimius Severus divided the northern parts of *Syria Palaestina* between the new *Syria Coele* and *Syria Phoenice* and at the end of the third century, Diocletian detached the Negev, Southern Transjordan and Sinai from *Arabia Petraea* and attached them to *Syria Palaestina*.
41. The death of Emperor Theodosius I in 395 CE marked the final and permanent division of the Roman Empire. Thrace, Asia Minor, Egypt, Syria and Palestine were ruled by Theodosius' elder son Arcadius, while his younger son Honorius succeeded as ruler in Rome of Italy, North Africa, Spain and Britain.
42. Patrich, 1995, p. 470.

Chapter 25 Christology

1. Rufus, *Peter the Iberian* §39.
2. Ibid §52. No identifiable ruins of Passarion's monastery have been discovered, raising the possibility that rather than it being located on Mount Zion, it was elsewhere with the term 'Zion' denoting all Jerusalem (Cornelia B. Horn, 2006, pp. 284–285).
3. Rufus, *Peter the Iberian* §64. The Monastery of the Iberians, near the Tower of David, was built in the early 440s.
4. Sivan, 2008, p. 222.
5. In 301 CE, Armenia had been the first nation to adopt Christianity as its state religion.
6. See chapter 18, *Herod's Legacy*, note 21.
7. The gate became known as St Stephen's Gate, until being renamed the Damascus Gate in the fourteenth century.
8. Tzaferis et al., 2000, pp. 287–289.
9. For the previous 23 years, the relic bones of St Stephen had been kept at the Church of Mt Zion. Also, it has been suggested that possibly an older Church of St Stephen had been built by Juvenal (see Honigmann, 1950, pp. 226–227).
10. Rufus, *Peter the Iberian* §49.
11. Sivan, 2008, p. 213
12. Feasibly, the break-up of the marriage was contrived by Chrysaphius, a eunuch who became Theodosius' chamberlain and effective ruler of the Byzantine empire.
13. See Chapter 24, *The Beginnings of a Christian City*, note 3.

Notes

14. Metropolitan bishop of Nisibis (Present-day Turkish Nusaybin, near the border with Syria).
15. Menze, 2016, pp. 231–240.
16. Cyril of Scythopolis, *Vita Euthym* 35. (The churches of St Peter and St Stephen are mentioned).
17. Cornelia B. Horn, 2006, p. 369. See also Socrates, *HE* VII, xlvii.
18. Honigmann, 1950, p. 258.
19. Shalev-Hurvitz, 2015, p. 52 and p. 78.
20. *Chron. Pasch*, Olympiad 306, 444 and Evagrius *EH* I, 22 refer to restoration work, rather than extending the circuit of the walls. *Anon. Plac.* XXV relates 'the Empress Eudocia herself added these walls', which if true may have been because, until Mount Zion became of significant religious-economic interest, it might have been left outside the original Late Roman/Byzantine wall. See, however, *NEAEHL 2*, p. 771.
21. Cyril of Scythopolis, *Vita John the Hesychast* 4.
22. Cyril of Scythopolis, *Vita Euthym* 35.
23. See *Anon. Plac.* XXIII, note 3 on pp. 19–20 (annotation Sir C. W. Wilson); Also, Donner, 1992, p. 93.
24. There had been an earlier 'Council of Ephesus' in 431 CE.
25. Chalcedon is now the present-day Turkish city of Kadiköy.
26. *The Chalcedon Definition of Faith* (reproduced in *NAPNF 2*, volume XIV, pp. 262–265).
27. Dioscorus, Archbishop of Alexandria since 444, was deposed by the Council of Chalcedon in 451.
28. Honigmann, 1950, p. 244.
29. *Decree on the Jurisdiction of Jerusalem and Antioch* (reproduced in *NAPNF 2*, volume XIV, p. 266).
30. Zach. Rhet. *Chron.* III, 3, c; Evagrius, *EH* II, 5.
31. Cornelia B. Horn, 2006, p. 3.
32. Rufus, *Peter the Iberian* §77.
33. (Pope) Leo I, *Epist.* 117, iii.
34. After 451, the term 'patriarch' denoted the head of a diocese who was independent (autocephalous). As the territory subject to Juvenal's jurisdiction now comprised all three Palestinian provinces, and he had acquired the right of consecrating the metropolitans of their capitals, he could be referred to as a patriarch, although perhaps never officially called so during his lifetime. (Honigmann, 1950pp. 271–275).
35. Eudocia's daughter and granddaughters were amongst the hostages taken by the Vandals after the sack of Rome in 455 CE, and their potential rescue by the forces of Constantinople influenced Eudocia's decision.

36. Rufus, *Theodosius of Jerusalem,* §9.
37. Cyril of Scythopolis, *Vita Euthym* 30.
38. Ibid., 35.
39. The distance from Jericho to Jerusalem is about 14 miles, varying with the different sites of Canaanite, Hasmonean/Herodian and Roman Jericho. The road is extremely steep rising from 825 feet below to 2,500 feet above sea level. In antiquity it was known as 'the way of blood' due to the prevalence of violent robbers.
40. The *Henotikon* endorsed many of the pronouncements made at Chalcedon, but avoided the dispute over whether Christ had one or two natures.
41. Cyril of Scythopolis, *Vita Sabas* 16. Now known as *Mar Saba,* the *Great Laura* has been inhabited almost uninterruptedly (except for a brief period in the Middle Ages) until the present day.
42. Like Sabas, Martyrius was born in Cappadocia and earlier in the fifth century, both had been disciples of the monk, Euthymius, at his *Laura* on the Jericho–Jerusalem road. (Cyril of Scythopolis, *Vita Euthym.* 31–32).
43. Cyril of Scythopolis, *Vita Sabas* 19.
44. Anastasius was the name of two Byzantine emperors (Anastasius I, 491–518 and Anastasius II, 713–715 CE) and two Patriarchs of Jerusalem (Anastasius I, 458–478 and Anastasius II, c.692–706 CE).
45. Cyril of Scythopolis, *Vita Sabas* 30. At the same time, the leading monk, Theodosius, was appointed archimandrite in charge of the monks living in communities (*coenobitic*).
46. Cyril of Scythopolis, *Vita Sabas* 31.
47. Theodosius, *De Situ Terrae Sanctae 44–45*; Donner, 1992, p. 22.
48. Frend, 1979, pp. 205 and 230.
49. Known as the feast of Encaenia.
50. Cyril of Scythopolis, *Vita. Sabas* 35–36.
51. Byzantine emperor Constantine had imposed the *collatio lustralis* tax on tradesmen, craftsmen and prostitutes. The *superflua discriptio* transferred tax liabilities from the insolvent to those of means, particularly the Church of the Holy Sepulchre.
52. Cyril of Scythopolis, *Vita. Sabas* 52.
53. Ibid., 56. *Acephaloi* referred to extremist anti-Chalcedonians.
54. The episcopacies of previous bishops of Jerusalem named John were c.117–118 CE and 386–417 CE.
55. Cyril of Scythopolis, *Vita. Sabas* 56.
56. Ibid. Presumably, the governor Zacharias, not mentioned in this context, also returned to Caesarea.
57. Ibid., 57.

Notes

Chapter 26 Justinian

1. Cyril, *Vita Sabas* 67.
2. Much of North Africa, Spain and Italy had all succumbed to Germanic invasions.
3. In the fifth and sixth centuries the Samaritans in Palestine initiated and/or reacted to disputes with Jews, Christians and the Byzantine authorities, often with bloody violent consequences, the culpability for which can be disputed. For a useful summary see Sivan, 2008, pp. 107–142.
4. Cyril, *Vita Sabas* 70.
5. Ibid., 72–73.
6. Including the pre-existence of souls, the superiority of Christ's soul, and that upon resurrection, mortal bodies may not be exactly the same as they were before death.
7. Cyril, *Vita Sabas* 72.
8. In 545 CE, a truce was agreed, following which hostilities were mainly confined to an area east of the Black Sea known as Lazica (a strategic Byzantine vassal kingdom that occasionally fell under Persian domination).
9. Procopius, *Hist.* II, xxii, 1.
10. Ibid., *Hist.* II, xxiii, 1–2.
11. (Pseudo-)Dionysius, *Chron. III, Plague* 4.
12. Evagrius, *EH* IV, 29.
13. (Pseudo-)Dionysius, *Chron. III, Plague* 5. ['Justinian's plague' continued to recur for just over 200 years].
14. Evagrius, *EH*, IV, 29.
15. Michael the Syrian, *Chron.* 100.
16. Procopius, *Hist.* II, xxii, 28.
17. (Pseudo-)Dionysius, *Chron. III, Plague* 1.
18. 'In Constantinople, it has been calculated, around 250,000 people died, perhaps a little over half the population,' Louth, 2009, p. 122.
19. Barsanuphius, 'Letter 569.'
20. (Pseudo-)Dionysius, *Chron. III, Plague* 1.
21. Avigad, 1983, pp. 213–229. Reich, 1987, pp. 164–167.
22. Procopius, *de aedificiis* 5:6.
23. Ibid.
24. Cyril, *Vita Sabas* 73.
25. Procopius, *de aedificiis* 5:6.
26. Cyril, *Vita Sabas* 73.
27. *Anon. Plac.* XXIII.
28. Avigad, 1977. The monastery of Abba Constantinus (Constantine) is mentioned by Moschos, *Pratum Spirituale* 218.
29. Gelasius was Superior of the Great Laura from 537 until his death in 546 CE.
30. Cyril of Scythopolis, *Vita Sabas* 84–89.

31. As a previous bishop of Aelia Capitolina (325–333 CE) was also named Macarius, it is often convenient to refer to this later Patriarch as Macarius II.
32. Cyril of Scythopolis, *Vita Sabas* 90.
33. The First Council of Constantinople (The Second Ecumenical Council) took place in 381 CE. This Second Council of Constantinople in 553 CE came to be known as The Fifth Ecumenical Council.
34. The more important motivation of Justinian, who had convened the Council, was the validation of his earlier edict condemning the writers of the so-called 'Three Chapters.' See *NAPNF 2*, vol. XIV, pp. 315–316.
35. The Second Council of Constantinople, Canon XI. [*NAPNF 2*, vol. XIV, p. 314].
36. Cyril of Scythopolis, *Vita Sabas* 90. The replacement *New Laura* monks included Cyril of Scythopolis. It is possible that this event occurred in February 555, but 554 CE seems more likely.
37. Broshi, 1978, pp. 12–15.
38. Cf. Tsafrir and Di Segni, 1999, p. 264.
39. Brewer, 2005, pp. 127–128. Justinian's *Novella CXXXI* (545 CE) declared the canons of the four Councils to be laws and their dogmas to be sacred writings.
40. 543 CE, Edict against Origen (see Cyril of Scythopolis, *Vita Sabas* 85–86) and *Novellae VI* (535 CE), *CIX* (541 CE), *CXXXI* (545 CE) and *CXXIII* (546 CE).

Chapter 27 The Persians

1. The respective dates of these Byzantine emperors were: Justin II (565–578), Tiberius Constantine (578–582) and Maurice (582–602).
2. Michael the Syrian, *Chron.* 117; *Chron. Pasch.* 591 [p. 691]; Whitby, 1988, p. 304.
3. *Chron. Pasch.* 602 [p. 693]; Michael the Syrian, *Chron.* 117.
4. Sebeos, *Armenian Hist.* 106 [Chap. 31].
5. Rubin, 2009, p. 136; Whittow, 2012, pp. 87–88.
6. Bury, vol. 2, 1889, p. 200.
7. *Chron. Pasch.* 609 [p. 697]. Strategius, *Jerusalem*, p. 504 asserts that Bonosus' intention was to kill Issac.
8. The various obstacles encountered by the new emperor are explained by Bury, vol. 2, 1889, p. 212.
9. Strategius, *Jerusalem*, p. 503; Sebeos, *Armenian Hist.* 115 [Chap. 34]. The Persian occupation of the Palestinian city of Caesarea in 113/114 CE, took place two years after their 111/112 CE occupation of the similarly named city of Caesarea in Cappadocia, during the Persian campaign in Anatolia (Howard-Johnston, 1999, pp. 202–203).
10. Sebeos, *Hist. Heraclius*, XXIII (p. 63).
11. Avi-Yonah, 1976, pp. 259–260. According to Eutychius (*Annals* II, p. 36) as the Persians were on their way to Jerusalem they were joined by Jews from Tiberias, Galilee, Nazareth and the surrounding areas.

Notes

12. Tsafrir and Di Segni, 1999, p. 261.

13. Sebeos, *Armenian Hist.* 115 [chap. 34].

14. Roman Chariot racing originally had supporters of Blue, Green, Red, and White teams, but by the sixth century, the Greens had assimilated the Reds and the Whites had merged into the Blues.

15. E.g. Constantinople's 532 CE Nika riots, during which buildings were burnt and tens of thousands of people were killed (*Chron. Pasch.* 531, but actually year 532 [pp. 620–628]).

16. Jos. *War* II, 44 and Jos. *Ant.* XVII, 255.

17. The deity of fortune or luck, of particular relevance to sporting fans, and of the prosperity of a city.

18. Dan, 1981, page 111.

19. Strategius, *Jerusalem*, p. 503.

20. *Chron. Pasch.* 614 [p. 704] 'in about the month of June' is perhaps when the news reached the Chronicler.

21. Strategius, *Jerusalem*, p. 505.

22. Sebeos, *Armenian Hist.* 115 [chap. 34].

23. Ibid.

24. Strategius, *Jerusalem*, p. 506.

25. Ibid. Ballistae were siege engines/catapults that could propel pointed projectiles or stones weighing up to around 45 kilos.

26. Sebeos, *Armenian Hist.* 115 [chap. 34].

27. Strategius, *Jerusalem*, pp. 506–507.

28. Ibid., pp. 507–508.

29. Most likely the remaining survivors of those Christians most associated with the attack on the Jews before the fall of Jerusalem (Howard-Johnston, 1999, p. 208).

30. Strategius, *Jerusalem*, p. 508; Michael the Syrian, *Chron.* 119. The ancient Christian reports of this atrocity perpetrated by Jews against Christians have been challenged by some more recent Jewish writers: 'a pure fiction' claims Graetz, 1894, p. 19, and Avi-Yonah, 1976, p. 266 queries 'if it is a fact.'

31. Sebeos, *Armenian Hist.* 116 [chap. 34]; *Chron. Pasch.* 614 [p. 704].

32. E.g. Eutychius, *Annals* II, p. 36: *the Persians and Jews together slew innumerable Christians. These are the corpses which lie in the place called Mamela.*

33. Sebeos, *Armenian Hist.* 116 [chap. 34].

34. Strategius, *Jerusalem*, pp. 507–509.

35. Ibid., pp. 514–516. An incredible death-toll of 90,000 is mentioned by Michael the Syrian, *Chron.* 119.

36. Avni, 2010, pp. 36–44.

37. Broshi, 1978, pp. 12–15 guesstimates the late-Byzantine population of Jerusalem at 55,000–60,000. Also, cf. Wilkinson, 1974, who calculations arrive at a population 'ceiling' of 76,130 for *Aelia Capitolina*.

38. The symbolic name of the Jewish commander, *The Book of Zerubbabel*, apud Avi-Yonah, 1976, p. 266.
39. Cf. Avi-Yonah, 1976, p. 268–269 and Howard-Johnston, 1999, p. 208.
40. Howard-Johnston, 1999, p. 209.
41. Eutychius, *Annals* II, pp. 39–40.
42. Sebeos, *Armenian Hist.* 116 [chap. 34]; Avi-Yonah, 1976, p. 269; Michael the Syrian, *Chron.* 119.
43. Strategius, *Jerusalem*, pp. 507–509.
44. Sebeos, *Armenian Hist.* 115 [chap. 34].
45. *Chron. Pasch.* 614 [p. 704].
46. Sebeos, *Armenian Hist.* 116–118 [chaps. 34–35].
47. Eutychius, *Annals* II, p. 36.
48. Ibid. p. 38.
49. Avni, 2010, pp. 40–44.
50. *Chron. Pasch.* 626 [pp. 715–726].
51. Siroes adopted the dynastic name Kavad after imprisoning his father and proclaiming himself Shah of Persia in February 628. Just over six months later he had died after contracting the plague.
52. Bury, vol. 2, 1889, pp. 243–244.
53. Despite divergent views, Mango and Scott's commentary to Theophanes, *Chron.* AM 6120 [ad 627/8], note 3, pp. 459–460 advances the reasoning behind the correct date being almost certainly 21 March, 630.
54. Strategius, *Jerusalem*, p. 516; Eutychius, *Annals* II, pp. 37 and 50; Theophanes, *Chron.* AM 6123 [ad 630/1], notwithstanding differences given for the duration of Modestus' reign as Patriarch. He died late in 630 CE.
55. Strategius, *Jerusalem*, p. 516. For a tale of misuse of the Cross see pp. 510–511.
56. Sebeos, *Armenian Hist.* 131 [chap. 41]; Howard-Johnston, 1999, p. 226.

Bibliography

Religious Texts

Christian Bible   *The Holy Bible*, Revised Standard Version [Second Catholic Edition, San Francisco, 2006].

Greek Septuagint *(LXX)*   *The Septuagint with Apocrypha* [Sir Lancelot Brenton (trans), London, 1851, reprinted United States of America 2009].

Tanakh (Jewish) Bible   *Hebrew-English Tanakh* [The Jewish Publication Society, Second Edition, Philadelphia, 1999].

Babylonian Talmud   *The Babylonian Talmud: A Translation and Commentary* [edited and translated by Jacob Neusner, Peabody, Massachusetts, 2011].

Jerusalem Talmud   Center for Online Judaic Studies. http://cojs.org/ accessed 07/02/2018.

Mishnah   The Mishnah [Herbert Danby (trans.), Oxford, 1933, reprinted 2008].

Primary Sources

Ambrose, *Theodosius*   Ambrose, *On the Death of Theodosius* [*The Fathers of the Church, Funeral Orations by Saint Gregory Nazianzen and Saint Ambrose* (trans. Roy J. Deferrari), New York, 1953]. https://ia802706.us.archive.org/4/items/fathersofthechur012812mbp/fathersofthechur012812mbp.pdf Accessed 20/05/2019.

Ammian, *History*   Ammianus Marcellinus, *The Later Roman Empire (ad 354–378)* [trans. Walter Hamilton, London, 2004].

Athanasius, *De Synodis*   Athanasius of Alexandria, *De Synodis*. http://www.newadvent.org/fathers/2817.htm Accessed 21/05/2019

Anon. Plac.	Antoninus of Piacenza, *Placentini Itinerarium (Of the Holy Places Visited by Antoninus Martyr)* [Palestine Pilgrims' Text Society, Vol. 2, A. Stewart (trans.), London, 1896, reprinted New York, 1971].
App. *Mithridatic Wars*	Appian, *The Mithridatic Wars*. http://www.livius.org/sources/content/appian/appian-the-mithridatic-wars/appian-the-mithridatic-wars-24/#117
App. *Roman Civil Wars*	Appian, *The Roman Civil Wars*. http://penelope.uchicago.edu/Thayer/E/Roman/Texts/Appian/Civil_Wars/5*.html
App. *Syrian Wars*	Appian, *The Syrian Wars*. https://www.livius.org/sources/content/appian/appian-the-syrian-wars/appian-the-syrian-wars-14/ Accessed 14/04/2019
Aristeas	*The Letter of Aristeas* (or *Letter to Philocrates*) [R. H. Charles (trans.), Oxford, 1913. Scanned and edited by Joshua Williams, Northwest Nazarene College, 1995]. http://www.ccel.org/c/charles/otpseudepig/aristeas.htm Accessed 20/12/2018
Barsanuphius	Barsanuphius' Letters [*Fathers of the Church, Barsanuphius and John Letters*, John Chryssavgis (trans.), Vol. 2, Washington, 2007].
Bordeaux Pilgrim, *Jerusalem*	The Anonymous Pilgrim from Bordeaux (333 CE), *Jerusalem*. [Aubrey Stewart (trans.), Palestine Pilgrim's Text Society, 1887, with a few additions and amendments].
Cic. *Flac.*	Cicero, *pro Flacco*. Latin texts and translations. http://perseus.uchicago.edu/perseus-cgi/citequery3.pl?dbname=LatinAugust2012&getid=1&query=Cic.%20Flac.%2067 Accessed 28/04/2019.
Chron. Pasch.	*Chronicon Paschale 284–628 ad* [Michael Whitby and Mary Whitby (trans. and notes), Liverpool, 2007].
(Pseudo-)Cyril Harvard Syriac 99 folios 188b–190a.	apud S. P. Brock, 'A letter Attributed to Cyril of Jerusalem on the Rebuilding of the Temple' *SOAS*, Vol. 40, No. 2, 1977, pp. 267–286.
Cyril of Scythopolis, *Vita Euthym Vita John the Hesychast Vita Sabas*	Cyril of Scythopolis [*The Lives of the Monks of Palestine*, translated by R. M. Price, Kalamazoo, MI, 1991].
Dio *Hist.*	Dio Cassius, *Roman History* [Loeb Classical Library, 1914–1927].

Bibliography

Diodorus, *Lib. hist.*	Diodorus Siculus, *Library of History* [Loeb Classical Library, 1947].
(Pseudo-) Dionysius, *Chron, III.*	(Pseudo-)Dionysius of Tel-Mahre, *Chronicle, Part III* [Witold Witakowski (trans.), Liverpool, 1996].
Epiphanius, *Panarion*	The *Panarion* of Epiphanius of Salamis. http://www.masseiana.org/panarion_bk1.htm#29 Accessed 19/10/2017
Euseb. *EH*	Eusebius, *Ecclesiastical History* [NAPNF, Second Series, Vol. 1, Edinburgh and Grand Rapids, 1997 reprint].
Euseb. *Chron*	Eusebius *Chronicle* [Beloved Publishing 2015].
Euseb. *PE*	Eusebius, *Praeparatio Evangelica* [E. H. Gifford (trans., 1903), reprinted in two volumes, Eugene, Oregon, 2002].
Euseb. *VC*	Eusebius, *Vita Constantine* [NAPNF, Second Series, Vol. 1, Edinburgh and Grand Rapids, 1997 reprint].
Eutychius, *Annals II*	Eutychius, *Annals*, Book II [Aubrey Stewart (trans.), Palestine Pilgrim's Text Society, Vol. XI, London, 1897].
Evagrius, *EH*	*The Ecclesiastical History of Evagrius Scholasticus* [Michael Whitby (trans.), Liverpool, 2000].
Gregory of Nyssa *Letter on Pilgrimages*	Gregory of Nyssa, *Dogmatic Treaties* [Nicene and Post-Nicene Fathers, series 2, Vol. V, William Moore and Henry Austin Wilson (trans.), 1893, reprinted New York, 2007].
Heidelberg Epitome	Anonymous [Felix Jacoby (edit.) *Fragmente der Griechischen Historiker* (FGrH 155), Berlin, 1923–1959]. www.attalus.org/translate/fgh.html#155.0 Accessed 30/01/2015
Herodotus, *The Histories*	Herodotus, *The Histories* [Robert B. Strassler (ed.), *The Landmark Herodotus*, London, 2008].
Jerome	St Jerome, Letters and Select Works [Nicene and Post-Nicene Fathers, series 2, Vol. VI, W. H. Fremantle (trans.), Oxford, 1893].
Jos. *Ant.*	Josephus, *Jewish Antiquities* [Loeb Classical Library, 2001 reprint].
Jos. *War*	Josephus, *The Jewish War* [Loeb Classical Library, 1997 reprint].
Jos. *Apion.*	Josephus, *Against Apion* [Loeb Classical Library, 2004 reprint].
(Pope) Leo I	*The Letters and Sermons of Leo the Great* [Nicene and Post-Nicene Fathers, series 2, Vol. XII, Rev. C. L. Feltoe (trans.), 1895, reprinted New York, 2007].

Livy, *Hist.* — Livy (Titus Livius), *History of Rome (Periochae)* https://www. livius.org/sources/content/livy/livy-periochae-51-55/#55.1 Accessed 13/04/2019

Michael the Syrian, *Chron.* — The Chronicle of Michael the Great, Patriarch of the Syrians [Translated from Classical Armenian by Robert Bedrosian, Long Branch, N.J., 2013]. https://ia801802.us.archive.org/23/ items/ChronicleOfMichaelTheGreatPatriarchOfTheSyrians/ Chronicle_Michael_Syrian.pdf Accessed 05/06/2019

Moschos, *Pratum Spirituale* — John Moschos, *Pratum Spirituale* [John Wortley (trans), 'The 'Spiritual Meadow'* Michigan, 1992].

Nicholas of Damascus, *Autobiography* — Nicholas of Damascus, *Autobiography* [C. M. Hall (trans.), Felix Jacoby (edit.), *Fragmente der Griechischen Historiker* (FGrH 90), Berlin, 1923]. http://www.attalus.org/translate/ nicolaus2.html Accessed 02/03/2018

Palladius, *Hist. Laus.* — Palladius of Galatia, *The Lausiac History*. http://www. tertullian.org/fathers/palladius_lausiac_02_text.htm#C46 Accessed 07/11/2018

Philo, *Spec. Laws* — Philo, *The Special Laws* [C. D. Yonge (trans.), *The Works of Philo*, Hendrickson Publishing, USA, 1993, reprinted 2016].

Philo, *Flaccus* — Philo, *In Flaccum* [C. D. Yonge (trans.), *The Works of Philo*, Hendrickson Publishing, USA, 1993, reprinted 2016].

Philo, *Leg. Ad Gaium* — Philo, *Quod Est De Legatione Ad Gaius* [C. D. Yonge (trans.), *The Works of Philo*, Hendrickson Publishing, USA, 1993, reprinted 2016].

Pliny, *Nat. Hist.* — Pliny the Elder, *Natural History* [Loeb Classical Library, 1942].

Plutarch, *Antony* — Plutarch, *Mark Antony* [Ian Scott-Kilvert (trans.), *The Makers of Rome*, Dorset Press, 1985].

Polybius, *Hist.* — Polybius, *The Histories* [Loeb Classical Library, revised 2012].

Procopius, *de aedificiis* — Procopius, *The Buildings of Justinian* [Palestine Pilgrims' Text Society, Vol. 2, Aubrey Stewart (trans.), London 1896, reprinted New York, 1971].

Procopius, *Hist.* — Procopius, *History of the Wars* [H.B. Dewing (trans.), Loeb Classical Library, Jeffrey Henderson (ed.), Cambridge, MA., 1914].

Bibliography

Rufus, *Peter the Iberian* Rufus, *Theodosius of Jerusalem*	John Rufus [*Lives of Peter the Iberian, Theodosius of Jerusalem, and the Monk Romanus*, Cornelia B. Horn and Robert R. Phenix Jr. (eds and trans.), Atlanta, 2008].
Sebeos, *Armenian Hist.*	Sebeos, *Armenian History* [*The Armenian History attributed to Sebeos*, Part I, R. W. Thomson (trans.), Liverpool, 1999].
Sebeos, *Hist. Heraclius*	Sebeos, *Histoire d' Heraclius* [F. Macler (trans.), Paris, 1904]. https://ia802908.us.archive.org/32/items/ HistoireDheracliusParLevequeSebeos/Sebeos_French.pdf Accessed 16/06/2019
(Sulpitius) Severus, *SH*	Sulpitius Severus, *Sacred History* [Nicene and Post-Nicene Fathers, series 2, Vol. XI, *The Works of Sulpitius Severus*, Rev. Alexander Roberts (trans.), Oxford, 1894].
SHA, Hadrian	Scriptores Historiae Augustae, *The Life of Hadrian.* http:// penelope.uchicago.edu/Thayer/E/Roman/Texts/Historia_ Augusta/Hadrian/1*.html Accessed 07/02/2018.
Socrates, *EH*	Salaminius Hermias Sozomen, *Ecclesiastical History* [Nicene and Post-Nicene Fathers, series 2, Vol. II, A. C. Zenos (trans.), Oxford, 1891].
Sozomen, *EH*	Socrates Scholasticus, *Ecclesiastical History* [Nicene and Post-Nicene Fathers, series 2, Vol. II, C. D. Hartranft, Oxford, 1891].
Strabo, *Geog.*	Strabo, *Geography.* http://penelope.uchicago.edu/Thayer/E/ Roman/Texts/Strabo/ Accessed 14/04/2019.
Strategius, *Jerusalem*	Antiochus Strategos' Account of the Sack of Jerusalem in ad 614 [Frederick C. Conybeare (trans.), *EHR*, Vol. 25, No. 99 (1910), pp. 502–517].
Suetonius	Suetonius, *The Lives of the Twelve Caesars.* http://penelope. uchicago.edu/Thayer/E/Roman/Texts/Suetonius/12Caesars/ home.html Accessed 05/02/2018
Tac. *Annals*	Tacitus, *The Annals.*
Tac. *Hist.*	Tacitus, *The Histories.* http://penelope.uchicago.edu/ Thayer/E/Roman/Texts/Tacitus/ Accessed 02/05/2019
Theophanes, *Chron.*	Theophanes, *The Chronicle of Theophanes Confessor. Byzantine and Near Eastern History ad 284–813* [trans. Cyril Mango and Roger Scott, Oxford, 1997].

| Theodoret, *EH* | Theodoret, *Ecclesiastical History* [Nicene and Post-Nicene Fathers, series 2, Vol. II, Rev. Blomfield Jackson (trans.), Oxford, 1891]. |

| Theodosius, *De Situ Terrae Sanctae* | Theodosius, *The Topography of the Holy Land* [Palestine Pilgrims' Text Society, Vol. 2, J. H. Bernard (trans.), London, 1893, reprinted New York, 1971]. |

| Zach. Rhet. Chron. | The Chronicle of Pseudo-Zachariah Rhetor [*Church and War in Late Antiquity*, Geoffrey Greatex (ed.), Phenix and Horn (trans), Liverpool, 2011]. |

Secondary Sources

Aharoni, Yohanan

1962   'Expedition B – The Cave of Horror, in Expeditions to the Judean Desert' *IEJ* 12, No. 3/4, pp. 186–199.

Aharoni, Yohanan and Avi-Yonah, M.

1978   *The Macmillan Bible Atlas*, New York and London.

Alon, Gedaliah

1980   *The Jews in their Land in the Talmudic Age (70–640 ce)* [Reprint, translated and edited by Gershon Levi, Cambridge, MA, 1996].

Ahlström, Gösta

1993   *The History of Ancient Palestine*, Sheffield.

Arnould, Caroline

1997   'The "Ecce Homo" Arch in Jerusalem: Analysis of the Architecture and New Evidence for Dating' *WCJS*, Vol. Div. B: History of the Jewish People, pp. 45–48.

Avigad, Nahman

1970a   'Excavations in the Jewish Quarter of the Old City of Jerusalem, 1969/70' (Preliminary Report), *IEJ*, Vol. 20, No. 1/2, pp. 1–8.

1970b   'Excavations in the Jewish Quarter of the Old City of Jerusalem, 1970' (Second Preliminary Report), *IEJ*, Vol. 20, No. 3/4, pp. 129–140.

1972   'Excavations in the Jewish Quarter of the Old City of Jerusalem, 1971' (Third Preliminary Report), *IEJ*, Vol. 22, No. 4, pp. 193–200.

1977   'A Building Inscription of the Emperor Justinian and the Nea in Jerusalem' (Preliminary Note), *IEJ*, Vol. 27, No. 2/3, pp. 145–151.

1983   *Discovering Jerusalem*, Nashville.

Avigad, Nahman et al.

1961/62 'Expeditions to the Judean Desert' *IEJ*, Vol. 11, No. 1/2, pp. 6–62 and *IEJ* Vol. 12, No. 3/4, pp. 167–262.

Bibliography

Avi-Yonah, M.

1968   'The Third and Second Walls of Jerusalem' *IEJ*, Vol. 18, No. 2, pp. 98–125.

1976   *The Jews of Palestine, A Political History from the Bar Kokhba War to the Arab Conquest*, Oxford.

Avni, Gideon

2010   'The Persian Conquest of Jerusalem (614 CE) – An Archaeological Assessment' *BASOR*, No. 357, pp. 35–48.

Bar, Doran

1998   'Aelia Capitolina and the Location of the Camp of the Tenth Legion' *PEQ*, 130:1, pp. 8–19.

Barstad, Hans M.

2003   'Myth of the Empty Land: Major Challenges in the Study of Neo-Babylonian Judah' in *Judah and the Judeans in the Neo-Babylonian Period*, Lake Winona, Indiana, pp. 3–20.

Bedford, Peter Ross

1995   'Discerning the Time: Haggai, Zechariah and the Delay in the Rebuilding of the Jerusalem Temple' in S. W. Holloway and L. K. Handy (eds), *The Pitcher is Broken*, Sheffield, pp. 71–94.

Bosworth, A. B.

1974   'The Government of Syria under Alexander the Great' *The Classical Quarterly*, Vol. 24, No. 1 (May), pp. 46–64.

Brewer, Catherine

2005   'The Status of the Jews in Roman Legislation: The Reign of Justinian 524–565 CE' *Eu. Jud.*, Vol. 38, No. 2, pp. 127–139.

Broshi, Magen

1975   'La Population De L'Ancienne Jérusalem' *Revue Biblique*, No. 1, pp. 5–14 (French).

1978   'Estimating the Population of Ancient Jerusalem' *BAR* 4.02, pp. 10–15.

Bryan, Betsy M.

2000   'The Eighteenth Dynasty before the Amarna Period (c.1550–1352 BC)' in Ian Shaw (ed.), *The Oxford History of Ancient Egypt*, Oxford, pp. 218–271.

Bury, J. B.

1889   *A History of the Later Roman Empire*, Vol. 2, reprinted Cambridge, 2015.

Cahill, J. M. and Tarler, D.

2000   'Excavations Directed by Yigal Shiloh at the City of David, 1978–1985' in H. Geva (ed.), *Ancient Jerusalem Revealed*, Jerusalem, pp. 31–45.

Cotton, H. M. and Eck, W.

2005   'Roman Officials in Judaea and Arabia and Civil Jurisdiction' in R. Katzoff and D. Schaps (eds), *Law in the Documents of the Judaean Desert*, Leiden, pp. 23–44.

Coüasnon, Charles

1974   *The Church of the Holy Sepulchre Jerusalem*, London.

Dan, Yaron

1981   'Circus Factions (Blues and Greens) in Byzantine Palestine' in L. I. Levine (ed.), *The Jerusalem Cathedra*, Vol. 1, Jerusalem, pp. 105–119.

Di Segni, Leah

1990   'The Life of Chariton' in V. L. Wimbush (ed.), *Ascetic Behavior in Greco-Roman Antiquity*, Minneapolis.

Donner, Herbert

1992   *The Mosaic Map of Madaba: An Introductory Guide*, Palaestina antiqua 7, Kampen: Kok Pharos.

Duncan-Jones, R. P.

1963   'City Population in Roman Africa' *JRS*, Vol. 53, Parts 1 and 2, pp. 85–90.

Eck, Werner

1999   'The Bar Kokhba Revolt: The Roman Point of View' *JRS*, Vol. 89, pp. 76–89.

Faust, Avraham

2015   'On Jerusalem's Expansion During the Iron Age II' in E. Van der Steen, et al. (eds), *Exploring the Narrative*, London, pp. 256–285.

Frend, W. H. C.

1979   *The Rise of the Monophysite Movement*, Cambridge.

Gelinas, Margaret M.

1995   'United Monarchy-Divided Monarchy: Fact or Fiction' in S. W. Holloway and L. K. Handy (eds), *The Pitcher is Broken*, Sheffield, pp. 227–237.

Geva and Bahat

1998   'Architechural and Chronological Aspects of the Ancient Damascus Gate Area' *IEJ*, Vol. 48, No. 3/4, pp. 223–235.

Gibbon, Edward

1776/88 *The History of the Decline and Fall of the Roman Empire*, London [Folio Society fifth printing, Oxford, 1997].

Gibson, Shimon

2014   'Charles Warren's Kidron Valley Tunnels. Bir Ayyub, and the Location of Biblical En Rogel' in E. van der Steen et al. (eds), *Exploring the Narrative –Jerusalem and Jordan in the Bronze and Iron Ages*, London, pp. 351–393.

Bibliography

Gill, Dan

1991   'Subterranean Waterworks of Biblical Jerusalem: Adaptation of a Karst System' *Science*, Vol. 254 (5037), pp. 1467–1471.

Graetz, Heinrich

1891/98 *History of the Jews*, Vols I–VI, Philadelphia [Reprinted by The Jewish Publication Society of America, Philadelphia, 1946].

Grainger, J. D.

2010   *The Syrian Wars*, Leiden.

Grayson, A. Kirk,

2000   *Assyrian and Babylonian Chronicles*, Winona Lake, Indiana.

Haldon, John

2012   'The resources of Late Antiquity' in C. F. Robinson (ed.), *The New Cambridge History of Islam*, Vol. 1, Cambridge.

Harris, Rendel

1926   'Hadrian's Decree of Expulsion from Jerusalem' *HTR*, Vol. 19, No. 2, pp. 199–206.

Honigmann, Ernest

1950   'Juvenal of Jerusalem' *DOP*, Vol. 5, pp. 209–279.

Horn, Cornelia B.

2006   *Asceticism and Christological Controversy in Fifth-Century Palestine*, Oxford.

Horn, Siegfried H,

1964   *The Chronology of King Hezekiah's Reign*, Andrews University, Berrien Springs, Michigan. http://www.auss_publication_file.php?pub_id=374 [accessed 17/12/2015].

Howard-Johnston, James

1999   *The Armenian History Attributed to Sebeos: Part II, Historical Commentary*, Liverpool.

Jeremias, Joachim

1967   *Jerusalem in the Time of Jesus* [trans. F. H. and C. H. Cave, London, 1969].

Kanael, B.

1971   'Notes on the Dates Used During the Bar Kokhba Revolt' *IEJ*, Vol. 21, No. 1, pp. 39–46.

Kenyon, Kathleen M.

1967   *Jerusalem. Excavating 3000 Years of History*, London.

1975   *Digging Up Jerusalem*, London.

Kokkinos, Nikos

2010   *The Herodian Dynasty*, London.

Levine, Lee I.

2002   *Jerusalem: Portrait of the City in the Second Temple Period (538 BCE –
70 CE)*, Philadelphia.

Lipiński, Edward

2000   *The Aramaeans. Their Ancient History, Culture, Religion*, Leuven, Belgium.

Liverani, Mario

2014   *The Ancient Near East*, Abingdon.

Louth, Andrew

2009   'Justinian and his legacy (500–600)' in Jonathan Shepard (ed.), *The
Byzantine Empire (c. 500–1492)*, Cambridge, pp. 99–129.

Mackowski, R. M.

1980   *Jerusalem City of Jesus*, Grand Rapids, Michigan.

Magen, Menahem

2000   'Excavations at the Damascus Gate, 1979–1984' in H. Geva (ed.), *Ancient
Jerusalem Revealed*, Jerusalem, pp. 281–286.

Mantel, Hugo

1968   'The Causes of the Bar Kokba Revolt' *JQR*, Vol. 58, No. 3, pp. 224–242
and No. 4, pp. 274–296.

Mazar, Benjamin

1975   *The Mountain of the Lord*, New York.

1982   'Jerusalem in Biblical Times' in L. I. Levine (ed.), *The Jerusalem
Cathedra*, Vol. 2, Detroit, pp. 1–24.

McFall, Leslie

1989   'Did Thiele Overlook Hezekiah's Coregency?' *Bibliotheca Sacra*,
Vol. 146, No. 584, pp. 393–404.

1991   *Has the Chronology of the Hebrew Kings Been Finally Settled?* 25 May,
1990 (Revised 29 January 1991).
prophetess.lstc.edu/~rklein/Doc10/Themelios.pdf Accessed 22/15/2015

McGing, Brian

2002   'Population and Proselytism: How Many Jews Were There In the Ancient
World?' in J. R. Barlett, *Jews in the Hellenistic and Roman Cities*, London,
pp. 88–106.

Mendelsohn, I.

1942   'State Slavery in Ancient Palestine' *BASOR*, No. 85, pp. 14–17.

Menze, Volker

2016   'The Dark Side of Holiness: Barsauma the 'Roasted' and the Invention of
a Jewish Jerusalem', in J. Kreiner and H. Reimitz (eds), *Motions of Late
Antiquity*, Turnhout, Belgium, pp. 231–247.

Bibliography

Meshorer, Ya'akov

1967   *Jewish Coins of the Second Temple Period*, Tel Aviv.

Miller, J. M. and Hayes, J. H.

1986   *A History of Ancient Israel and Judah*, Philadelphia.

Patrich, Joseph

1982   'A Sadducean Halakha and the Jerusalem Aqueduct' in L. I. Levine (ed.), *The Jerusalem Cathedra*, Vol. 2, Jerusalem, pp. 25–39.

1995   'Church, State and the Transformation of Palestine – the Byzantine Period (324–640 CE)' in T. E. Levy (ed.), *The Archaeology of Society in the Holy Land*, London, pp. 470–487.

2002   'Herod's Theatre in Jerusalem: A New Proposal' *IEJ*, Vol. 52, No. 2, pp. 231–239.

Pioske, D. D.

2013   'David's Jerusalem: A Sense of Place' *NEArch*, Vol. 76, Issue 1, pp. 4–15.

Pritchard, J. B.

1969   *Ancient Near East Texts Relating to the Old Testament*, Princeton.

Reich, Ronny

1987   'Four Notes on Jerusalem' *IEJ*, Vol. 37, No. 2/3, pp. 158–167.

Reich, Ronny and Billig, Ya'akov

2000   'A Group of Theatre Seats Discovered near the South-Western Corner of the Temple Mount' *IEJ*, Vol. 50, No. 3/4, pp. 175–184.

Reinhardt, Wolfgang

1995   'The Population Size of Jerusalem and the Numerical Growth of the Jerusalem Church' in Richard Bauckham (ed.), *The Book of Acts in its First Century Setting*, Vol. 4, Grand Rapids, Michigan.

Rocca, Samuele

2018   'City-Coin of Aelia Capitolina Depicting the Head of Hadrian and the Ceremonial Foundation of the City (130 ce)' *Judaism and Rome*, 31 August, http://judaism-and-rome.cnrs.fr/city-coin-aelia-capitolina-depicting-head-hadrian-and-ceremonial-foundation-city-130-ce accessed 6/9/2018

Ross, William

1942   'The Four Northern Walls of Jerusalem' *PEQ* 74, Vol. 2, pp.72–75.

Rubenstein, J. L.

2002   *Rabbinic Stories*, New Jersey.

Rubin, Ze'ev

2009   'Eastern Neighbours: Persia and the Sasanian Monarchy (224–651)' in Jonathan Shepard (ed.), *The Cambridge History of the Byzantine Empire c.500–1492*, Cambridge, pp. 130–155.

Safrai, Ze'ev

1998   *The Missing Century*, Leuven.

Sartre, Maurice

2005   *The Middle East Under Rome*, Cambridge, Massachusetts.

Schürer, Emil

1890   *The History of the Jewish People in the Age of Jesus Christ.* Reprint, Peabody, MA, 2012.

Shalev-Hurvitz, Vered

2015   *Holy Sites Encircled (The Early Byzantine Concentric Churches of Jerusalem)*, Oxford.

Shanks, Hershel

2014   'After Hadrian's Banishment: Jews in Christian Jerusalem' *BAR*, Vol. 23, Issue 6, pp. 34–43, 45, 72.

Sharon, Nadav

2010   'The Title "Ethnarch" in Second Temple Period Judea' *JSJ*, Vol. 41, No. 4, pp. 472–493.

Shick, C.

1887   'Herod's Amphitheatre' *PEQ*, 19, Vol. 3, pp. 161–166. Published online 20/11/2013. http://dx.doi.org/10.1179/peq.1887.19.3.161 accessed 19/01/2017

Shotwell, Willis A.

1964   'The Problem with the Syrian Akra' *BASOR*, No. 176, pp. 10–19.

Simons, J.

1952   *Jerusalem in the Old Testament*, Leiden.

Sivan, Hagith

2008   *Palestine in Late Antiquity*, New York.

Smallwood, E. Mary

1959   'The Legislation of Hadrian and Antoninus Pius against Circumcision' *Latomus*, T. 18, Fasc. 2, pp. 334–347.

Smith, George Adam

1907   *Jerusalem: The Topography, Economics and History from the Earliest Times to AD 70*, London.

Smith, William (ed.)

1844   *Dictionary of Greek and Roman Biography and Mythology*, London.

Stern, Menahem

1982   'Social and Political Realignments in Herodian Judaea' in L. I. Levine (ed.), *The Jerusalem Cathedra*, Vol. 2, Jerusalem, pp. 40–62.

Taylor, John

2000   'The Third Intermediate Period (1069–664 BC)' in Ian Shaw (ed.), *The Oxford History of Ancient Egypt*, Oxford, pp. 330–368.

Tcherikover, Victor

1959   *Hellenistic Civilization and the Jews* (trans. S. Applebaum), Philadelphia, 1966.

Thiele, Edwin R.

1983   *The Mysterious Numbers of the Hebrew Kings*, Grand Rapids, MI.

Tsafrir, Yoram and Di Segni, Leah

1999   'The Ethnic Make-Up of Jerusalem's Population in the Byzantine Period' in Y. Tsafrir and S. Safrai, *The History of Jerusalem – The Roman and Byzantine Periods (70–628 ce)*, Jerusalem, pp. 261–281 (Hebrew).

Tzaferis, V. et al.

2000   'Excavations at the Third Wall, North of the Jerusalem Old City' in H. Geva (ed.), *Ancient Jerusalem Revealed*, Jerusalem, pp. 287–292.

Vermes, Geza

1997   *The Complete Dead Sea Scrolls in English*, London.

Walker, Peter

2000   *The Weekend that Changed the World: The Mystery of Jerusalem's Empty Tomb*, London.

Whitby, Michael

1988   *The Emperor Maurice and his Historian: Theophylact Simocatta on Persian and Balkan Warfare*, Oxford.

Whittow, Mark

2012   'The Late Roman/early Byzantine Near East' in Chase F. Robinson (ed.), *The New Cambridge History of Islam*, Vol. 1, Cambridge, pp. 72–97.

Wilkinson, John

1974   'Ancient Jerusalem: Its Water Supply and Population'
        PEQ, Vol. 106, No. 1, pp. 33–51.

Index

Index

Index

Index

Index

Index